Applied Sufism:

Classical Teachings for the Contemporary Seeker

Shaykh Ahmed Abdur Rashid

The Circle Group

WingSpan Press

Printed in the United States of America

Published by WingSpan Press, Livermore, CA
www.wingspanpress.com

The WingSpan name, logo and colophon are the trademarks of WingSpan Publishing.

ISBN 978-1-59594-121-3

First edition 2007

Library of Congress Control Number 2006938188

Inquiries:
The Circle Group
1329 Prosperity Drive
Bedford, VA 24523 USA
e-mail: mail@circlegroup.org

www.circlegroup.org

Dedication

This book is dedicated to Allah *(Subhaanahu wa ta'aalaa),* Who is *Rabbi-l-ʿAalameen;*

... and to Shaykh al-Tariqat Hazrat Azad Rasool, my Pir o Murshid, guide to the inner realities and awakener of my spiritual heart. May Allah protect his soul and give him the blessings that accrue to true saints. His presence that accompanied and inspired me for over 30 years remains today, even though he has moved beyond this world. He is the pole-star of my journey and my service. Although my heart yearns for his physical presence, I recognize the presence of his love and his hand guiding me from beyond this world.

... my children Sabreen and Samah, who are destined to inherit a world sorely in need of Sufism and in need of people of Compassion, Love, Patience and Peace. May Allah *(Subhaanahu wa ta'aalaa)* protect them and guide them in right and good ways. And to their mother, my wife Mitra, and to their grandmother Sayeeda Fakhri Aghamiri, who are preparing them for the world of tomorrow.

... the students who inspire me and strive in the way of Allah. May Allah *(Subhaanahu wa ta'aalaa)* protect all of them.

I ask for forgiveness from Allah *(Subhaanahu wa ta'aalaa)* for any errors that I have made in attempting this task.

Acknowledgments

My gratitude first goes to Salima Christie Burke, who as my editor for 20 years worked tirelessly on the lectures and independent booklets which form the basis of this text.

Also to Maryam Brown who has assumed the demanding position of editor and has re-edited and clarified this text.

And to my researchers and proofreaders Kareemah Mullen and Arifa Thompson, and to Abu'l Hasan Rubin who did the manuscript and Arabic preparation, and to Safiyya Palmer who designed the cover.

May Allah *(Subhaanahu wa ta'aalaa)* shower countless blessings on them.

Various English translations of the Qur'an have been used throughout the text, in some cases for the same *ayat* appearing in different essays. These include the work of Yusef Ali, Muhammad Asad, Abdalhaqq and Aisha Bewley, A. Noorudeen Durkee, F. Malik, and Mohammad Marmaduke Pickthall. May Allah *(Subhaanahu wa ta'aalaa)* reward them all for their efforts to make the meaning of the Qur'an accessible to English-speakers.

We also owe a great debt to the many men and women responsible for preserving the *hadith* (statements of the Prophet Muhammad) and passing this priceless wisdom on to future generations. In *hadith* citations in this volume, the name before the slash (/) is the person who committed the Prophet's saying to memory and narrated it. The name following the slash is the scholar who compiled it.

Contents

About the Author

SHAYKH AHMED ABDUR RASHID was first accepted as a student of Shaykh ul Tariqat Hazrat Azad Rasool of New Delhi in 1976, and was authorized as his representative *(khalifah)* and an authorized teacher of the Naqshbandiyya, Mujaddadiyya, Qadriyya, Chistiyya, and Shadiliyya orders of Sufism on February 20, 1984. This unusually brief period of time was due to Shaykh Abdur Rashid's two previous decades of meditation and study.

An American by birth, Shaykh Abdur Rashid is also known by his English name, J.E. Rash. In all of his endeavors he strives to apply the essence of Islam and *Tasawwuf.* His career includes studies in law and religion; work in professional theater and advertising; coalition-building for interfaith dialogue, peace building and conflict-resolution efforts; and the design of training programs and curricula for educators, parents, and youths. He is also a trained homeopath.

Shaykh Ahmed Abdur Rashid founded the World Community (1970) to provide a supportive environment in which individuals could study the ancient methods of spirituality in which he is authorized to teach, and strive to refine their inner state. The Circle Group was established shortly thereafter as a publication center and outlet for disseminating books, audio resources, and other materials (www.circlegroup.org). As an educator trained in the Montessori Method by the St. Nicholas Training Centre in London, he has established a number of Montessori preschools, as well as a small private school serving students of the community, which came to be known as the World Community Education Center (1971).

In 1979, Shaykh Abdur Rashid and a group of colleagues established a non-profit secular organization Legacy International that has been instrumental in creating domestic and international programs in leadership training, sustainable development, cross-cultural relations, and inter-community dialogue (www.legacyintl.org). One of its longest-running and well-recognized programs, the Global Youth Village (www.globalyouthvillage.org), has hosted over 3000 participants from more than 105 countries including Israeli Jews and Palestinians; Northern Irish Catholics and Protestants; Cambodians; Vietnamese; Albanians, Bosnian Muslims, Croats, and Serbs from Bosnia and Herzegovina, Croatia, Macedonia, and other former Yugoslavian republics; Central and South Americans; citizens of various ethnicities from the former Soviet republics; as well as Native Americans and Americans of all backgrounds. As a result of Legacy's innovative environmental work with Mediterranean youths and young adults, he received the *UNEP 500 Award* from the United National Environment Programme in 1985

Shaykh Abdur Rashid is a member of the Board of Advisors to the Islamic Studies and Research Association (ISRA). He lectures frequently at universities, interfaith forums, and conferences on topics ranging from the life of the Prophet Muhammad *(ṣalla-Llaahu ʿalayhi wa sallam)* to faith and democracy. He is a sought-after presenter at conferences on Sufism, Islam, and international studies. His students include people of all ages and walks of life in many countries around the world.

Shaykh Abdur Rashid's works have been translated into Arabic, Turkish, Russian, and Kazakh. They have appeared in both domestic and international publications including *World Affairs, Education and Urban Society*, *Sufism Journal*, *The American Muslim*, the Turkish publication "*Bugday*," and *Man and Development.* His book *Islam and Democracy: A Foundation for Ending Extremism and Preventing Conflict* (Legacy International, 2006) was published under his English name, J.E. Rash.

Other books to which he has contributed:

- *Democracy and Religion: Free Exercise and Diverse Visions* (Kent State University Press, 2004), recently recognized as an Outstanding Academic Title, *Choice: Current Reviews for Academic Libraries* (January 2006).
- *Taking Back Islam: American Muslims Reclaim Their Faith*, edited by Michael Wolfe (Rodale Press, 2002).
- *Turning Toward the Heart: Awakening to the Sufi Way* by Hazrat Azad Rasool (Fons Vitae, 2002)

Introduction

In his role as a scholar, educator, and spiritual mentor Shaykh Ahmed Abdur Rashid (J. E. Rash) has for over thirty years exemplified the highest ideals and aspirations of humanity's shared legacy. His intimate knowledge of the intellectual and intuition-based traditions of the East and West has made him a director of conscience, so needed in our times. The collected lectures presented in this volume provide us with a living document that testifies to the principles and attitudes that comprise the traditional Islamic ethical discourse and the relevance this discourse has to a multitude of issues facing us all today; from education to family values; from ethics to making peace. These principles, which include certitude, gratitude, and correct inner and outer comportment, are the essential aspects of the pedagogic method of Islam's process of spiritual transformation, known as the Sufi Path. The present volume frames these teachings in the form of a response to those seeking, in the midst of a world torn by social and political turmoil, a whole and integral path, a unity of form and meaning, self-effacing comportment, and intimate knowledge of God. The intimate portrayal of conscience afforded the reader in the exposition of these principles imbues these lectures with a light that is at once familiar and rare. In short, Shaykh Ahmed Abdur Rashid, in his person, as an exemplar and spiritual mentor, and in his teaching legacy, to which these lectures testify, has provided us with a timeless criteria, clear and coherent, of the theoretical and practical aspects of the timeless spiritual discourse of traditional Islam.

Dr. Kenneth Honerkamp
Associate Professor of Religion
University of Georgia

Author's Preface

A great deal has been written about Sufism from perspectives ranging from the scholarly to the eclectic, the classical to the post modern. Translations, interpretations, and personal experiences have been published. Adding to this compendium of information is difficult. However, many of these texts have been written about Sufism and few attempt to portray a Sufic point of view when discussing everyday subjects that affect each of us as we attempt to live our lives in the context of Islam and Sufism. Perhaps what characterizes my effort over the past three decades is the intention to make practical that which many see as philosophical, presenting the practices enjoined by our predecessors as a catalyst for inner and outer change, and moment-to-moment understanding. My spiritual journey began when I was quite young. Enchanted by the celestial bodies above my suburban lawn in Pennsylvania, I lay for hours pondering the origins of the Universe, the purpose of life, the destiny of humanity, and most especially my own destiny. Every journey begins with selfishness and desire, and as we proceed we begin to learn that the journey is in fact about gaining a humble understanding of the inseparable relationship between oneself and one's Creator. Allah is present: if you truly know yourself, you know Allah.

After half a century of wondering, wandering, studying, meditating, and meeting truly astounding people, I find myself listening, often in wonder, to the words that emerged from my heart and mind during *dars* (lectures) and conversations with students. In the presence of my students and peers, some epiphanic stream of inner visuals and meanings surface. I find these words center around certain recurrent themes. Chief among these is that of the practical application of classical teachings and methods to the life of a modern seeker. Another is the firm belief, based in experience, that there is a possibility of living (at least most of the time) in a way that makes the transition between the *dhaahir* (outer realm) and *baatin* (inner realm) seamless. The third theme is the necessity of spiritual companionship, which I touch on in this book and intend to address more fully in a future volume, *inshaa'a-Llaah.*

As I am called upon to speak at conferences and in the *dars* (lectures) that I often give at our *Khanaqah* or with small groups of students, I find I return again and again to trying to create an "aha!" moment of awakening in the hearts and minds of listeners, the sense that, "he was speaking directly to me." Through emphasizing the practicality and the subtle transformational effects of meditation and *dhikr* (remembrance of Allah *[Subhaanahu wa ta'aalaa]*), I strive to encourage seekers to apply Sufic and Islamic principles and practices, and to affirm universal values. With effort, sincerity, and inner yearning, one can bring more balance and peace into one's day-to-day life, despite vicissitudes, tests, and challenges. From the liberating perspective of Sufism, there is a way of understanding Islam—its historical and modern manifestations, its traditional and progressive aspects—that assists the sincere seeker in navigating the often murky waters, the reefs, the hidden obstacles if you will, of the sea of difficulties that is today's troubled world.

Whether I am discussing health or conflict, the Prophet Muhammad *(salla-Llaahu 'alayhi wa sallam)* or the *shuyukh* (mystical teachers) of our orders, politicized Islam or revealed Islam and the truth and security at its root, or modern society and democracy, my contributions are rooted in the understanding I've detailed above. My writing is prefaced by a heartfelt gratitude to Allah *(Subhaanahu wa ta'aalaa)*, my Shaykh Hazrat Azad Rasool, and the *shuyukh* of our orders. I attempt to present a compressed, rich form of prose that allows the reader to return again and again to find something new and exciting. This is a style of teaching that has characterized our tradition for over a millennium, a method transmitted internally from one *murshid* (guide) to the next as a means of reaching people at diverse levels of comprehension and ability, as they seek knowledge and the means of attaining inner and outer awakening.

This book is based on lectures given in various venues from 1998 to 2004. The audiences were varied: some were interfaith gatherings, some were Sufic gatherings, and some were gatherings of Muslims who had little or no knowledge of Sufism. Some of the references may be dated in terms of recent events, but the content remains valid. In my lectures, at times I exhort; at times reflect, question, and attempt to answer; and at other times, I point to what is concealed and can only be discovered by the individual seeker through his or her effort and trust. As is true for all tried and tested spiritual traditions, it takes a mature and responsible seeker to plumb the depths of Sufism, which begins with and is encompassed by Islam. Islam today can only benefit, as it has for centuries, from comprehensive Sufic thought and practices. Indeed Sufism may be called the hope of Islam.

It becomes necessary at times to step back and realize that this personal journey of seeking the Truth has unique characteristics. Although it is indeed a personal journey, it cannot be realized without the *ummah* (community). It is an individual experience achieved through individual effort, but also requires an egalitarian and a self-oriented balance where individualist tendencies are transformed into social and personal responsibilities. One who begins this journey and is guided rightly will not be the same person who completes the journey. Indeed any attempt to remain that "same person"—the one we are comfortable being, the one who depends on past definitions, conditioned attitudes, and habitual patterns of evaluating information and experiences—finds only barriers and impediments to progress. The journey demands discipline, but does not elevate it to the status of proof of advancement; it is detoured by elitism; it flourishes in an environment of simplicity, but does not reject addressing complexity. Sufism is deeply religious in essence, but not preoccupied with ritualistic behavior to such an extent that it becomes an excuse for avoiding the joys of Allah's creation. Consistency is essential as we strive to be the servants of Allah *(Subhaanahu wa ta'aalaa)*, not seekers of "enlightenment."

As the journey applies to all of us—*mureed* and *murshid* alike—I have therefore tried my best over the years to speak in terms of "we" not "you" as often as possible. This journey is, as I have said time and again, an open-ended one that we must come to embrace and enjoy even at times of difficulty.

I hope and pray that my years of studying and sharing will benefit the reader and the seeker. I have dedicated many years to assisting others to realize (as well as striving to remember myself) that Allah is truly Present through the *Asmaa' al-Husnaa* (attributes of Allah *[Subhaanahu wa ta'aalaa]*) in our moment to moment existence, and that we must learn how to see and hear by awakening the subtle organs of perception *(lataa'if)*. The virtually automatic transformation that accompanies the practices of our Orders on the part of a sincere and humble seeker is truly amazing. Through awakening the *lataa'if*, we may begin to find the resonant frequency with the outer organs of perception, and realize that, as Allah revealed in the Qur'an: ***To Allah belongs the East and the West. And in whichever direction you turn, there is the presence of Allah. Truly Allah is Vast, and All-Knowing*** (2:115).

One realizes that Justice, Peace, and Security as well as fairness, guidance in daily actions, tolerance, balance, and love are found in the Holy Qur'an and Hadith of the Prophet *(salla-Llaahu 'alayhi wa sallam)*. Furthermore, all this simply touches on the fullness of the Divine Truth as seen in the heart and manifest in the daily life of a Sufi. Indeed the Whole (Allah) is greater than the sum total of the apparent parts (qualities) but nonetheless present in each one of us regardless of our human definitions of self and other. We are the Children of Adam, and as such, we are brothers and sisters, related and responsible for each other's fulfillment and success. As the Prophet *(ṣalla-Llaahu ʿalayhi wa sallam)* said in his farewell *khutbah*, "...an Arab has no superiority over a non-Arab nor a non-Arab has any superiority over an Arab; a white has no superiority over a black nor a black has any superiority over a white except by piety and good action. Learn that every Muslim is a brother to every Muslim and that the Muslims constitute one brotherhood..."

I hope and pray that this book will be of use to sincere seekers, and to curious readers who are drawn by their hearts toward the Divine Presence, by whatever Name they refer to Her/Him.

Ahmed Abdur Rashid

بسم الله الرحمن الرحيم

Islam: The Reality, Not the Myth

Bismi-Llaah, Alhamduli-Llaah
Allaahumma salli wa sallim ʿalaa sayyidinaa Muhammadin,
wa ʿalaa aalihi wa sahbih

Human Nature and the Call Towards Islam

Understanding Islam begins with understanding the human being. Every infant is born good, in submission to a Higher Power, and with a yearning to develop knowledge. Every human being has an innate urge to seek truth, harmony, and unity. Every person's inborn instinct is to love the Supreme, the Absolute, the beauty and perfection of the Divine. Allah *(Subhaanahu wa taʿaalaa)* tells us in the Holy Qur'an:

> ***Laqad khalaqana-l-'iñsaana fee ahsani taqweem.***
>
> **Surely We created the human being of the best stature** (95:4).

The Prophet Muhammad *(salla-Llaahu ʿalayhi wa sallam)* said:

> **Every person is born in *fitrah*** (in a state of essential goodness and submission) (Abu Darda'a/ Muslim).

However, the innate qualities of the human being become obscured by the circumstances and experiences of daily life. Our inner light dims under the veils of emotional and mental conditioning; of diseases, desires, and fears; of greed and doubt.

Islam is based on removing the veils that stand between our inherent nature and our self. It responds to a call for bringing out the innate goodness in people. In Arabic, the root of the word "Islam" refers to peace, safety, wholeness, and well-being. Rather than being seen as a religion, Islam is better understood as a guidebook to finding peace, security, and wellness through fulfilling and realizing our essential nature, our *fit̲rah.*

Muslims believe that the same guidance was brought by the great leaders and prophets of the Torah, by Jesus as recorded in the Gospels, and by other divinely inspired messengers. The Qur'an instructs us:

> ***Sharaᶜa lakum-mina-d-deeni maa was̲s̲aa bihee Nuuhañw-wa-l-ladhee aw-h̲aynaa ilayka wa maa was̲s̲aynaa bihee Ibraaheema wa Muusaa wa ᶜEesaa an aqeemu-d-deena wa laa tatafarraquu feeh.***
>
> **Allah has ordained for you the faith that He commended to Noah, and that which We inspired in you [Muhammad], and that which We commended to Abraham and Moses and Jesus, saying: "Establish the religion, and be not divided therein."** (42:13)
>
> ***Inna-l-ladheena aamanuu wa-l-ladheena haaduu wa-n-Nas̲aaraa wa-s̲-S̲aabi'eena man aamana bi-Llaahi wa-l-yawmi-l-'aakhiri wa ᶜamila s̲aalih̲añ fa-lahum ajruhum ᶜiñda Rabbihim wa laa khawfun ᶜalayhim wa laa hum yah̲zanuun.***
>
> **Those who believe, and those who follow the Jewish [scriptures], and the Christians, and the Sabaeans—whoever believes in God and the Last**

> **Day and does what is right—surely their reward is with their Lord; no fear shall come upon them, nor shall they grieve** (2:62).

The Qur'an includes major events of the Torah and the Gospels: the stories of Moses, Pharaoh, and the Exodus; David and Goliath; Joseph and his brothers; Mary and the immaculate conception; and Jesus and his disciples (may Allah's blessings be upon all these noble prophets and saints).

Common Ground for Multi-faith Partnerships

Muslims, Christians, and Jews share common history. We tell stories of the same events and people, all unified around the theme of dedication to worship of the same God, and all affirming fundamental human values: fundamental values of family, the search for knowledge, compassion, peace, justice, respect for all life and for the Creator of that life.

Let me pause here for a moment to clarify the term "fundamental," which we see and hear frequently in the media. To the average Muslim, "fundamental" refers to the basic beliefs of the *shareeʿah* and the *sunnah* that all Muslims share, just as fundamental Christian beliefs and fundamental Jewish beliefs are shared by all Christians and all Jews, respectively. Real fundamentalist Islam is a far cry from the negative implications of fundamentalism based on extremist, narrow-minded, and ultra-orthodox thinking that does not take into consideration other schools of thought. It is equally distant from the so-called fundamentalism that uses Islamic principles for political ends. Many of these ends are questionable, and some fall entirely outside of the *shareeʿah*: for example, killing innocent people, manipulating political situations in the name of Islam, and even oppressing contrasting expressions of Islam. No matter how often such attitudes and activities are labeled "fundamentalist," they do not reflect the fundamental principles of Islam, principles that are universal and constructive.

Muslims call upon God as the Compassionate and the Merciful at least thirty-four times a day, reciting *ar-Rahmaan ar-Raheem* twice in every cycle of prayer. They value the establishment of a peaceful society, the well-being of the family, respect for elders, freedom to worship, efforts to create a better world for future generations—values that are dear to all people of faith, whether they are called Jews, Christians, Muslims, Hindus, Buddhists, or by any other name.

Through dialogue, all our communities of faith can work together to affirm these values. We can become better able to meet the needs of the society we share.

In August 1999, I participated in a unique meeting in Cordoba, Spain, that brought together Jewish and Muslim scholars and religious leaders. In-depth discussions revealed a substantial agreement in goals that is often overlooked due to historical inaccuracies, cultural bias, and the politicization of Jewish-Islamic relations. We all agreed on the need for mutual respect and for developing common ground for the future, especially with regard to the deterioration of values and ethics in today's society.

Many opportunities exist for sincere peoples of faith in the United States to form partnerships for mutual goals. Together, we can help this society reverse the trends towards violence, materialism, the breakdown of communities and families, drug and alcohol abuse, and other social ills.

Islam as a Framework for Practical Approaches

For Muslims, one of the most exciting aspects Islam has to offer is a way of looking at life not only in its esoteric, philosophical forms, but also in its practical forms. Islam is a dynamic movement to re-establish certain principles and values in daily life.

The day-to-day responsibilities of a Muslim are shaped by a trust that was given to us by God. In the Qur'an, Allah *(Subhaanahu wa ta'aalaa)* says:

> ***Innaa ʿaradnaa-l-'amaanata ʿala-s-samaawaati wa-l-'ardi wa-l-jibaali fa-abayna añy-yahmilnahaa wa ashfaqna minhaa wa hamalaha-l-'iñsaan; Innahuu kaana dhaluumañ jahuulaa.***
>
> **Lo! We offered the *amaanaat* (trust) to the heavens and the earth and the hills, but they shrank from bearing it and were afraid of it. And the human being assumed it. Lo! the human being has proved a tyrant and a fool** (33:72).

The mechanisms for upholding the *amaanaat* are revealed to us in the Qur'an, exemplified in the *sunnah* (the way) of the Prophet Muhammad *(salla-Llaahu ʿalayhi wa sallam)*, and manifest through qualified personal decisions on applied topics of life and worship. While I do not have time to enumerate all the ways that Muslims strive to fulfill the trust, I can at least list some of them.

- A Muslim must guarantee the rights of non-Muslims to practice their religions, and he or she must respect and preserve others' institutions.

- A Muslim has the duty to help those who are in need in the community, to the point where they can begin to assist themselves, if possible. Muslims regard bureaucratic welfare systems as less effective than the bonds of community and personal responsibility. The Prophet Muhammad *(ṣalla-Llaahu ʻalayhi wa sallam)* said:

He is not a man of faith who eats his fill when his neighbor is hungry. (Bukhari)

(Note that the Prophet *(ṣalla-Llaahu ʻalayhi wa sallam)* said "his neighbor," not "his Muslim neighbor.")

- A Muslim is enjoined to be fair and just. The Prophet Muhammad *(ṣalla-Llaahu ʻalayhi wa sallam)* said:

  There are three attributes, which, if they are found in a person, will complete his faith: giving charity despite abject poverty, spreading peace throughout the world, and giving people their acknowledged rights without the use of a judge.

- Muslims are enjoined to be loyal to the countries that they live in, whether they have Islamic governments or not.

- Muslims are enjoined not to distinguish on the basis of race, ethnicity, or nationality. In one of his last public sermons, the Prophet Muhammad *(ṣalla-Llaahu ʻalayhi wa sallam)* said:

  God says: "Verily in [My] sight, the most honored among you is the most God-fearing. There is no superiority for an Arab over a non-Arab and for a non-Arab over an Arab, nor for the white over the black nor for the black over the white, except in piety" (Faizi 145).

- Islam believes strongly in the rights of women, both in the areas of law and justice, and in the areas of religious rites and practice. Islam also acknowledges differences between men and women that are considered to be positive and constructive for society.

- A truly Islamic community is inherently pluralistic and democratic.

In addition, Islam has a system of thought and self-evaluation that enables it to adapt to the ongoing changes in the world. It embraces and encourages the evolution of human understanding. For example, the Qur'an describes Abraham (Ibrahim *(ʿalayhi-s-salaam)*) as a *ḥaneef*—a believer in one God—not a Jew, nor a Christian, nor a practicing Muslim, other than in the literal sense of being one who submits to a higher authority. Later, the doctrines and practices of the three Abrahamic religions evolved through the teachings of the prophets of the Torah, the Bible, the Qur'an: through Isaac, Jacob, and Joseph; Moses, David, and Solomon; through Jesus; and through Muhammad, whom we consider to be the final prophet (may Allah's peace and blessings be upon all the prophets and messengers).

The evolution of human understanding is a core principle of Islam. In the Qur'an, Allah *(Subḥaanahu wa taʿaalaa)* tells us:

> ***...lahum quluubul-laa yafqahuuna bihaa, wa lahum aʿyunul-laa yubsiruuna bihaa, wa lahum aadhaanul-laa yasmaʿuuna bihaa...***
>
> **...they have hearts that do not understand, and eyes that do not see, and ears that do not hear...** (7:179).

Our faculties can be developed through conscious effort, in accordance with the saying often attributed to the Prophet Muhammad *(ṣalla-Llaahu ʿalayhi wa sallam)*:

Seek out knowledge from cradle to grave. [1]

To catalyze the growth of understanding, Allah *(Subḥaanahu wa taʿaalaa)* gave human beings the capacity for choice within parameters. For the Muslim, the parameters of choice are *shareeʿah.*

Shareeʿah is based on revelation: its sources are the Qur'an and the *sunnah*, meaning the living commentary on the Qur'an that the Prophet Muhammad *(ṣalla-Llaahu ʿalayhi wa sallam)* conveyed through his words and acts. By observing *shareeʿah* in all his or her activities, the Muslim places everything that he or she does within the context of revelation.

This framework is evolutionary, not constraining. In Arabic, *shaariʿ* means "a broad street or boulevard"; *shareeʿah*, therefore, is a broad boulevard of activity. It is like a raga in Indian music. A raga is a precise musical form, but endless improvisation is possible within that form. *Shareeʿah* gives us clear guidelines about life; yet, it also allows ongoing innovation, as long as each innovation serves the purpose of Islam.

Islam is a dynamic, vibrant way of life that is well able to address the issues of today and tomorrow. But for many non-Muslims, it remains a mystery, if not a threat.

Sources of and Responses to Misunderstandings of Islam

Every day, non-Muslims in the West hear about Islam, whether through news of an earthquake in Turkey or the conflict in Kashmir, through negative publicity about so-called Muslims like Osama Bin Laden or through sympathetic stories of

Kosovar refugees. With all this exposure, no educated person can claim to know nothing about Islam. On the other hand, this deluge of impressions can seem hopelessly confusing, if not outright contradictory. Most difficult to understand are the misinterpretations of Islam that exist among Muslims themselves, as I mentioned earlier. Such misinterpretations have fed misunderstandings of Islam among non-Muslims, playing into stereotypes of the religious fanatic or terrorist.

We cannot avoid addressing these misunderstandings of Islam both from within and without, for they reflect on all Muslims. More seriously, they undermine the contributions that Islam can and should make to today's society.

We can tackle misunderstandings by reflecting on history: for example, on the role of Muslim scholars and scientists in preserving and transmitting the discoveries of classical civilizations and in extending humanity's knowledge of chemistry, medicine, astronomy, human rights, law, organizational development, government, philosophy, education, navigation, and architecture.

But we can learn about the historical role of Muslims from books. I prefer to speak about the role of the Muslim in today's society. How can we best illustrate the progressive aspects of Islam? How can we most effectively interface with the needs of today's world?

One important step being taken by educated, practical Muslims is to address the most difficult cultural and heretofore accepted practices which have reflected poorly on Islam or which have not been considered in the light of modern times. Contemporary scholars are discussing and finding ways in which the *sharee'ah*/ Qur'an and the *sunnah* can guide us in the present and future, without compromising the essentials of the faith or betraying the trust that Allah has given us.

For example, some of the most destructive cultural overlays that have been imposed on Islam are customs that oppress or limit the activity of women. The integral role of women in Islamic society is evident in the historical examples of Khadija *(raḏiya-Llaahu ʿanhaa)*, the first wife of the Prophet *(ṣalla-Llaahu ʿalayhi wa sallam)*, who was his employer before she was his wife. It is equally evident in accounts of Muslim women who fought in battle, who served as some of the earliest archivists of Islamic teachings, and who, throughout the history of Islam, ranged from saints to scholars. However, I do not want to give the impression that Islam looks at women in the same terms as Western political feminism. Islam offers a whole other view of women, which many Muslim women are actively exploring as they extend Islamic understanding of women's roles inside and outside of the home.

In addition to addressing cultural overlays, Muslims today face the need to adjust for modern times. An example may be drawn from the field of medicine. An ultra-orthodox Muslim may regard organ transplants as an offense against God's natural order, arguing that the violation of a body is forbidden in Islam. But other contemporary Muslims point to the Qur'anic passage:

> ***...man aḏyaahaa fa-ka'annamaa aḏyaa-n-naasa jameeʿaa.***
>
> **...whoever saves a life, it would be as if he [or she] saved the life of all the people** (5:32).

They note that according to Islamic law, "the lesser of two evils is to be chosen if both cannot be avoided." From their perspective, an organ transplant is permissible if it will make the difference between life and death (Organ).

By carefully examining both age-old cultural customs and the latest technological and social advances, scholars are using the light of *shareeʿah* to see and to relate to today's world in better ways for individuals and for the community at large. They are expanding opportunities for Islam to be a major force, working together with other faiths and forces in society to re-affirm the fundamental values that we share.

Fulfilling the Amaanaat Here and Now

Scholarly explications are just the beginning. Ultimately, it is up to each individual Muslim to contribute something of his or her value system to society at large.

Many Muslims in the United States are first-generation Americans. They have come to this country for various reasons: some are refugees; many are seeking a better life, a higher standard of material well-being for themselves and their children. Like other immigrants and religious minorities, they have often found support in cultural enclaves or sub-communities of people from the same background.

Perhaps the most important challenge facing Muslims in this country today is to integrate more fully into American society as Muslims. We need more Muslim teachers, more Muslim curriculum developers, more Muslim sociologists and psychologists, more Muslim urban planners, more Muslims throughout diverse professions. We need professionals who are Muslims in the true sense of the word: living and working in submission to God, accepting our *amaanaat*. Muslims must be full participants, individually and collectively, actively seeking means and venues for applying Islamic values and mechanisms to the needs of our times.

CONCLUSION

Family issues, greed in the marketplace, falling educational standards, prejudice in the workplace, inter-religious and intercultural conflicts: these and many other issues cry out for the attention of all people of faith. By responding to such needs, we can build mutual understanding and partnerships among our diverse religious communities. We can become better Muslims, better Christians, better Jews, better Hindus, better Buddhists, better believers by any name. We can help to re-awaken the essential goodness that resides within every human being. We can fulfill the trust that we bear. As Allah *(Subḫaanahu wa ta'aalaa)* instructs us in the Holy Qur'an:

> ***Wa li-kulliñw-wijhatun huwa muwalleehaa fa-stabiqu-l-khayraat; ayna maa takuunuu ya'ti bi-kumu-Llaahu jameeᶜaa; inna-Llaaha ᶜalaa kulli shay'iñ qadeer.***
>
> **And every [community] faces a direction of its own, of which God is the focal point. Vie, therefore, with one another [as in a race] towards all that is good. Wherever you may be, God will bring you together; for God has power over all things** (2:148).

Thank you very much.

* * *

O Allah, guide us to build better understanding among people of all religions, working together to help our society and to build a safe, nurturing environment for our children to be able to carry forward our beliefs and values of tolerance, peace, harmony, and compassion.

...sallamu ʿalaa jamiʿi-l-'anbiya'i wa-l-mursaleen
wa jamiʿi-l-malaaa'ikati-wa-l-muqarrabeen...
wa jamiʿi mashaikheena wa murrabeena wa murshideena illa-Llaahi taʿala
bi-iẖsaanin wa eemaanin wa islaamin ilaa yowmi-d-deen
yaa Arẖama-r-raaẖimeen.

...peace be upon all of the Prophets and Messengers
and all of the Angels and Those Brought Near...
and all our Venerable Masters and those who foster us
and our Guides to God the Most High
with abiding goodness and faithful belief
and peaceful self-surrender until the Day of Judgment,
O Merciful Bestower of Compassion.[2]

Notes

1 The saying, "Seek knowledge from cradle to grave," is typically attributed to the Prophet Muhammad *(salla-Llaahu 'alayhi wa sallam)*, although this specific wording is not found in *hadith* literature. However, other *hadith* are quite similar in language and meaning, such as, "Seeking knowledge is incumbent upon every Muslim," which was reported as a saying of the Prophet *(salla-Llaahu 'alayhi wa sallam)* by Ibn Majah, Bayhaqi, and other scholars. Consequently, the former statement is regarded as part of the general wisdom of Islam, whether it was uttered by Muhammad *(salla-Llaahu 'alayhi wa sallam)* or one of his early followers.

2 The author acknowledges Shaykh Noorudeen Durkee for the transliteration and translation of the closing Arabic *du'aa*, drawn from Noon Hierographers printing of *Hizbu-l-Bahr (The Orison of the Sea).*

References

Faizi, S.F.H. *Sermons of the Prophet (Peace Be Upon Him).* New Delhi: Kitab Bhavan, 1991.

Organ Donation and Transplantation. Printed by the University of Northumbria (UK) Islamic Student Society. Available on the Internet at <http://www.unn.ac.uk/societies/islamic/about/modern/organ.htm>.

بسم الله الرحمن الرحيم

The Status of Tasawwuf in Islam

Bismi-Llaah, Alhamduli-Llaah
Allaahumma salli wa sallim ʿalaa sayyidinaa Muhammadin,
wa ʿalaa aalihi wa sahbih

The Boulevard of Shareeʿah and the Lane of Tasawwuf: One Reality

The status of *Tasawwuf* in Islam is clear. Sufism is Islam; and at the core of Islam, one finds Sufism.

One need not be an Arabic scholar to detect clues to this interrelationship in the roots of the words *shareeʿah* and *tareeqah*. *Shaariʿ* means a wide boulevard. In European terms, we might visualize it as a lovely thoroughfare, spacious and lined with trees. In American terms, we might think of it as a superhighway, with vehicles traveling in different lanes at different speeds. The word *tareeq* means a way or method, road or path. *Tareeqah* is like a high occupancy vehicle (HOV) lane on the superhighway of *shareeʿah*. It comes from the same place and goes to the same place as *shareeʿah*. It is open to anyone who qualifies, just as the HOV lane is open to anyone with at least two passengers.

The outer law *(shareeʿah)* and the inner way *(tareeqah)*, the orthodox Muslim and the ecstatic lover of God, are one. This is far more than a congruence of definitions. It reflects the essential construct of the human being. Allah *(Subhaanahu wa taʿaalaa)* instills in each human soul a memory of having once been united with the Creator, and a desire to reunite.

This yearning is accompanied by the recognition of the need for outer structures and standards: that is, for *shareeʿah*. Shah Waliyullah, the eighteenth century Muslim scholar, observed:

> *Shareeʿah* is...the result of the requirement of the [human] species itself. It has not been thrust upon [human beings] against their will but has been given to them at their request (Jalbani 120).

Shareeʿah provides the framework whereby a working relationship can be established between humankind and the Divine Reality.

Observance of *shareeʿah* is uplifting and meaningful. For many Muslims, it is sufficient. Others are more acutely aware of their separation from the Source, and long to hasten their approach to the Divine. *Taṣawwuf* addresses their need.

Taṣawwuf has been described as "the internalization and intensification of Islam." This intensification is not incumbent upon believers, but rather an opportunity available to those who pursue it. Even at the time of the Prophet Muhammad *(ṣalla-Llaahu ʿalayhi wa sallam)*, only a select few among the Muslims inclined towards the more intensive, supererogatory practices (Lings 211). The Qur'an states:

> ***Inna Rabbaka yaʿlamu annaka taquumu adnaa miñ thuluthayi-l-layli wa nisfahuu wa thuluthahuu, wa ṯaaʾifatum-mina-l-ladheena maʿak...***
>
> **Verily thy Lord knowest that thou [Muhammad] keep vigil well nigh two thirds of the night, and sometimes half of it or a third of it, thou and a group of those that are with thee...** (73:20).

In all times and places, there have been individuals whose deep yearning (*himma*) and inner restlessness have led them to the Path of *Tasawwuf.*

Islam reveals that Sufism is not something outside of itself, but something contained within itself. When sincere spiritual yearning and practice are combined, the depth and breadth of Islam are revealed. Inner restlessness becomes profound fulfillment.

The Inseparability of Shareeᶜah and Tareeqah

Both the founders of the Sufic Orders and the founders of the Islamic *madh-habs* (schools) recognized the value of *Tasawwuf* to gain ever fuller understanding of Islam, its inner and outer dimensions, and its relevancy to personal development and social order.

Shah Naqshband *(radiya-Llaahu ʿanhu)* said: "The correct way to the Path is to follow the Prophet *(salla-Llaahu ʿalayhi wa sallam).*" According to Shaykh Ahmed al Rifa'i *(radiya-Llaahu ʿanhu)*: "The *tareeqah* is the same as the *shareeᶜah*; and the *shareeᶜah* is the same as the *tareeqah.*" Abu al Hasan Shaadhili *(radiya-Llaahu ʿanhu)* cautioned students: "If extraordinary matters happen with you that contradict the laws of religion, the Book of Allah *(Subhaanahu wa taᶜaalaa)*, or the *sunnah* of the Messenger *(salla-Llaahu ʿalayhi wa sallam)*, then definitely leave them out and follow the rules of religion." Imam Malik *(radiya-Llaahu ʿanhu)*, to whom the Maliki *madh-hab* owes its origins, wrote: "[One] who practices *Tasawwuf* without learning Sacred Law corrupts his faith, while one who learns Sacred Law without practicing *Tasawwuf* corrupts himself. Only [the person] who combines the two proves true." All of these individuals investigated and acknowledged the transformative effect of pursuing the Path of *tareeqah* on the broad boulevard of *shareeᶜah* (Kabbani).

False Divisions Between Tasawwuf and Islam

The fact that any human being can experience the synthesis of outer and inner—and that this experience has been verified by personal testimonies throughout the millennia—should ensure recognition of the status of *Tasawwuf* in Islam. Unfortunately, it has not. Instead, we find so-called Sufis who disassociate themselves from Islam, and we find Muslims who have no understanding of Sufism and who, in their ignorance, judge it to be antithetical to Islam.

From this perspective, the status of *Tasawwuf* in Islam has been weakened: not because of any genuine schism between the two, but because of widespread illusions of barriers between them. (Indeed, the very phrase "*Tasawwuf* in Islam" implies distinction where none exists.)

Our Responsibility to Re-Link the Chain

False barriers between Islam and *Tasawwuf* reflect the overall fragmentation of Westernized society. By the design of Allah *(Subhaanahu wa ta'aalaa)*, our *himma* (yearning), *ikhtiraam* (sacredness and respect), *ihsaan*, and innate predisposition towards discipline, values, and ethics are all linked to one another in the core of our being. As societies have become fragmented, these links have been broken. We have started to compartmentalize our lives. We distinguish between individual and community; we imagine conflicts between our spiritual, physical, emotional, and intellectual natures; we break knowledge into narrow disciplines; we disconnect our minds from our hearts.

When a chain is intact, lifting any one link lifts the whole chain. Once a chain is broken, it becomes possible to pick up a single link.

Individuals have been able to pick up fragments of *sharee'ah* and *tareeqah* because the chain is broken. It is up to us to repair it.

People's ears, eyes, and minds need to be re-attached to their hearts, their sense of sacredness, and their *jadhbah* (attraction) to the Divine.

The place to begin is by re-asserting the unity of our *ummah* (community) and the breadth and depth of *shareeʿah* and *sunnah*.

DIVERSITY WITHIN UNITY

Allah *(Subhaanahu wa taʿaalaa)* says in the Holy Qur'an:

> ***Inna haadhihee ummatukum ummatañw-waahidatañw-wa ana Rabbukum fa-ʿbuduun***
>
> **Verily, this *ummah* of yours is a single *ummah*, and I am your Lord and Cherisher: therefore, serve Me [and no other]** (21:92).

We are a single *ummah* encompassing tremendous diversity. In recent decades, scientists have made discoveries that point to unity within diversity. In the case of the *ummah*, it is more accurate to speak of diversity within unity.

Human beings naturally seek to gather around shared beliefs. Ironically, this urge to come to unity—to form communities—becomes a source of division when carried to an extreme. Unity becomes confused with uniformity, and uniformity entails removing all that is "different."

The Qur'an tells us:

> ***Laa ikraaha fee-d-deen...***
>
> **There is no compelling in religion...** (2:256).

There is no compelling in religion, but there are those who seek to compel. Compelling takes many forms. It is not just insisting that a person recite the *shahaadah* (profession of faith). Compelling also takes the form of distrust; of making *takfeer* (accusing other Muslims of disbelief); of asserting one's own school of thought to the exclusion of any other. All such forms of compelling impose narrow and restrictive definitions of *shareeʻah* and *sunnah*.

From Reality to Name

While some confuse unity with uniformity, others mistakenly assert that unity means that anything is acceptable in the realm of spirituality.

The great Sufi master al-Hujwiri *(radiya-Llaahu ʻanhu)* quoted Abu'l Hasan Fushanja *(radiya-Llaahu ʻanhu)* as saying, "Today, *Tasawwuf* is a name without a reality, but formerly it was a reality without a name" (al Hujwiri 44). What does it mean for *Tasawwuf* to be "a name without a reality"? As a consistent spiritual experience emerges into a name, people tend to use its name to embrace other forms that appeal to their *nafs-i-ammaarah* (desire nature).

So it is that we find the name "Sufism" associated with attitudes that would astonish the founders of the *tareeqahs*. Individuals take it upon themselves to twist the *shareeʻah*, the *sunnah*, and the accepted practices to suit their desires, so that they themselves will not have to change. They have little or no apprehension in doing so, because they have little or no sense of wrong. Rather, their modifications are justified in the name of "modernizing" Islam and *Tasawwuf*.

Consequently, our *ummah*—once the leader in knowledge and thought—has deteriorated to the point that its essence lies scattered across the desert of the world. The result is either passivity or aggression, expressed in aberrated forms of Islam and degraded forms of *Tasawwuf*.

In the Holy Qur'an, Allah *(Subhaanahu wa taʻaalaa)* speaks of those who

> ***...iñy-yattabi**ᶜ**uuna illaa-dh-dhanna wa maa tahwa-l-'añfusu: wa laqad jaaa'ahum-mir-Rabbihimu-l-hudaa***
>
> **...follow nothing but mere conjecture and the whims which their souls incline to, although the guidance has come to them!** (53:23).

In an age when whims and conjecture predominate, is it any wonder that the intra-relationship of *Tasawwuf* and Islam should be largely misunderstood?

UNDERSTANDING THE NATURE AND BENEFITS OF OUR DIVERSITY

Between the extremes of false orthodoxy and self-indulgent secularism lies a middle way. This is the way of appreciating and making the most of the diversity within our unity. According to a *hadith* (of which the *isnaad* is *da*ᶜ*eef*, but the *hadith* itself is *saheeh)*, the Prophet *(salla-Llaahu* ᶜ*alayhi wa sallam)* said:

> **The differences among my *ummah* are a mercy** (Ibn ᶜAbaas/Khateeb).

We need diversity in order to come to unity. Diversity sets a developmental process in motion. It stimulates purification, *tazkiyah*. An analogy can be made to *zakat*. *Zakat* is much more than a way of helping those in need. It is a way of purifying the community. A pond of still water becomes stagnant; a running stream remains pure. *Zakat* keeps resources flowing within the community.

Similarly, diversity within the *ummah* enables us to develop true compassion, forgiveness, patience, and affection. It enables us to make the best possible use of our resources and our knowledge for the benefit of the world we inhabit. Only such wise use of the bounties of Allah *(Subhaanahu wa ta'aalaa)* will guarantee our spiritual survival.

In addition, diversity challenges culturally-based interpretations and prompts us to return to the universal truths of Islam.

According to the Holy Qur'an:

> ***...qat-tabayyana-r-rushdu mina-l-ghayy. Fa-mañy-yakfur bi-t-taaghuuti wa yu'mim-bi-Llaahi fa-qadi-s-tamsaka bi-l-ᶜurwati-l-wuthqaa lañ-fisaama lahaa...***
>
> **...Henceforth the Truth stands out clear from error. And he who rejecteth false deities and believeth in Allah hath grasped a firm handhold which will never break...** (2:256).

If we trust that Truth stands out clearly from error, then it follows that the best way to help individuals evolve an understanding of Truth is to let them hear and weigh different views. Diversity cannot obscure *Al-Haqq*. Rather, it makes the Truth all the more evident.

Allah *(Subhaanahu wa ta'aalaa)* has created us as a diverse community inspired by the highest common denominators: shared faith, shared practice, and shared responsibility with one purpose.

> ***Wa kadhaalika jaᶜalnaakum ummatañw-wasatal-li-takuunuu shuhadaaa'a ᶜala-n-naasi wa yakuuna-r-Rasuulu ᶜalaykum shaheedaa.***
>
> **Thus We made you a community of the center (*ummata wasata*) that you might be a witness**

> **to the people, and the Messenger, a witness to you** (Qur'an 2:143).

As Muslims, we all believe in Allah *(Subhaanahu wa ta'aalaa)*; we all affirm that Muhammad *(salla-Llaahu 'alayhi wa sallam)* is Allah's *(Subhaanahu wa ta'aalaa)* Messenger; we all pray; we all do *wuduu';* we all believe in all the prophets—whether we are *Shi'a*, *Salafiya*, Sufi, or any other label. Based on the strength of these common bonds, we can address even the most difficult questions. We can share differing viewpoints with openness and tolerance, rather than fearfully defending our views and attacking others'.

A Call to Action

Everyone who calls himself or herself a Sufi or Muslim needs to speak as a representative of the *ummata wasata:* the community of the center. We need to work together to recapture Islam and *Tasawwuf* from extremist thinking. We need to redirect our focus to the core responsibilities that we are enjoined to fulfill: to feed the poor, house the homeless, educate the ignorant, and assist others in the attainment of *al hayaat-i-tayyibah* (the good life). Real unity begins when we place ourselves second.

We must be the models of the high status of *Tasawwuf* in Islam. This entails examining our own state. Allah tells us in the Holy Qur'an:

> ***Iñ kullu mañ fi-s-samaawaati wa-l-'ardi illaa aati-r-Rahmaani 'abdaa.***
>
> **None is there in the heavens and the earth that does not come to the All Merciful as a servant *('abd)*** (19:93).

Let us consciously embrace our roles as *'abd Allaah*, as people of *'ibaadah* (worship). Let us be "in the world and not of the world," gaining skills and fulfilling our duties in a balanced and appropriate manner, and preparing the generations after us to take responsibility. Let us purposefully re-make our *shahaadah* and re-affirm our Islam.

Conclusion

In sum, the status of Sufism in Islam is central and unquestionable. However, consciously or unconsciously, individuals have erected false divisions between *sharee'ah* and *tareeqah*, between the broad boulevard and the special lane. These divisions are symptomatic of the overall fragmentation of our *ummah*, a fragmentation that has its roots in the failure to appreciate the benefits of our diversity.

I come from the Mujaddadiyya Order—the line of the *mujaddids*, the revivers. Each person present here today has a responsibility to be a reviver: to restore vitality to Islam where deterioration has set in. The status of *Tasawwuf* in Islam will be made clear as each of us becomes a model of *'ibaadah*.

'Ibaadah is a love of Allah and of all His creatures. It leaves no room for exclusivity, rejectionism, or condemnation of others. It allows only compassion, hope, effort, truth, and prayer—prayer even for those who are lost, blind, and deaf to the Divine admonitions of Allah *(Subhaanahu wa ta'aalaa)*. These are our tools for repairing the chain. Our task is to apply them. The rest is up to Allah *(Subhaanahu wa ta'aalaa)*.

Jazaaka-Llaah khayr. Thank you very much.

* * *

Shaykh Ahmed Abdur Rashid

Wa Llaahu lahu-l-haqqi wa huwa yahdi-s-sabeel.
Hasbuna Llaahu wahdahu wa ni'ma-l-wakeel.
Wa salli 'alaa Sayyidinaa Muhammadin
wa aalihi wa sahbihi ajma'een
wa-l-hamdu li-Llaahi Rabbi-l-'aalameen.

Truth belongs to Allah; it is He who shows the way.
Allah, alone, suffices us, and what a fine Guardian is He!
Blessings upon our Master Muhammad
and his family and companions altogether
and praise is due to Allah, Lord of the Worlds.

References

al Hujwiri, Ali b. Uthman al Jullabi. *The Kashf al-Mahjub.* Translated and edited by Reynold A. Nicholson. London: Luzac and Company, 1976.

Jalbani, G.N. *Teachings of Shah Waliyullah of Delhi.* Third edition. Lahore: Sh. Muhammad Ashraf, 1979.

Kabbani, Muhammad Hisham. What the Scholars Say about Tasawwuf. *The Muslim Magazine.* April 1998: 50-51.

Lings, Martin. *Muhammad: His Life Based on the Earliest Sources.* Kuala Lumpur: A.S. Noordeen, 1983.

Organ Donation and Transplantation. Printed by the University of Northumbria (UK) Islamic Student Society. Available on the internet at http://www.unn.ac.uk/societies/islamic/about/modern/organ.htm.

Serageldin, Ismail. Mirrors and Windows: Redefining the Boundaries of the Mind. *The American Journal of Islamic Social Sciences.* Volume 11, Number 1, Spring 1994: 79-107.

al-Suhrawardi, Abu al-Najib. *A Sufi Rule for Novices (Kitab Adab al-Muridin).* Translated by Menahem Milson. Cambridge, MA: Harvard University Press, 1975.

al-Sulami, Muhammad ibn al-Husayn. *The Book of Sufi Chivalry: Lessons to a Son of the Moment (Futuwwah).* Translated by Sheikh Tosun Bayrak al-Jerrahi al-Halveti. New York: Inner Traditions International, 1983.

Therapies in Health and Medicine 1998 Mar 4(2):67-70. University of Maryland School of Medicine, Baltimore. Precis posted online at http://home.tampabay.rr.com/lymecfs/abstract98.htm.

بسم الله الرحمن الرحيم

THE NECESSITY OF SPIRITUALITY FOR DAʿWAH WORK

Bismi-Llaah, Alh̲amduli-Llaah
Allaahumma s̲alli wa sallim ʿalaa sayyidinaa Muh̲ammadin,
wa ʿalaa aalihi wa sah̲bih

THE ESSENTIAL ATTRACTIVENESS OF ISLAM

The journey to Islam is a journey to *salaam:* to peace, safety, security, wholeness, well-being. It is an inherently personal and internal journey, for true peace, safety, security, wholeness and well-being are not to be found outwardly, but rather by releasing the innermost essence of our being. To embrace Islam—to come to submission—is to stop resisting and start allowing ourselves to find our ultimate security and peacefulness in reliance on Allah *(Subh̲aanahu wa taʿaalaa)*.

This is, by definition, a spiritual journey. The word "spirituality" implies an active process based on the progressive realities of Islam (as opposed to the limited definitions that have been imposed on Islam).

The journey towards Islam is a clear and proven path that any person can traverse. Indeed, every human being naturally inclines towards this journey from birth. A *h̲adith* of the Prophet *(s̲alla-Llaahu ʿalayhi wa sallam)* states:

> **Every person is born in *fit̲rah*** [in a state of essential goodness and submission]**. It is his**

> **parents who make him a Christian, Jew, or Magian** (Abu Hurayra/Bukhari).

Throughout nature, we witness Allah's *(Subhaanahu wa ta'aalaa)* creation acting in accordance with the Divine will. The flowers do not have to be coerced to bloom, nor the birds to migrate, nor the fruit to ripen. So, too, our inner nature is governed by certain laws. As the seed is called to push forth from the earth, we are called to follow the directives and fulfill the responsibilities for which human beings were created: to serve as the *khalifahs* (vice-regents) of Allah *(Subhaanahu wa ta'aalaa)*.

The journey towards Islam is therefore best understood as an inner, spiritual *jihaad* (struggle) to stop erecting obstacles to our own awakening. Islam is not so much a religion as a guidebook to our essence, a codebook that breaks the code to the secret of our beingness. It is a light that reveals that which is hidden in the most hidden place. It is a process of removing the accretions within us that have obscured the essential peace that is *Al-Islaam*.

THERE CAN BE NO COMPELLING IN ISLAM

Once we recognize the continuing, unbreakable relationship between our beingness and Allah's *(Subhaanahu wa ta'aalaa) niyyah* (intention) for us, it becomes clear that the message of Islam contains within itself the ability to call people. Allah tells us in the Holy Qur'an:

> ***Laa ikraaha fee-d-deen...***
>
> **There is no compelling in religion...** (2:256).

Compulsion is incompatible with *deen*, for *deen* depends on an individual's trust, love, and willingness to participate. Trust, love, and will can no more be forced than the seed can be forced to grow. Allah *(Subhaanahu wa ta'aalaa)* instructed the Prophet *(salla-Llaahu 'alayhi wa sallam)*:

> ***Qul haadhihee sabeelee ad'uu ila-Llaah: 'alaa baseeratin ana wa mani-t-taba'anee ...***
>
> **Say: "This is my way: I call to Allah [resting] upon conscious insight – I and those who follow me"...** (12:108).

This *ayat* presents a litmus test for *da'wah*. It tells us that *da'wah* is a call or an invitation that appeals to "conscious insight." It can never be an act of outward coercion.

Timeless Appeal; Timely Applicability

The timeless appeal of *al-Islaam* is reinforced by its applicability to the particular needs of each day and age.

What are the needs of our society today? In light of the scandals here in Washington, DC, we may well conclude that our most serious problems are ethical and moral. Consider also the confused (and frequently detrimental) ends towards which new technologies, scientific discoveries, and advances in knowledge are being applied. It would seem that many human beings lack clear understanding of the meaning of their existence. Devoid of a sense of higher purpose, these individuals settle for something lower: lives centered around the fulfillment of material desires.

Other individuals sense the limitations of materialism. For them, the issue is where to turn for an alternative. In centuries past, religious institutions spoke to people's longing for a sense of meaning. Today, many Americans (particularly highly-educated professionals) find little significance in traditional religious forms.

They are disinclined to pray regularly, to ascribe importance to religion, or to affirm belief in God. Instead, they acknowledge a "universal spirit or life-force" (Post-Modernity Project).

In an era when ethical issues loom large and organized religion is seen as out-dated, spirituality is likely to appeal to a broad range of people. Evidence bears this out in the case of Islam and *Taṣawwuf.* In the mid-1980's, two authors interviewed numerous European and American Muslims who had embraced Islam in adulthood. They concluded that "almost all educated converts to Islam come in through the door of Islamic spirituality"—that is, *Taṣawwuf* (Murad 20).

Westerners are searching—not for a moral path, not for a political ideology, not even for a spiritual identity—but for some element that they feel they are lacking. They are searching for a sense of spiritual meaning (Murad 20). *Taṣawwuf* addresses this inner longing.

Some argue that being drawn to Sufism is a far cry from becoming a Muslim. This is certainly true in the case of individuals who enjoy tasting many options from the buffet of teachers and mystical schools that are accessible in the West today. However, as my Shaykh, Hazrat Azad Rasool *(Raḥmatu-Llaahi ʿanhu)* of New Delhi, pointed out, the person who is sincere in his or her pursuit of Sufism will be drawn to Islam (and, conversely, the Muslim who sincerely pursues Islam will discover Sufism). In fact, there is only one Islam. There is only one *Nuur-i-Allaah*, only one real knowledge. It is internal knowledge *and* external knowledge. There is no difference between Islam and *Taṣawwuf.*

DAʿWAH AL-KUBRAA

The role of spirituality in *daʿwah* is reflected in the power of inviting by personal example. Early Sufis spread Islam as far as Central Asia, India, Pakistan, China, Mongolia, and Indonesia through the model of their goodness, honesty, and humble lifestyle.

Many Muslims have interpreted *da^cwah* as an obligation to issue calls *to* Islam. *da^cwah* may be better understood as hearing the calls *for* Islam—and responding. Needs for peace, for justice, for equitable economic growth, and for education are all calls for Islam. The *da^cwah al-kubraa* (greater *da^cwah*) is to respond to these calls for Islam practically, generously, and thoughtfully, while allowing the call to Islam to come from Allah *(Subhaanahu wa ta^caalaa)*. As the Holy Qur'an reminds us:

> ***...Allaaha yahdee mañy-yashaaa': wa huwa a^clamu bi-l-muhtadeen.***
>
> **...it is Allah who guides him that wills [to be guided]; and He is fully aware of all who would let themselves be guided** (28:56).

Allah *(Subhaanahu wa ta^caalaa)* does not need us. We need Allah *(Subhaanahu wa ta^caalaa)*. Allah *(Subhaanahu wa ta^caalaa)* has not hired us.

Moreover, Allah *(Subhaanahu wa ta^caalaa)* makes clear that not everyone is expected to respond to His call.

> ***...in huwa illaa dhikruñw-wa Qur'aanum-mubeen. Liyuñdhira mañ kaana hayyañw-wa yahiqqa-l-qawlu ^calaa-l-kaafireen.... Wa-t-takhadhuu miñ duuni-Llaahi aalihatal-la^callahum yuñsaruun.... Fa-laa yahzuñka qawluhum. Innaa na^clamu maa yusirruuna wa maa yu^clinuun.***

> **...this is no less than a reminder and a Qur'an making things clear: that it may give admonition to any [who are] alive and that the charge may be proved against those who reject [Truth].... Yet they take [for worship] gods other than Allah [hoping] that they might be helped!... Let not their speech grieve thee. Verily We know what they hide as well as what they disclose** (Qur'an 36:69-70, 74, 76).

Numbers Versus Effects

Da'wah does not aim to attract huge numbers of followers to the Way. Indeed, the Prophet *(salla-Llaahu 'alayhi wa sallam)* predicted that:

> **The day will come when the Muslims will be numerous, but will be froth and flotsam, carried along by a flash flood** (Abu Dawuud).

Islam is not a matter of building institutions, and Sufism is not based on having millions of students. Rather, Islam and *Tasawwuf* are about changing society in accordance with Islamic principles for the benefit of everyone: Muslim and non-Muslim, human and animal, insect and plant, here in *dunyaa* and in those worlds that we have yet to visit.

In the Naqshbandiyya Order, we speak about the importance of the *naqsh* (design). What does it mean to be a Naqshbandiyya: a designer? How do we design? We design by striving to draw forth the blueprint of Reality and Truth that Allah *(Subhaanahu wa ta'aalaa)* has seeded within every human heart. We design by assisting in the transformation of the potentials for beauty, service, creativity, and worship within each individual into realities. We design by addressing the complexity of life with the simplicity of the Qur'an, the *sunnah*, and the *ḥikmah* (wisdom) of those who truly know the Way.

The average human being today feels overwhelmed by the complexities of post-modern society. People speak of the "good old days" when "life was simpler." But even the most apparently complex system may be influenced by the circumstances that surround it. We can influence the phenomena that emerge out of today's complex issues by shaping the environment around them.

Consciousness is the most critical factor in that environment. The more aware we are of the order of the universe and of Allah's *(Subḥaanahu wa taʿaalaa)* intention for our interaction with that order, the more we will be able to see with new eyes, hear with new ears, and operate in new ways. Allah *(Subḥaanahu wa taʿaalaa)* asks us:

> *...afalaa tasmaʿuun?...afalaa tubṣiruun?*

> **...Will ye not, then, hear?....Will ye not, then, see?** (Qur'an 28:71-72).

We will hear and we will see as we remove the plugs from our ears and the veils from our eyes. The more we regard the mystery of life within the context of the simplicity of the message of *Al-Islaam*, the less mystifying it will be. In short, the more we will be able to affect change for the better—to respond to the calls for Islam.

To attain clarity amidst complexity, we must submit. Submission means setting aside conflicts and focussing on the unifying elements of Islam. It means diving deeply into ourselves, shifting our perceptions away from I-centeredness towards "Allah-centeredness." It means letting go of vested interests and possessive attitudes towards people, institutions, and methodologies.

The guru orientation is not necessarily suited to today's needs. Worthwhile students are seeking ways to apply spirituality in day-to-day life. They are not interested in god-like figures who own their students and who claim that only their teachings are relevant.

Teachers who want to facilitate change in individuals, in communities, and in society at large focus on the refinement of character, on *akhlaaq* (ethics), on *tazkiyah* (purification). Yes, there are those who love the *barakah* (blessing); but only those who love the *tarbiyah* (education) will make the constructive changes in the world.

Our efforts need to be focused around Allah *(Subhaanahu wa ta'aalaa)*, not around any particular personality. To focus one's efforts around Allah means to focus them around *al-Asmaa' al-Husnaa*: the Ninety-Nine Beautiful Names. We succeed in transmitting an Islamic point of view to the degree that we manifest the qualities of the Divine, the Names seeded within our hearts: *ar-Rahmaan* (the Compassionate), *ar-Raheem* (the Merciful), *al-Ghaffar* (the Forgiver), *al-Hafeedh* (the Protector), *al-Kareem* (the Generous), *as-Sabuur* (the Patient). How many times a day do we have the opportunity to dip our cups into the ocean of compassion, forgiveness, love, effort, justice, protection? How often can we distribute this ambrosia to others through our communications, our businesses and enterprises, our teaching, our commitment to our families, our devotion to our Creator?

The greatest *da'wah* is the way we act. If we have something to offer, then people will seek us out. If our example of faith is inviting, then we will inspire others to examine their own relationships with the Divine. If we speak in the language that people can understand—without the cultural overlays that either confuse or attract Westerners so much that they mask the essence of Islam—we will awaken people to the benefits of our way of life.

Ultimately, if we are to convey the truth of Islam, we must have a clear inner understanding of its significance. It has been said that "man is an enemy of what he does not know." To know Islam requires more than observing its outward forms. It requires that we turn all aspects of our lives into *ʿibaadah* (worship).

ʿIbaadah means to fulfill our responsibility as human beings—developing one's skills in society; being "in the world and not of it"; fulfilling one's duties in a balanced and appropriate manner, and preparing the next generation to do the same. It is heeding the calls for Islamic approaches in ways that are creative, flexible, and open-minded, while at the same time firmly grounded in *shareeʿah.*

Conclusion: Fulfilling the Call to Return

Our capacities to submit, to find peace, and to develop our potential reflect the resonance of our soul with its Divine Source. Allah *(Subhaanahu wa taʿaalaa)* calls us, and we call Him.

> ***Wa 'idhaa sa'alaka ʿibaadee ʿannee fa-innee Qareeb: ujeebu daʿwata-d-daaʿi idhaa daʿaani fa-l-yastajeebuu lee wa-l-yu'minuu bee laʿallahum yarshuduun.***
>
> **And when My servants ask you concerning Me, then verily I am near. I answer the call of the supplicant when he calls on Me, so let them answer Me and believe in Me so that they may walk in the right way** (Qur'an 2:186).

Daʿwah takes place in two directions. Allah *(Subhaanahu wa taʿaalaa)* calls us to Himself, and we call upon Him. Our *duʿaas* to Allah *(Subhaanahu wa taʿaalaa)* are a response to his *daʿwah* to us. "Your call is My reply" is a well-known saying among the people of *Tasawwuf.*

This mutual relationship cannot be forced. It cannot be created out of the material of this world. It is not even the result of our effort. Whatever we accomplish is part of an inexorable journey that we have been on since pre-existence—a gravitational, celestial pull to remember Allah *(Subhaanahu wa ta'aalaa)* within and outside the nexus of time and space. Just as the monarch butterflies know how to migrate thousands of miles, navigating along magnetic field lines, so, too, we are attracted by forces whose inception in pre-eternity began with the injunction *"Kun"* (Be). It is a journey of fulfillment: not just fulfillment in the material sense, but fulfillment in the sense of fulfilling our trust, the *amaanaat* bestowed upon us by Allah *(Subhaanahu wa ta'aalaa)*.

> **...My servants continue to draw near to Me with supererogatory works so that I shall love them. When I love them, I am the ears with which they hear, the eyes with which they see, the hands with which they strike, and the feet with which they walk** *(hadith qudsi)*.

This is the true *daa'i*. This is the spirituality of *da'wah* work. Until we can call one another to unity, we cannot call anyone to Islam; and we cannot call anyone to unity until each one of us respects all others in our hearts. No one is greater than anyone else, and no one deserves worship but Allah *(Subhaanahu wa ta'aalaa)*.

Jazaaka-Llaah khayr. Thank you.

* * *

Wa Llaahu lahu-l-haqqi wa huwa yahdi-s-sabeel.
Hasbuna-Llaahu wahdahu wa ni'mal-wakeel.
Wa salli 'alaa sayyidinaa Muhammadin wa aalihi wa sahbihi ajma'een
wa-l-hamdu li-Llaahi Rabbi-l-'aalameen.

Truth belongs to Allah; it is He who shows the way.
Allah, alone, suffices us, and what a fine guardian is He!
Blessings upon our Master Muhammad
and his family and Companions altogether
and praise is due to Allah, Lord of the Worlds.

References

Murad, Abdal Hakim. "Islam and the New Millennium, Part I." BICNews <afifi@iol.ie>. Posted 21 January 1998. From a lecture delivered at the Belfast Mosque, March 1997.

The Post-Modernity Project at the University of Virginia. Executive Summary, 1996 Survey of American Political Culture. Charlottesville, VA: In Medias Res Educational Foundation, 1996.

Organ Donation and Transplantation. Printed by the University of Northumbria (UK) Islamic Student Society. Available on the internet at http://www.unn.ac.uk/societies/islamic/about/modern/organ.htm.

Serageldin, Ismail. Mirrors and Windows: Redefining the Boundaries of the Mind. *The American Journal of Islamic Social Sciences.* Volume 11, Number 1, Spring 1994: 79-107.

al-Suhrawardi, Abu al-Najib. *A Sufi Rule for Novices (Kitab Adab al-Muridin).* Translated by Menahem Milson. Cambridge, MA: Harvard University Press, 1975.

al-Sulami, Muhammad ibn al-Husayn. *The Book of Sufi Chivalry: Lessons to a Son of the Moment (Futuwwah).* Translated by Sheikh Tosun Bayrak al-Jerrahi al-Halveti. New York: Inner Traditions International, 1983.

بسم الله الرحمن الرحيم

ISLAM:
AN EXPRESSION OF THE SOUL'S LONGING

Bismi-Llaah, Alhamduli-Llaah
Allaahumma salli wa sallim ʿalaa sayyidinaa Muhammadin,
wa ʿalaa aalihi wa sahbih

We have been on an inexorable journey since pre-existence—pulled by a gravitational, celestial force to remember Allah within and outside the nexus of time and space. Just as the monarch butterflies know how to migrate thousands of miles, navigating along magnetic field lines, so too we are attracted by forces whose inception in pre-eternity began with the injunction *"Kun"* (Be). It is a journey toward fulfillment: toward completion in uniting with that which the soul longs for.

What does the soul most long for? Home. Reunion. A return to its origins in the Divine Unity, the One Truth. Mevlana Jalaladdin Rumi said of that return:

> To be one with the Truth for just a moment
> Is worth more than the world—more than life itself!

From the moment we are born into this separation known as "life," Allah *(Subhaanahu wa taʿaalaa)* calls us, and we call Him.

> ***Ujeebu daʿwata-d-daaʿi, idhaa daʿaani; fa-l-yastajeebuu lee, wa-l-yu'minuu bee, laʿallahum yarshuduun.***
>
> **I answer the call of the supplicant, when he**

> **[or she] calls on Me; let them, then, respond to Me, and believe in Me, so that they may walk in the right way** (Qur'an 2:186).

Allah *(Subhaanahu wa ta'aalaa)* calls us to come back. This process of turning back to our origins describes religion in its fundamental meaning: the process of *"religare,"* meaning "to return to the source."

Allah *(Subhaanahu wa ta'aalaa)* not only calls us to return, but provides the means to increase both the speed and the awareness of that journey. That means is Islam.

Islam did not "begin" when the Prophet Muhammad *(salla-Llaahu 'alayhi wa sallam)* first received revelation in 610 C.E. Long before the name "Islam" became identified with a particular set of practices and teachings, Islam existed as a truth: the truth of unity and surrender.

Throughout nature, we witness Allah's creation acting in accordance with the Divine will. The flowers do not have to be coerced to bloom, nor the fruit to ripen. So, too, inwardly we are called to discover the peace that is Islam, the security that is Islam, the safety that is Islam, the reconciliation that is Islam.

But sometimes, we get distracted. As much as we long for Allah *(Subhaanahu wa ta'aalaa)*, we have certain characteristics that cause us to lose track of Him, as if we are in a department store, and suddenly we turn around and realize we have lost our child. Only in this case, we are the child, and we have wandered off, and now we are looking for the One Who created us.

Do you remember what it is like being two feet tall? You can walk right through the racks of clothing. You easily get lost, because you can be inside the rack, and no one even notices you, you're so small. There you are, surrounded by all these big people's knees, and you can't possibly know where your mother is, because you can't see over anything.

So, you start wandering. Every once in a while, you stumble onto an aisle, the *siraata-l-mustaqeem*. You go down that aisle, crying and wailing, "Mommy! Mommy!" The store clerks come to help you, saying, "Don't worry, we'll take care of you." But do you want them to take care of you? No. You don't want anyone taking care of you. You want to go out on your own and find your mother. And that is what got you in trouble in the first place—wanting to go out on your own.

You wander down more aisles, then wander through the racks again, off the beaten path, with no pattern to your search, except calling out to Allah *(Subhaanahu wa ta'aalaa)*.

But you have to learn how to listen. When you learn how to listen, you hear your mother calling. Can you see her? No. Does it make you feel happier? No. You feel more miserable. Why? Because you cannot get to her. The more you hear her, the greater your *himma* (yearning).

Finally, you run across your mother. She opens her arms, gives you a big hug, and tells you sternly, "Don't ever do that again!" But do you remember what you did? No. You have no idea what you did. You were taken to this wonderful place of so many attractions, and all you did was go look at them. What's wrong with that? You forgot who brought you here. You forgot who would take you home. You forgot the purpose of coming here in the first place.

Allah *(Subhaanahu wa ta'aalaa)* informs us in the Qur'an:

> ***Wa man a'rada 'añ dhikree fa-inna lahuu ma'eeshatañ dañkañw-wa nah-shuruhu yawma-l-qiyaamati a'maa.***

> **The one who turns away from remembering Me shall live a meager life, and We shall raise that one up blind on the Day of Resurrection** (20:124).

"Meager" in this *ayat* means not only impoverished, but cramped, confined, weak and exhausted, in distress or hardship.

Remembering Allah *(Subhaanahu wa ta'aalaa)* in this minute is much more important than anything else we think is important. If we remember God this moment, we will find happiness; if we forget, we will find only desolation. The Prophet *(salla-Llaahu 'alayhi wa sallam)* said:

> **The likeness of the one who remembers his Lord and the one who does not remember Him is like that of a living person to a dead person** (Abu Hurayra/Bukhari).

Remembering Allah *(Subhaanahu wa ta'aalaa)* means meditating on His commands, His promises, and His warnings; contemplating the design and order of life; and attempting to grasp inner dimensions of the mystery hidden behind the veil of *dunyaa* (the material world) by plumbing the depths of His Divine science through spiritual efforts and practices.

It is not enough to feel longing. We must make effort. A person may have strong yearning, but minimal willingness to cooperate. They yearn, but do nothing to fulfill that yearning. If I yearn for you, and you yearn for me, and I pursue you, but you do not do anything to help the process, where will the relationship end up?

Submission is essential to the process of fulfilling our longing. Allah *(Subhaanahu wa ta'aalaa)* guides us in the Qur'an:

> ***Yaa ayyuha-l-ladheena aamanu-s-tajeebuu***

li-Llaahi wa li-r-Rasuuli idhaa da^caakum li-maa yuhyeekum! Wa-^clamuuu anna-Llaaha yahuulu bayna-l-mar'i wa qalbihee, wa annahuu ilayhi tuhsharuun.

O you who believe! respond to Allah and to the Messenger when He calls you to what will bring you to life! Know that Allah intervenes between a person and his heart, and that you will be gathered to [Him] (8:24).

In the relationships of *dunyaa*, we long for the beloved until we are with the beloved, and then—as soon as we are with the beloved—we start to fear that we will lose that love or be rejected. But if we draw near to Allah *(Subhaanahu wa ta^caalaa)*, then Allah *(Subhaanahu wa ta^caalaa)* never rejects us. Allah *(Subhaanahu wa ta^caalaa)* never distances Himself from us.

Nahnu aqrabu ilayhi min habli-l-wareed.

We are nearer to a person than the jugular vein (Qur'an 50:16).

Allah *(Subhaanahu wa ta^caalaa)* is near, but we veil the nearness of the Divine with distraction. It is up to us to strive to lift the veil. We do so by fulfilling the obligations of *sharee^cah*, by trusting in those who guide us, and by being willing to reflect upon ourselves.

Most people run from seeing themselves because they do not want to feel criticized, to feel humiliated, to succumb to self-deprecation. But for the Muslim/Sufi, self-reflection is constructive and clarifying. Seeing the discrepancy between what we know and what we do, we yearn to change so much that we feel frustrated. We worry that we might never change. If, in that frustration and worry, we persevere, and keep yearning, and sincerely do the practices, then that, in and of itself, is progress. If we start off not seeing our faults, then see them, then get frustrated, then yearn, then strive all the harder, we have progress from complacency to effort, from forgetting to remembering. Just as a cold, barren winter makes us long for spring, so, too, that sense of distance from our goal catalyzes us to seek the Truth more diligently.

Allah *(Subhaanahu wa ta'aalaa)* commands:

> ***Wa-dh-kur-Rabbaka fee nafsika tadarru'añw-wa kheefataa...bi-l-ghuduwwi wa-l-'aasaali wa laa takum-mina-l-ghaafileen.***
>
> **Remember your Lord in yourself, humbly and fearfully...in the mornings and evenings. Do not be one of the unaware** (Qur'an 7:205).

Allah *(Subhaanahu wa ta'aalaa)* also describes the people of understanding as "**those who remember Allah standing, sitting, and reclining...** ***(alladheena yadhkuruuna-Llaaha qiyaamañw-wa qu'uudañw-wa 'alaa junuubihim...)"*** (Qur'an 3:191).

Morning and evening, in activity and rest, everything we do can be done with remembrance. Every aspect of life—our relationships, work, search for knowledge—can be made part of a positive, constructive process of development, if we do it with consciousness of the Divine.

We go through life wanting, wanting, wanting to experience the nearness to Allah *(Subhaanahu wa ta'aalaa)*, out there, looking for fulfillment this way and that way, always facing disappointment—until finally, we break through to the other side. Finally, we awaken and realize that the Divine Presence is near. We detach ourselves from our fears, from our limited definitions of security in *dunyaa*, from our self-centered attitudes, from doubt, from feeling the world owes us something. We make Allah *(Subhaanahu wa ta'aalaa)* the center, accepting, submitting, and finding our peace and security in Islam; and in so doing, we transform all situations into opportunities to fulfill the soul's longing. When someone harms us, we draw near to Allah *(Subhaanahu wa ta'aalaa)* through forgiveness. When someone helps us, we draw near to Allah *(Subhaanahu wa ta'aalaa)* through gratitude. When we are misunderstood, we draw near to Allah *(Subhaanahu wa ta'aalaa)* through patience. When we are understood, we draw near to Allah *(Subhaanahu wa ta'aalaa)* through recognizing the source of the *hikmah* (wisdom).

Islam is the key to remembrance, and remembrance is the key to spiritual success, for it brings us to a state of continual, conscious tranquility in the presence of the Divine, no matter what else is happening in our lives.

According to a tradition,

> **Musa *('alayhi-s-salaam)* said, "O my Lord! Are You near, so that I may speak to You intimately, or are You far, so that I may call out to You?" God inspired to him, "I am sitting next to the one who remembers Me."**

When our heart is turned to Allah, when we fully concentrate on Allah, when we seek refuge in Allah—we establish a relationship with Allah *(Subhaanahu wa ta'aalaa)*. We whisper to Allah, pouring out our hearts to Allah, and Allah answers our call. When this *munaasabah*, this congenial relationship, is re-established with Allah *(Subhaanahu wa ta'aalaa)*, then we are imbued with a special kind of peace, and our eyes fill with tears of joy, and our ears hear His reply in our own language, in our own breath, in our own voice.

This is the experience that comes from Islam. This is the path through which longing finds completion.

> ***Yaa ayyatuha-n-nafsu-l-muṯma'innah, irjiᶜee ilaa Rabbiki raaḏiyatam-marḏiyyah.***
>
> **O soul at rest! Return to your Lord, well-pleased and well-pleasing [to Him]!** (Qur'an 89:27-28).

* * *

Wa-Llaahu lahu-l-ḫaqqi wa huwa yahdis-sabeel.
Ḫasbuna-Llaahu wahdahu wa niᶜmal-wakeel.
Wa ṣalli ᶜalaa Sayyidina Muhammadin wa aaalihi wa saḫbihi ajmaᶜeen.
wal-ḫamdu li-Llaahi Rabbi-l-ᶜaalameen.

Truth belongs to Allah; it is He who shows the way.
Allah, alone, suffices us, and what a fine guardian is He!
Blessings upon our Master Muhammad
and his family and Companions altogether
and praise is due to Allah, Lord of the Worlds.

بسم الله الرحمن الرحيم

The Journey of Surrender

Bismi-Llaah, Al-hamdu li-Llaah
Allaahumma salli wa sallim ʿalaa Sayyidinaa Muhammadin,
wa ʿalaa aalihi wa sahbih

Misconceptions of Surrender

The journey of surrender is, literally, the journey to Islam—for the Arabic word "Islam" itself means surrender. Allah *(Subhaanahu wa taʿaalaa)* reveals in Qur'an:

> ***Wa mañy-yabtaghi ghayra-l-islaami deenañ fa-lañy-yuqbala..., wa huwa fi-l-'aakhirati mina-l-khaasireen.***
>
> **If one seeks a religion other than the surrender [to Allah], it will not be accepted..., and one will be a loser in the Hereafter** (3:85).

Being told that surrender is the only way to success may pose a challenge. After all, "surrender" is a pejorative concept in the West, equated with weakness, loss of identity, failure, and insecurity.

Yet, surrender is part of all our daily lives. We surrender to our emotions, intellects, and mental and physical states. Often we seek out some thing or somebody to surrender to: a diet plan, a motivational or physical trainer, a doctor, therapist, lawyer, or life partner! Certainly, with given needs or symptoms, such "trust" is justifiable and even beneficial.

But these day-to-day modes of surrender differ from the submission required for spiritual growth. The difference between the two is a source of much confusion. Too often, people approach surrender to the Divine as if it were the latest diet or therapy: take it or leave it, stick to it or give it up, etc. As a result, they lose their sense of spiritual direction.

The ultimate surrender demands a different criteria. It comes from inner necessity, and requires the character that is developed through prayer, remembrance, selfless service and patience.

This is the surrender that liberates us. It frees us from the layers of unconscious behavior and semi-conscious responses—from the self-referencing, self-centered, self-protective elements that we interpose on our decisions and opinions, goals and relationships. In surrender to the Divine, we rediscover our true nature. The Prophet *(salla-Llaahu ʿalayhi wa sallam)* said,

> **Every child is born in *fitrah*** (in a state of essential goodness and submission) (Abu Hurayra/Bukhari).

We were born at peace, trusting in Allah *(Subhaanahu wa taʿaalaa)*, enjoying the security and safety of peace. No newborn ever asked, "Do I really want to be here? Do I have to submit to being fed by my mother?" Questions and doubts only arise later, in the course of growing up.

As we strive to bring forth our *fitrah*, we must learn to submit like the infant, but with the consciousness and maturity of adulthood. If we pursue this submission, we will fulfill our purpose in life. All else either supports or degrades this process.

Tasleem: Presenting Ourselves to Allah (Subhaanahu wa taʿaalaa)

Conscious surrender is described by the Arabic word *tasleem*, from the same root as "*islaam*." *Tasleem* means "handing over" or "presenting." It also means "greeting"; "concession"; "assent and approval." We see, then, that surrender involves coming forward, greeting, purposefully handing ourselves over to Allah *(Subhaanahu wa ta'aalaa)*—and then consenting to whatever Allah *(Subhaanahu wa ta'aalaa)* wishes for us.

This form of surrender is a very high state, because it is not forced. Allah *(Subhaanahu wa ta'aalaa)* says in the Qur'an: **"*laa ikraaha fi-d-deen* (there is no compelling in religion)"** (2:256). On the journey of *Tasawwuf*, nothing compels us to surrender but our own self. We willingly reconcile our thoughts, actions, and aspirations with Allah *(Subhaanahu wa ta'aalaa)*. We surrender not out of blind faith, but based on real faith: faith that has been struggled for and proven. We surrender because we understand ***"Rabbi innee dhalamtu nafsee, wa aslamtu*** **(O my Lord! Truly, I have wronged my soul; and I do [now] submit...)"** (Qur'an 27:44). We surrender because, in the midst of crises, we choose to submit; or because an undeniable moment of humility and gratitude overwhelms our minds and enlivens our hearts.

Surrendering to Love

Surrender becomes easy when we realize that our relationship with the Creator is one of love. We read in the Qur'an:

> ***...fa-sawfaya'ti-Llaahubi-qawmiñy-yuhibbuhum wa yuhibbuunahuu...***
>
> **...Allah will bring forward a people whom He loves, and who love Him...** (5:54).

Love is the consummate surrender. Love succumbs; love adjusts; love bears the burden. When the beloved calls, the lover forgets all else in the rush to respond.

No Beloved calls more sweetly than Allah *(Subḥaanahu wa taʿaalaa)*.

"Wa-Llaahu yadʿuu ilaa daari-s-salaam (Allah summons to the abode of peace)" (10:25), we are told in the Qur'an—and what an abode that is!— an abode of *salaam*, of safety, security, and well-being, where our soul becomes *saleem*: free, flawless, healthy, whole.

Are we responding to the call of the Beloved, or turning a deaf ear? One way to tell is by pausing now and then to ask a series of questions, like, "Why am I doing what I'm doing right now? Is it to serve myself...or someone else? Is it to get something... or to give? Is it feeding my anger and doubts...or refining my higher qualities?"

If we are not guided by clear parameters and forms, we will find ourselves acting haphazardly—sometimes for the good, sometimes not. If instead we embrace certain parameters, we will progress steadily along the path to fulfillment. For Allah *(Subḥaanahu wa taʿaalaa)* **"...yahdee mañy-yashaaa'u ilaa ṣiraaṭim-mustaqeem (...guides the one who wills [to be guided] onto a straight way)"** (Qur'an 10:25).

ACCEPTING THE PARAMETERS OF SUFIC-ISLAM

Have you ever said to someone you love: "Listen, there's some advice I'd like to offer that might help you be successful and happy"? This is the way Allah *(Subḥaanahu wa taʿaalaa)* loves us; and the gift of Allah's love is *shareeʿah*. *Ṭareeqah* also is the love of Allah *(Subḥaanahu wa taʿaalaa)*, saying, "For those of you who are selected and who select, here is a specific form and environment that will help you go deeper."

Becoming adept in applying the parameters of *shareeʿah* and *tareeqah* requires that we absorb them. We cannot just say, "I'm a Muslim; I'm a Sufi." We have to accept the teachings.

Unfortunately, as well-educated individuals, we want to understand something before we accept it. This is the opposite of the attitude needed for spiritual progress. If we insist on understanding *sharee'ah* and *tareeqah* before applying their guidance, we will never develop the tools to be able to understand them. Rather, we must accept first—knowing that certainty will grow as we begin to see through different eyes, from the core of the heart.

Mevlana Jalaladdin Rumi said:

> Whatever you wish to unite with, go absorb yourself in that Beloved....if you wish to find a way out of this ruined prison, don't turn your head away from the Beloved, but bow and worship and draw near.

We are part of a larger and longer story than the dramas of *dunyaa* that imprison us. If we refuse to surrender, we become victims of a life that feels incomplete. If instead we realize ***"Laa haula wa-laa quwwata ilaa bi-Llaah*** **(there is no power nor strength but in Allah** ***[Subhaanahu wa ta'aalaa]*****)"** (Qur'an 2:256) then we will discover meaning in our existence, and strength in our dependency.

Finding Confidence in Surrender

Sometimes when my three-year-old daughter is climbing out of the car, she says, "Daddy, take my hand. I can't do it by myself." Faced by a circumstance of helplessness, she turns towards trust. There is an honest appraisal that she cannot do it alone. Simultaneously, she has confidence that she can do it... with me. Confidence comes in the moment of surrender. Allah *(Subhaanahu wa ta'aalaa)* says,

> ***...mañy-yattaqi-Llaaha...yarzuqhu min haythu laa yahtasib.***
>
> **...who guards himself for Allah,...[Allah] provides for him from sources he could never imagine** (Qur'an 65:2-3).

By relying on Allah *(Subhaanahu wa ta'aalaa)*, by committing to and confiding in Him, by saying, "Okay, this is my life, and I give it," we become able to tap other resources of energy. We find sustenance, and grow, and expand our ability to give. We reach a stage where we can direct our prayers and energies towards a problem or need, and effect positive change. It is almost as if the design or flow of events starts to adjust to our good intentions. Why? Because, having accepted that we are not the doers, we have stopped rowing against the current. We are rowing with the current. We have relinquished our I-centered universe for a Thou-centered universe.

The Journey from "I" to "Thou"

"Knock, knock"—"Who is there?" goes the ancient Sufi story. "It is I." "Go away!" "Knock, knock"—"Who is there?" "It is Thou." "Come in!"

Through our practices, through our *adab*, through struggling to follow *sharee'ah* and *sunnah*, this self we call "I" takes its most fulfilling place: as the servant of the Divine Presence in every circumstance. How do we serve Allah *(Subhaanahu wa ta'aalaa)*? When compassion is needed, we give compassion. When forgiveness is needed, we forgive. When mercy is called for, we show mercy. When peace must be made, we make peace.

As we center our lives around love and effort, submission and trust, we open the doorway to a conscious relationship with Allah that never stops.

> **My servant continues to draw near to Me with supererogatory works so that I shall love him [or her]. When I love him [or her], I am the hearing with which he [or she] hears, the seeing with which he [or she] sees, the hand with which he [or she] strikes and the foot with which he [or she] walks** *(ḥadith qudsi).*

Note the prerequisite: to draw near to Allah, we must make our effort first. ***"Fa-dhkuruunee adhkurkum* (Remember Me and I will remember you),"** Allah *(Subḥaanahu wa taʿaalaa)* tells us in the Qur'an (2:152). We remember Allah when we praise Allah *(Subḥaanahu wa taʿaalaa)*, when we recite the Names of Allah *(Subḥaanahu wa taʿaalaa)*, when we sit in contemplation of Allah *(Subḥaanahu wa taʿaalaa)*, in *muraaqabah,* quieting the mind.

Indeed, until the mind becomes quiet, we really cannot surrender for more than brief moments, and we cannot see the long-term value of surrender.

We can quiet our minds and experience spiritual submission, peace, and security, with someone who is trained to help us do that, by studying the methods and drawing from the *madad* (assistance) of Allah *(Subḥaanahu wa taʿaalaa)*, the Prophet *(ṣalla-Llaahu ʿalayhi wa sallam)*, the *awliyaa'*, the *shuyukh,* our guides. We progress along the path of surrender in the company of those who have made greater progress than we—those who are the lovers of the Beloved.

The journey of surrender will take us up mountains and through valleys, across meadows and over oceans, even if we never leave the land where we were born. Eventually, the journey leads to the *dar-as-salaam*—the abode of peace—the security that is peace, the well-being that is peace, the reconciliation that is peace. As we were born in surrender and *salaam*, so too, *inshaa'a-Llaah*, we will return to surrender and *salaam*.

> ***Wa ud-khila-l-ladheena aamanuu wa ᶜamilu-s-saaliḫaati jannaatiñ tajree miñ taḫtiha-l-'anhaaru khaalideena feehaa bi'idhni Rabbihim; taḫiyyatuhum feehaa salaam.***
>
> **Those who had *imaan* (belief) and did right actions will be admitted into Gardens with rivers flowing under them, remaining in them timeless, forever, by the permission of their Lord. Their greeting there is "Peace!"** (Qur'an 14:23).

* * *

O Allah *(Subḫaanahu wa taᶜaalaa)*, grant that we may attain a high state of understanding, consciousness and purity, aware of our own helplessness and weaknesses as well as our strengths, and able to trust totally in Your power and strength. O Allah *(Subḫaanahu wa taᶜaalaa)*, enable me to accept, even when I do not understand with my mind; and help me change myself so that I may expand my understanding of the Truth.

Wa-Llaahu lahu-l-ḫaqqi wa huwa yahdis-sabeel.
Ḫasbuna-Llaahu wahdahu wa niᶜmal-wakeel.
Wa salli ᶜalaa Sayyidina Muhammadin
wa aaalihi wa saḫbihi ajmaᶜeen.
wal-ḫamdu li-Llaahi Rabbi-l-ᶜaalameen.

Truth belongs to Allah; it is He who shows the way.

Allah, alone, suffices us, and what a fine guardian is He!
Blessings upon our Master Muhammad
and his family and Companions altogether
and praise is due to Allah, Lord of the Worlds.

بسم الله الرحمن الرحيم

Iẖsaan: Being Present in the Divine Presence

Bismi-Llaah, Al-hamdu-li-Llaah
Allaahumma s̱alli wa sallim ʿalaa sayyidinaa Muẖammadin,
wa ʿalaa aalihi wa saẖbih.

Miʿraaj and Iẖsaan: Lessons in Seeing

In *Israa'* and *Miʿraaj*, we are told that Allah *(Subẖaanahu wa taʿaalaa)*:

> ***...asraa bi-ʿabdihee laylam-mina-l-masjidi-l-ẖaraamiilaa-l-masjidi-l-'aqs̱a-l-ladheebaaraknaa ẖawlahu li-nuriyahuu min aayaatinaa....***
>
> **...did take His servant for a journey by night from the Sacred Mosque to the Farthest Mosque, whose precincts We did bless in order that We might show him some of Our signs...** (Qur'an 17:1).

The Qur'an further narrates:

> ***Wa laqad ra'aahu nazlatan ukhraa, ʿiñda sidrati-l-muñtahaa; ʿiñdahaa jannatu-l-ma'waa, idh yagh-sha-s-sidrata maa yaghshaa. Maa zaagha-l-bas̱aru wa maa ṯaghaa, laqad ra'aa min aayaati Rabbihi-l-kubraa!***
>
> **For indeed he [the Prophet] saw him [Jibreel] at a second descent, near the Lote tree beyond which none may pass: near it is the Garden of**

> **Abode. Behold the Lote tree was shrouded [in mystery unspeakable!] [His] sight never swerved nor did it go wrong, for truly *did he see* of the signs of his Lord the greatest!** (53:13-18).

The experience of seeing lies at the core of *mi'raaj*. What kind of seeing? A kind that penetrates shrouds and mysteries without wavering—that penetrates the veils of human limitation to see "the greatest" of "the signs of [the] Lord." But with what did the Prophet *(salla-Llaahu 'alayhi wa sallam)* see these signs? With his physical eyes? Did he just see them, or was there an element of hearing, as well? According to a hadith, the Prophet *(salla-Llaahu 'alayhi wa sallam)* said that during the *mi'raaj*,

> **I was taken straight to an open place wherein I heard the sound of pens** (Karim 391).

Such hearing and vision surpass our comprehension. But as hard as it may be to fathom the experience of the *mi'raaj*, one lesson seems clear: in it, we find a model of coming to see in new ways, to observe and hear Allah's signs clearly, to overcome distractions and be fully present in the Presence of the Divine.

Being present in the Presence brings me to my topic: *ihsaan*. The definition of *ihsaan* (as you know) is given in the following *hadith*, known as *Hadith Jibreel*, narrated by 'Umar ibn al-Khattaab (*radiya-Llaahu 'anhu*):

> **One day while we were sitting with the Messenger of Allah (may the blessings and peace of Allah be upon him) there appeared before us a man whose clothes were exceedingly white and whose hair was**

exceedingly black; no signs of journeying were to be seen on him and none of us knew him. He walked up and sat down by the Prophet (may the blessings and peace of Allah be upon him). Resting his knees against his and placing the palms of his hands on his thighs, he said: "O Muhammad, tell me about Islam." The Messenger of Allah (may the blessings and peace of Allah be upon him) said: "Islam is to testify that there is no god but Allah and Muhammad is the Messenger of Allah, to perform the prayers, to pay the *zakat*, to fast in Ramadan and to make the pilgrimage to the House if you are able to do so." He said: "You have spoken rightly," and we were amazed at him asking him and saying that had spoken rightly.

He said: "Then tell me about *imaan*." He said: "It is to believe in Allah, His angels, His books, His messengers and the Last Day, and to believe in divine destiny, both the good and the evil thereof." He said: "You have spoken rightly."

He said: "Then tell me about *ihsaan*." He said: "It is to worship Allah as though you are seeing Him, and while you see Him not yet truly He sees you."

He said: "Then tell me about the Hour." He said: "The one questioned about it knows no better than the questioner." He said: "Then tell me about its signs." He said: "That the slave-girl will give birth to her mistress and that

> **you will see the barefooted, naked, destitute herdsmen competing in the construction of lofty buildings."**
>
> **Then he took himself off and I stayed for a time. Then he said: "O 'Umar, do you know who the questioner was?" I said: "Allah and His Messenger know best." He said: "It was Jibreel, who came to you to teach you your religion"** (an-Nawawi 28-32).

What is *ihsaan*? To strive to create a real and sustainable living consciousness of the presence of God in our lives—a consciousness so strong, so clear, so vivid, that when we live it, we feel as if we were actually seeing God.

Ihsaan (along with *imaan* and *islaam*) is an essential part of the *deen* (religion) of Islam, for the Prophet *(salla-Llaahu 'alayhi wa sallam)* said, **"...That was Jibreel, who came to teach you your *deen*."** Indeed, we might say that *ihsaan* is the pinnacle of the *deen*. It is the vertex or nodal point of Islam. How can we surrender, if we are unaware of the Divine Presence to which we are surrendering? *Ihsaan* is a catalytic agent that allows submission to come about. *Ihsaan* also deepens our *imaan* (faith). It is difficult to maintain faith if we have no sense of seeing or knowing Allah *(Subhaanahu wa ta'aalaa)*. On the other hand, once we have *ihsaan*, it becomes difficult not to have *imaan*.

So, we have to avoid settling into being contented with ourselves, when we could be doing more to develop *ihsaan*. A person whose life revolves around wealth always wants more—more money, more things. What about us—do we feel as urgent a need to experience Allah's Presence as that person feels to get rich? Do we really realize that in that Presence of God, there is peace, happiness, understanding, and love? We have to take this as seriously as if our boss walked into our office and said, "The company is in trouble, and you won't have a job tomorrow unless you go out today and generate a lot of business for us."

After all, what could be more important than developing a living consciousness of Allah *(Subhaanahu wa ta'aalaa)* moment to moment—a consciousness so strong and so clear, it is as if one is actually seeing God? Not "as if" with a question mark. "As if" with a bond of attachment and loyalty to God that sweeps away every trace of doubt, every modicum of uncertainty.

Allah *(Subhaanahu wa ta'aalaa)* does not tell us that we have to be an *'alim*. He does not tell us we have to be a *hafiz*. He does not say we have to be a *shaykh* or an *ustadh*. Instead, Allah *(Subhaanahu wa ta'aalaa)* tells us that we can be and should be people who pursue insight. Allah *(Subhaanahu wa ta'aalaa)* tells us that the only thing He wants from us is to know Him.

> ***Fa-dhkuruunee adhkurkum...***
>
> **Remember Me, and I will remember you...** (Qur'an 2:152).
>
> ***Wa idhaa sa'alaka 'ibaadee 'annee fa-innee qareeb...***
>
> **And when My servants ask you concerning Me, then verily I am near...** (Qur'an 2:186).

It is said that during the *mi'raaj*, when the Prophet Muhammad *(salla-Llaahu 'alayhi wa sallam)* ascended to the highest heaven, Allah *(Subhaanahu wa ta'aalaa)* showed him an endless line of humanity, walking from the beginning of time. The Prophet *(salla-Llaahu 'alayhi wa sallam)* was told, "This is humankind. From the first moment to the last minute of creation, there have been and always will be human beings in this endless line, passing in front of Allah." These are all the souls, each soul in existence long before its physical body, each existing in the Presence and the Light of Allah *(Subhaanahu wa ta'aalaa)* from the beginning of time.

Allah *(Subhaanahu wa ta'aalaa)* asks in the Qur'an,

> ***Hal ataa 'ala-l-'iñsaani heenum-mina-d-dahri lam yakuñ shay'am-madh-kuuraa?***
>
> **Has there ever come upon a person any period of time in which he was a thing unremembered?** (76:1).

There never was a time in which we could not be remembered. We were always in the "mind" of the Creator. We were not even in the minds of our own parents before we were conceived, but we were in the "mind" of the Divine.

Allah *(Subhaanahu wa ta'aalaa)* has always been aware of us. Through *ihsaan*, we strive to become aware of Allah *(Subhaanahu wa ta'aalaa)* being aware of us.

How are we to do this?

"As If"

Part of the answer lies in a small Arabic phrase in the *Hadith Jibreel: "ka-anna." Ka-anna* means "as if," and it comes midway through the first part of the definition of *ihsaan*: ***"an ta'a'buda-Llaaha ka-annaka taraahu…*** **(Worship Allah as if you were seeing Him….)"**

This "as if" has significant implications. Obviously, we cannot literally "see" Allah *(Subhaanahu wa ta'aalaa)* with our eyes in this world. Even the Prophet *(salla-Llaahu 'alayhi wa sallam)* is described as having seen the signs of Allah *(Subhaanahu wa ta'aalaa)*. Nowhere does the Qur'an say he saw Allah *(Subhaanahu wa ta'aalaa)* directly. We, too, may aspire to see at least some of the signs of our Creator—and, having recognized them, to worship Him with the assumption, with the thought, that He is within our range of vision, although not visible to our outer eyes.

More than the thought, we must have the feeling of Allah's Presence. The Sufis say that we have eyes in our hearts. Our capacity to see through those eyes increases as we allow love to grow between ourselves and God, and between ourselves and one another. Through the eyes of the heart, through love, we respond differently to the world than we respond when we are acting only through the intellect, through reason, or through our normal emotional reactions. Our ability to be aware of the Presence of Allah *(Subhaanahu wa ta'aalaa)*, moment to moment, has to do with our heart and with how we feel toward Allah *(Subhaanahu wa ta'aalaa)* and His creation. To have one's external life totally suffused by the internal feeling *as if* we are seeing God: this is the goal.

"If Not"

But as we all know, feelings can be tricky. We cannot just say, "I think I'll love so-and-so now," and instantly fall in love. Nor can we say, "Starting this instant, I am going to continually feel as if I am seeing Allah."

Fortunately, the *Hadith Jibreel* seems to anticipate this challenge by adding a second part to the definition of *ihsaan*. We are guided to worship Allah *as if* we were seeing Him, but we are also given a back-up plan: ***"fa in lam takun taraahu fa-innahu yaraak* (if not, know that He is seeing you)."**

If the first part of the definition were possible for everyone, there would be no need for the phrase *"fa in lam"* (meaning, "if [you do] not") between the first and second parts. *"Fa in lam"* tells us that we might not feel as if we are seeing Allah *(Subhaanahu wa ta'aalaa)*. It also assures us that we should be able to at least have the thought that God is seeing us.

We cannot force ourselves to be in the state of *ihsaan*, but we can practice the things that make that state come forward. Through *dhikru-Llaah* and *tafakkur* (remembrance and contemplation), we can become more aware of the vital, living Reality of Allah's Presence in every moment. Especially important is *muraaqabah*.

Although *muraaqabah* sometimes refers to Sufic meditation, it is not just sitting on the floor, closing one's eyes and making recitations. The Arabic root "*raqaba*" literally means to watch, to pay attention, to be alert and vigilant. *Muraaqabah* refers to actively paying attention to the Divine Presence. In *muraaqabah* we sit...thinking that we are in the Presence of Allah *(Subhaanahu wa ta'aalaa)*, and Allah *(Subhaanahu wa ta'aalaa)* is with us...we love Him, and He loves us...wherever we look internally, He is there...in whatever is happening, He is present.

When you go to an optician for an eye exam, he or she starts clicking different lenses in front of your eyes to find out how you see best. When the right lenses are aligned correctly, you see clearly. Analogously, within us there are lenses—called the *lataa'if*—which can be and need to be aligned in the most efficacious way for us to experience *ihsaan*. Not only do they need to be aligned, but we need to learn how to perceive (to pay attention) through them.

We have within us a unique organ of perception with which we are familiar: our heart. If our heart—center of both our physical being and our spiritual being—attains its optimal potential, we become aware of both the *dhaahir* and the *baatin* (the seen and the unseen). Outwardly, our heart is not only physically linked to our emotional center, but it also supports the intellect and allows us to reflect upon ourselves. As a result, our insight is deepened. When our heart, *qalb,* is nurtured by our *muraaqabah*, by our *du'aa*, by our *dhikr*—in an environment that is not overly attached to worldly matters or things—then it will begin to turn (*qalaba*) naturally toward Allah *(Subhaanahu wa ta'aalaa)*. Like a mirror, it will reflect the "Truth." It will move to the state of *mushaahadah* (witnessing), and we will begin to witness what is really true. What is a witness? Someone who is able to testify regarding an event. If we really aspire to believe (to have *imaan*), if we really want to submit in *Islam*, then we need to develop the ability to witness.

We align the *qalb* and our other *lataa'if* through *muraaqabah* and the transmissions directed to us by our shaykhs. The more we polish and focus these inner lenses, the more we come to "worship Allah as if [we were] seeing Him." Our spiritual practices unlock the doors and allow the Divine Presence to be seen. They are not just techniques, but experiences, passageways, moments to extend in our lives, places where we would like to be within ourselves all the time, on our inner journey or *sayr-i anfus*, and that we would like to manifest on our outer journey, the *sayr-i aafaaq*.

Two kinds of distractions interfere with our awareness of the Creator. First are distractions of the external world that attract our interest, occupy our attention, and cause us to forget God. Such distractions are related to the self (*nafs*). Second are distractions that come from within us and are associated with the heart (*qalb*). To draw nearer to God, we must become free of both outer and inner distractions.

In a sense, I am speaking about achieving the *maqaam* (station) of *firaasa.* The root of *firaasa* is *farasa*, which means (among other things) "to tear or to scrutinize"; accordingly, *firaasa* is variously defined as perspicacity, acumen, discrimination, or minute observation. Spiritually speaking, it connotes "insight or intuitive perception [or] the…discernment of the internal, inward, or intrinsic state, condition, character or circumstances, by the eye (or by the examination of outward indications)." It may also refer to "a faculty which God puts into the minds of His favorites, in consequence whereof they know the states, conditions, or circumstances, of certain [people]…or the discovery of an internal quality in a [person] by right insight" (Lane 2308).

The Prophet *(salla-Llaahu 'alayhi wa sallam)* said,

> ***Ittaqu firaasata al-mu'min, fa-innahu yan<u>dh</u>uru bi-nuur-i-Llah.***
>
> **Beware of the *firaasa* of the believer, for he sees with the light of Allah** (Tirmidhi).

Beware—does that mean to be afraid? Watch out? Be - aware. *Ittaqu* comes from the same root as *taqwah.* Be aware of the sight of those who believe, who see with the eyes of piety, for they have torn away the veil of distraction and illusion ("to tear" is the first meaning of *farasa*). They see with what the fourteenth-century scholar Ibn Qayyim al-Jawziyyah called, "a light which Allah *(Sub<u>h</u>aanahu wa ta'aalaa)* deposits in the heart of His servant. By this light, the servant distinguishes between truth and falsehood and between right and wrong." The reality of *firaasa* is a thought that dominates our point of view, and overwhelms the heart. Perhaps we could call it the love of the enlightened heart: the *ma'iyat-i-<u>h</u>ubbi* (accompaniment with love). *Firaasa* is seeing things as they really are, with a pure heart and an uplifted *ruu<u>h</u>.*

When we have *firaasa*, then when we see something beautiful, there is an immediate connection between our eyes and our heart. We feel the magnificence of what we are witnessing. Think of how we feel when we look at a baby: so sweet and innocent, with eyes wide open, gazing at us, drinking in the moment and us along with it. *As if (ka-anna)* we are looking into the purity of Allah's own being through those innocent eyes. When we look with a gaze that has been refined through meditation, through study, through humility in prayer, then what appears before our eyes automatically touches our heart. Instantly our heart expands. This gift of Allah *(Subhaanahu wa ta'aalaa)* is so pure, so clear, that there is no question that we are in the presence of something miraculous.

Ihsaan is like the "Midas touch" that turns everything to gold, except in this case, it turns everything to light. What are we seeing in the face of the child? Light. How do we know? Because it enlightens us. It awakens us. It focuses us. It does not just make us feel good; it puts a special kind of light in our hearts. That light is the awareness of the Presence of Allah *(Subhaanahu wa ta'aalaa)*.

It is interesting to note that according to the hadith, Jibreel *('alayhi-s-salaam)* did not respond to the Prophet's *(salla-Llaahu 'alayhi wa sallam)* definition of *ihsaan*. He responded to *islaam* and *imaan*, but not *ihsaan*. Why not? One possibility is that the angels have no knowledge of *ihsaan*. Maybe human beings alone have been gifted with that state. Perhaps *ihsaan* can only be achieved through life in *dunyaa*; perhaps physical existence plays a critical role in learning to reflect upon the Presence of Allah *(Subhaanahu wa ta'aalaa)*; that in fact, the goal of *ihsaan* may only be achievable by human beings through life. *Ihsaan* is more than just paying attention to God. It is being so aware of God's Presence that whatever we experience, whatever we see, is a sign—a switch that turns on our remembrance (*dhikr*)—or perhaps a thorn that pricks us and wakes us up.

To actively interface with Allah's creation is a form of dialoguing with Allah *(Subhaanahu wa ta'aalaa)*. Have you ever been with a child outside, when they see some flowers, and suddenly the questions start: "Why are the flowers yellow? Who made the flowers? Why? Why does this flower have thorns, when that one doesn't? Why are some tall and some short? Why do some bloom now and some at other times?" *Inshaa'a-Llaah* we try to encourage that: we say, "Oh, look at that color! Look at these petals!...," trying to train the children in a certain way, so that they will continue to see life in that way. That is a way of looking that will reveal the *jamaal* and the *jalaal* of Allah *(Subhaanahu wa ta'aalaa)*—the beauty and the majesty of Allah *(Subhaanahu wa ta'aalaa)*. That way of looking brings us to the awareness of the Presence of Allah *(Subhaanahu wa ta'aalaa)*—to Islam based not on dogma, not on doctrine, not even technically on scripture, but on the Reality of the Presence of Allah *(Subhaanahu wa ta'aalaa)* in our lives—the Reality from which all the doctrines and teachings are derived.

"Seeing is believing," we say. This we have just spoken about in detail, but there is also the concept of being present; in the moment free of all else but that moment. The Sufi has been called "the slave of the moment." This means that he or she is always aware of the Real, of Allah *(Subhaanahu wa ta'aalaa)*, and is always recognizing what the Real has provided in that moment. Nothing impinges on that circumstance. When we see that the moment we are in was given to us by that which alone is Real, Who has brought us to that moment and brought that moment to us—it is like waking from a deep sleep. Our ordinary perceptions are supplanted by another way of perceiving.

Effects of Ihsaan on Our Outer Actions

This change in our inner capacity to see has an important corollary in our outer lives.

When we realize that something overwhelmingly beautiful is before our gaze—we start to think, "O my God, what a responsibility!" Let's go back to the experience with the baby. Suddenly we realize, "I have to protect this child," or "I have to raise this child properly." These derivative thoughts and feelings arise in that moment. We look at the child and see past the superficialities of the situation, into the future—not a theoretical future, but a future that we are building, here and now. We start to think, "O Allah *(Subhaanahu wa ta'aalaa)*, O You Who have placed me here, O You Who have created this child, please help me to mold her according to Your instructions. How can I understand Your instructions more clearly? How might I interpret them better?" Through *ihsaan*, we experience the overwhelming position in which we have been placed. We begin to reflect on the capabilities Allah *(Subhaanahu wa ta'aalaa)* has given us, and we become inspired to constantly search for better ways to be.

Once we have a sense of the love with which this world is created, and a sense of respect for everything in creation, we become more aware of how we are.

After all, Who is watching? *HU* is watching. One of the Ninety-Nine Beautiful Names of Allah *(Subhaanahu wa ta'aalaa)* is *ar-Raqeeb*: the Source of all regulating, all monitoring. Allah *(Subhaanahu wa ta'aalaa)* says in the Qur'an,

> ***...inna-Llaaha kaana ᶜalaykum raqeebaa.***
>
> **...verily, Allah ever watches over you** (4:1).

He also tells us,

> ***...maa yalfidhu miñ qawlin illaa ladayhi Raqeebun ᶜateed.***

> **...not a single word does [a person] utter but there is a Watcher, ready** (Qur'an 50:18).

In *ihsaan* we become aware of Allah *(Subhaanahu wa ta'aalaa)* as the One Who engages in *raqaba*—Who observes and watches. From where is Allah *(Subhaanahu wa ta'aalaa)* seeing us? Think about it. If Allah *(Subhaanahu wa ta'aalaa)* is present everywhere, then Allah *(Subhaanahu wa ta'aalaa)* is seeing us from everywhere. He sees us from the person standing in front of us. He sees us from the flowers before us. He sees us from the person who we do not see, who is behind us. He sees us from the computer monitor. He is seeing us through His creation. In that sense, I think it is Islamically correct to say that Allah *(Subhaanahu wa ta'aalaa)* is omnipresent. Not like a big cloud that is everywhere, but rather in the sense that He is a part of everything He has created, and His Consciousness permeates all that exists.

Now, extrapolate the derivatives from that. How do you want people to see you? How do you want to appear to other individuals? How would you like them to describe you?

The more we think in this way, the more we begin to watch our own self intently, because we know that in everyone and everything, we are being observed. On the simplest level, we are more motivated to refrain from wrong actions. The promptings of the lower self lose much of their charm when we realize *ar-Raqeeb* is watching.

On another level, we become aware that our eyes may not always perceive correctly, and our ears may not always hear correctly, and our mind may not always understand correctly. At some point in our lives, we may have had a tendency to assume that we were seeing, hearing, and understanding the reality of situations. Now we realize that we need to polish our self—to work on purification (*tazkiyah*)—before we can assume our perceptions are accurate. We need to engage in *muhaasabah*, the process of self-assessment encouraged by the Messenger of Allah *(salla-Llaahu 'alayhi wa sallam)*:

> ***Haasibuu anfusakum qabla an tuhaasabuu wa zinuu a'maalakum qabla an tuzanuu 'alaykum.***
>
> **Account for yourselves before you are accounted; weigh your actions before your actions become a weight upon you.** [1]

Muhaasabah is a way of rubbing our inner eye, which in turn will rub our inner "I." It is part of the process of breaching the wall that stands between the Truth which we could potentially be witnessing, and the way we usually see and interpret reality, filtered through our personality, our culture, our habits, our desires.

In a way, I advocate being old fashioned: in this case, returning to manual from automatic. We live in a world that has made everything automatic. When was the last time any of us used a camera that required us to set the F-stop, or to know anything about parallax? We like our point-and-shoot cameras. So, too, many of us like to live a good part of our lives without needing to think, reflect, adjust our focus, or change our lenses. As a result, we end up with empty spaces in our lives: spaces where instead of being conscious and aware of the Presence of Allah, we are just coasting along, on automatic.

We have a daily experience of seeing our physical self that can provide a metaphor to help us understand the attentiveness necessary to develop *ihsaan* (assuming, of course, that that we all look in a mirror at least once a day). There are three ways you can look in a mirror. You can study the mirror itself: "Here is a piece of glass with silver on the back of it." Or, you can look at yourself in the mirror. Finally, you can look at yourself looking at yourself in the mirror. The material world is a mirror, and we can train ourselves to recognize that it reflects the essential Truth of Allah *(Subhaanahu wa ta'aalaa)* seeing us seeing us. Then the *raqeeb* within us—the one who monitors the errors and regulates us internally—is attained. In other words, we attain a state of real consciousness.

This state of consciousness accompanies us on our journey through life. Typically we think of companionship in terms of other people, but we also have an inner companion or *qareen*: from the root *qarana* (to connect, join, unite, couple, bind together). In the Qur'an, Allah *(Subhaanahu wa ta'aalaa)* says that in the Afterlife,

> ***...wa qaala qareenuhuu, haadhaa maa ladayya ʿateed.***
>
> **...and his companion will say, "Here is my testimony, ready with me"** (50:23).

That inner companion reveals the record of our deeds and experiences to Allah *(Subhaanahu wa ta'aalaa)*. Who is that companion? It is the essential truth that is our self at any given moment—the seer, the seeing, and what is seen—the *shaheed*, the *mushaahadah*, the *mash-huud*.

We exist for two reasons: internally, to create harmony and attunement with Allah *(Subhaanahu wa ta'aalaa)*, in praise of Allah *(Subhaanahu wa ta'aalaa)*; and externally, to help to create harmony and attunement among people and creatures in this earth. We take this body in order to fulfill our destiny, which is for our spirit to ascend and come near to its Creator, like the Prophet *(salla-Llaahu 'alayhi wa sallam)* did during the *miʿraaj*. A critical means for ascending lies in fulfilling our responsibilities as Muslims to care for other human beings. If we lose track of our purpose, if we lose our center, if we are not cognizant of the difficulties facing those around us and the issues of our times, if we make no effort to address those difficulties, then we are not going to be able to dialogue with Allah *(Subhaanahu wa ta'aalaa)*. We are not able to allow the derivative to take place when our gaze falls on something beautiful, or on something no longer beautiful and we see how beautiful it is and should be. We are not going to realize that whatever we have is a gift from Allah *(Subhaanahu wa ta'aalaa)*. How, then, could we possibly know how to operate it correctly?

Tasawwuf is not just an inner process. Our realizations in the inner (the *baatin)* should find expression in the outer (the *dhaahir*). *Tasawwuf* runs through anything, if we let it. It runs through nothing if we keep it out.

If we want to understand and be in the Presence of Allah *(Subhaanahu wa ta'aalaa)*, if we want to practice *ihsaan* and thereby deepen our *imaan* and Islam—our faith and our submission, peace, and security—then we must pay attention. We must pay attention to our *lataa'if*, and look through the optical lenses of those *lataa'if* inwardly and outwardly. We have to pay attention to the teachings, to our teachers, to our work, the way we speak, the way we act, the way we portray ourselves. If we want to live as if we were seeing Allah *(Subhaanahu wa ta'aalaa)*, and know that Allah *(Subhaanahu wa ta'aalaa)* is seeing us, then we need to work at our meditation and to try consciously to translate our meditation, our recitations, our study into the tone of our voice, the intentions behind our thoughts, the meaning of our words, the way we listen, the way we verify what we hear. We have to keep reading Qur'an, keep making *muraaqabah*, keep making *du'aa*. We have to use the correct language, and correct ourselves when our language is incorrect. We go beyond saying, "I have to have the right *adab*," to actively nurturing the good *adab*. Constantly, we are drinking from the well, so that we will not become spiritually dehydrated. So, we must make a schedule for sitting in *muraaqabah*, we must set aside time to read the Qur'an, we must make more *du'aa*. We have to go even deeper than that. We have to refine our attitudes and affects, too: how we speak to other people, how we greet a person with love and affection, how we say goodbye, how we do our work. Who among us can claim perfection in even these basic things?

When we are seeing God more and more in our lives, because we are reflecting more and more, we deepen our understanding of what it means to live *fee sabeeli-Llaah*: in the way of Allah *(Subhaanahu wa ta'aalaa)*. We start to act totally and completely in the way of Allah *(Subhaanahu wa ta'aalaa)*. No matter what happens, immediately—*immediately*—God is present. Immediately a *du'aa* rises to our lips from our heart. There is thanks. There is gratitude, without hesitation. It is as seamless as the meeting of our in-breath and our out-breath. All the external acts of love and friendship, social dealings, business transactions, even enmity, anger, and disagreement, all are carried out for His sake, not for ours.

The Prophet *(salla-Llaahu 'alayhi wa sallam)* spoke of:

> **...a person whose state may be that when he loves, he loves for the sake of Allah. When he hates, he hates for the sake of Allah. When he withholds his hand from giving, he withholds it for the sake of Allah. And he has attained perfection in his faith** (Tirmidhi/Abu Dawood).

Allah *(Subhaanahu wa ta'aalaa)* tells us in a *hadith qudsi*:

> **...My servants continue to draw near to Me with supererogatory works so that I shall love them. When I love them, I am the ears with which they hear, the eyes with which they see,**

the hands with which they strike, and the feet with which they walk.

The aim of life is not to go through some long struggle to find a moment of contentment. Contentment is always there for us, for Allah *(Subhaanahu wa ta'aalaa)* is as near to us as our jugular vein. Finding fulfillment and contentment, being happy, being at peace: these are not the ultimate goals of life. They are readily available to us if we just go through the steps; if we do what we have been given to do. Contentment and fulfillment are easy to attain when we have love in our hearts, when we are serving Allah *(Subhaanahu wa ta'aalaa)*, when we aspire to serve Allah *(Subhaanahu wa ta'aalaa)* better by deepening our service to His creatures and by turning everything into *'ibaadah* (worship).

We need to strive with all our hearts and all our minds to come to that place where the spaces in our lives are filled; where we are never more than a thought away from Allah *(Subhaanahu wa ta'aalaa)*; where we are so accepting of Allah's nearness that our thoughts and words naturally lead directly to Him. We have swept away all doubt and uncertainty. Then we can have acceptance and contentment with what He is giving us, and we can really begin to appreciate our lives and our existence, our roles, our responsibilities, our gains, and our losses, with contentment and fulfillment.

Pilgrim, stop this useless wandering.
Stay awhile and listen to the sound of your own heart's call.
See the moment's beauty,
The diamond stars garlanding the sky.
O blind one, see.
Awaken to My Presence
Everywhere.

My window is open to invite your entry on the breeze.

My eyes and ears turn inward to search the worlds within.
I wait for night and silence,
and still you pass me by.
I have heard your footsteps on the path
and called your name aloud,
but still you passed me by.
Tomorrow my window will be open again,
my eyes and ears turned inward.
And I will listen once more for you
upon the inner road.

In closing, let us draw inspiration from the journey of *mi'raaj* and the possibilities of *i<u>h</u>saan*, keeping in mind that Allah has promised in a *<u>h</u>adith qudsi*:

> **I have prepared for My righteous servants what no eye has seen and no ear has heard, nor has it occurred to the human heart. Thus recite if you wish: "And no soul knows what joy for them has been kept hidden"** (Qur'an 32:17).

* * *

Wa-Llaahu lahu-l-haqqu wa huwa yahdi-s-sabeel.
<u>H</u>asbuna-Llaahu wahdahu, wa ni'mal-wakeel.
Wa <u>s</u>alli 'alaa sayyidina Mu<u>h</u>ammadin
wa aalihi wa sa<u>h</u>bihi ajma'een
wa-l-<u>h</u>amdu li-Llaahi rabb i-l-'aalameen.

Truth belongs to Allah; it is He who shows the way.
Allah, alone, suffices us, and what a fine guardian is He!
Blessings upon our Master Muhammad
and his family and companions altogether
and praise is due to Allah, Lord of the Worlds.

Notes

1 The statement which begins "Account for yourselves before you are taken into account…" is usually attributed to the companion of the Prophet *(ṣalla-Llaahu ʿalayhi wa sallam)* and later imam Umar Ibn Khattab *(raḏiya-Llaahu ʿanhu)*, as Imam Ghazali indicates in his book Ihya 'Ulum ad-Din. Although it lacks a clear chain or transmission, by tradition many Sufis and scholars have attributed the saying and/or the wisdom behind it to the Prophet *(ṣalla-Llaahu ʿalayhi wa sallam).*

References

Karim, Fazlul. *Al-Hadis: An English Translation and Commentary of "Mishkat-ul-Masabih."* Vol. IV. Lahore: The Book House, undated.

Lane, Edward W. *Arabic-English Lexicon, Part 6*. Libraire du Liban, Beirut, Lebanon, 1968

An-Nawawi. *Forty Hadith*. Translated by Ezzeddin Ibrahim and Denys Johnson-Davies. Beirut: The Holy Koran Publishing House, 1976.

al-Jawziyyah, Ibn Qayyim. "The Station of Firasah." Excerpt from *The Steps of the Followers*. Online at http://www.alinaam.org.za/LIBRARY/firasah.htm. Accessed 18 October 2002.

"The Reality of Tasawwuf and Ihsaan." Fordsburg, South Africa: Jamiatul Ulama Transvaal. Online at http:/ww.islamsa.org.za/library/pamphlets/reality_of_tasawwuf_and_ihsaan.htm. Accessed September 2002.

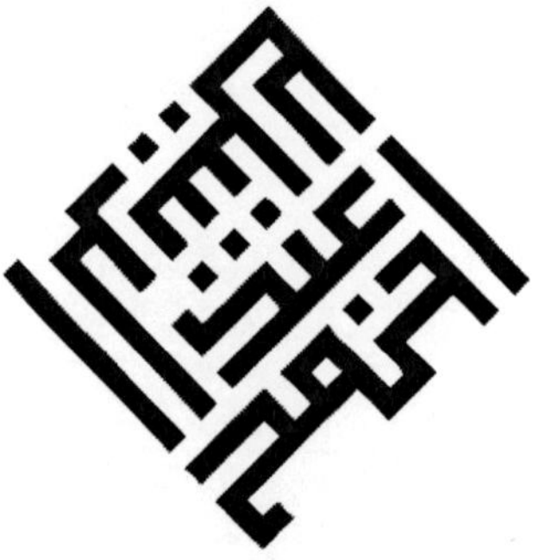

بسم الله الرحمن الرحيم

Relying on the Love and Mercy of Allah

Bismi-Llaahi-r-Rah̲maani-r-Rah̲eem

Al-h̲amdu-li-Llaahi, muqaliba-l-quluubi wa-l-abs̲aar.
Allaahumma thabit quluubana ʿalaa s̲iraat̲ika-l-qaweem,
Wa-jʿalnaa li-wajhika muttajiheen,
wa s̲alli ʿalaa-sh-shafeeʿi-l-h̲abeeb,
rah̲mati-l-ʿaalameen,
wa manaari-l-najiyeen, wa marsaa-l-ʿaarifeen

Praise be to Allah, the turner of the hearts and sight.
O Allah, fix our hearts on the best of Your ways,
and make us face You in our way,
and bestow blessings on the beloved intercessor,
the mercy of all the worlds,
the lighthouse of the survivors, the harbor of the knowers.

Bismi-Llaah, Al-h̲amdu-li-Llaah
Allaahumma s̲alli wa sallim ʿalaa Sayyidinaa Muh̲ammadin,
wa ʿalaa aaalihi wa sah̲bih

My topic today is the need for the Love and Mercy of Allah *(Subh̲aanahu wa taʿaalaa)* as it comes through the Prophet *(s̲alla-Llaahu ʿalayhi wa sallam)*, and about the process whereby one recognizes, responds to, and benefits from that love and mercy. My central theme is that we become aware of the ever-flowing mercy and love of the Prophet *(s̲alla-Llaahu ʿalayhi wa sallam)* through the process of responding to the intention and the call of Allah *(Subh̲aanahu wa taʿaalaa)* to become *muraad*—to align ourselves with Allah's design and purpose—and through the process of being *mureeduun* (those who aspire to draw near to Allah *(Subhaanahu wa ta'aalaa)*, Who is the ultimate *Muraad)*.

In every generation, Allah *(Subhaanahu wa ta'aalaa)* has called to human beings. Today is no different than in the past—except that today, individuals' responses to this call (or failures to respond) may have global repercussions. We have seen, for example, the rising forces of evil and of exclusivity—whether coming from Muslims themselves in their attacks on the People of the Book or on different sects within Islam, or from ideological aggressors outside of Islam, who have their own political, social, economic, or religious agendas. We have witnessed the effects of arrogance, hegemony, and empire-building, on the one hand, and of sectarianism and extreme religious ideologues among segments of the Christian, Jewish, Muslim, and Hindu populations, on the other.

Allah *(Subhaanahu wa ta'aalaa)* reveals in the Qur'an:

> ***Inna-Llaaha laa yughayyiru maa bi-qawmin hattaa yughayyiruu maa bi-anfusihim.***
>
> **Verily, God does not change [a] people's condition unless they change their own inner selves** (13:11).

But dare we hope for such change, when most people seem satisfied with submitting to the will of political leaders, self-proclaimed religious spokespersons, or the conclusions offered by media commentators? The average person is passive when it comes to social action or sustaining the principles of democratic pluralism, civil liberty, or spiritual freedom—and if not passive, then passive-aggressive and opportunistic. Consequently, people and nations find themselves controlled, even deceived, by the power agendas of the few who carefully promote a status quo mentality while undermining the freedom and the rights of the people themselves as guaranteed by Allah *(Subhaanahu wa ta'aalaa)* and by law.

I have given many lectures on democracy, Islam, and extremism in the past few years, and I would be happy to share my thoughts on those topics at another time. But on the occasion of the birthday of the Prophet *(salla-Llaahu 'alayhi wa sallam)*, I do not want to focus on these issues, but rather to mention them as a backdrop against which to consider the Prophet's role in terms of *araada* (to will or aim)—to respond to this call by coming to understand (to the extent that we are able) the will of Allah *(Subhaanahu wa ta'aalaa)*, the purpose of life, and the direction we are urged to move in. This is a discussion of seeking and being sought, and of ways of directing our will and our actions toward the one and only lasting goal: that of responding to the call of Allah *(Subhaanahu wa ta'aalaa)*.

> ***Wa idhaa sa'alaka ᶜibaadee ᶜannee fa-innee qareeb. Ujeebu daᶜwata-d-daaᶜi idhaa daᶜaani fa-l-yastajeebuu lee wa-l-yu'minuu bee laᶜallahum yarshuduun.***
>
> **When my servants question you about Me, tell them that I am near. I answer the call of every supplicant when he calls Me; therefore, they should respond to Me and put their trust in Me, so that they may be rightly guided** (Qur'an 2:186).

We sometimes might wonder if Allah's call is at risk of being drowned out by the din of modern communications technologies. Last week, I heard someone call into a talk-radio program to say that the reason the United States today has so many problems is that, instead of being taught to respond effectively and swiftly, Americans have been taught to be patient and tolerant. Our educational system has been subverted by a liberal conspiracy to make us all patient and tolerant, which translates into pacifism, which (to this caller) meant passivity. The ultra-conservative talk show host said, "You're absolutely right." That's the message of this day and age. "Stop being tolerant, and don't let anyone push you around."

Here we are, thinking that the strength of our *deen*, our religion, lies in *"Bismi-Llaahi-r-Rahmaani-r-Raheem"*—in compassion and mercy—in patience, tolerance, forgiveness, and understanding. We read in the Qur'an,

> ***Quli-dᶜu-Llaaha awi-d-ᶜu-r-Rahmaan; ayyam-maa tadᶜuu fa-lahu-l-'asmaaa'u-l-husnaa.***
>
> **Say: "Call upon Allah or call upon Rahman (the Merciful); by whatever name you call upon Him, to Him belong the Most Beautiful Names"** (17:110).

We are taught that **"every person is born in *fitrah*,"** as the Prophet *(salla-Llaahu ᶜalayhi wa sallam)* said—and so we think that most people naturally sense that it is right to be patient, tolerant, and forgiving. We try to convince non-Muslims that Islam is beneficial because it values patience and tolerance. But the message society wants to hear is changing. There are calls to "Crush the bullies" and to "Beat the enemy, because that's what a strong person or nation does." Even in local churches in rural Virginia, some preachers now are saying that Jesus was a warrior, not a peacemaker. This is a shift back to the attitudes of the Crusades, based on the saying attributed to Jesus: "Think not that I am come to send peace on earth: I came not to send peace, but a sword" (Matthew 10:34). If we were to put this forward about the Prophet Muhammad *(salla-Llaahu ᶜalayhi wa sallam)*, how much more would we be accused of? Are we being forced into defensive positions, or can we mobilize moderate Muslims, Christians, and Jews to counteract those who preach aggression in the name of religion?

I believe we can and must do the latter. We have a responsibility to live up to Allah's description of Muslims as an *ummata-wasata*—a community of the middle way as exemplified by our Prophet *(salla-Llaahu ʿalayhi wa sallam)* and his family and companions.

To find a path of moderation, mutual respect, and co-existence demands that people be educated to their true role in human society—that they recognize the reason that Allah *(Subhaanahu wa taʿaalaa)* created human beings, and are able to take this brief sojourn on earth to become aware of God's Divine Presence, to make their lives *ʿibaadah*, and to understand the real meaning of being a seeker of the Truth, a *mureed* or *mureeda*—one who seeks out knowledge or understanding of the inner world, who has a deep desire to serve Allah *(Subhaanahu wa taʿaalaa)* and His Creation and to develop the ultimate awareness of the Presence of God in every moment.

There are those who believe that life would be simpler if our relationship to Allah *(Subhaanahu wa taʿaalaa)* was, "God is over there somewhere. I worship God by doing my prayers, and that's it." Wouldn't it be easier not to think about worshiping God by serving others, or by refining oneself, or by questioning one's own intentions, or by accounting for one's actions? No. This is not ease; it is the cloud of ignorance and the fog of self-deception. It is an attitude that sentences us to live out our lives with the vague feeling that something is missing—that we can spend years making money, raising children, having pleasure and pain, health and illness—but what is it all about?

Like it or not, it is part of Allah's design that we have an innate spiritual capacity. No matter how unaware we may be, we are never outside of Allah's purpose, wishes, and will. Allah *(Subhaanahu wa taʿaalaa)* reveals in the Qur'an:

...wa-anna-Llaaha yahdee mañy-yureed

> **...Allah guides whom He will** (22:16).
>
> ***...wa iñy-yuridka bi-khayriñ fa-laa raaadda li-fa<u>d</u>lih....***
>
> **...if He desires good for you, there is none who can repel His bounty...** (10:107).
>
> ***Yureedu-Llaahu li-yubayyina lakum wa yahdiyakum sunana-l-ladheena miñ qablikum wa yatuuba ᶜalaykum; wa-Llaahu ᶜAleemun <u>H</u>akeem. Wa-Llaahu yureedu añy-yatuuba ᶜalaykum; wa yureedu-l-ladheena yattabiᶜuuna-sh-shahawaati añ tameeluu maylan ᶜadheemaa. Yureedu-Llaahu añy-yukhaffifa ᶜañkum: wa khuliqa-l-'iñsaanu <u>d</u>aᶜeefaa.***
>
> **Allah desires to clarify, and guides you to the ways which were followed by the righteous people before you, and turns to you in mercy. Allah is the Knowledgeable, Wise. Allah wishes to forgive you but those who follow their lusts wish to see you deviate far away [from the Right Way]. Allah wishes to lighten your burdens because humans have been created weak [by nature]** (4:26-28).
>
> ***...yureedu-Llaahu bikumu-l-yusra wa laa yureedu bikumu-l-ᶜusr....***
>
> **...Allah intends your well-being and does not want to put you to hardship...** (2:185).

Like a parent who wants to see a child attain his or her greatest potential, Allah *(Sub<u>h</u>aanahu wa taᶜaalaa)* wants us to know our spiritual potential. Out of Love, out of Compassion, Mercy, Kindness, and Generosity, out of Patience and Tolerance—for at least 99 reasons—

Allah *(Subhaanahu wa ta'aalaa)* strives to make every individual aware of what is possible in her or his life.

According to the Sufic tradition, God is transmitting signals to us all the time through our *kashf* (insight) beyond the *tajalli* (irradiation). Some of these signals come in the form of external events and circumstances. Some come through our bodies, minds, and emotions. Often they come through our hearts. (Now scientists are saying that there are several thousand brain cells in the heart.) From the moment we come into this world, Allah *(Subhaanahu wa ta'aalaa)* is trying to get our attention: through our mother's voice, through touch, through sounds, through smell and taste, through the beauty of nature.

All that we experience is an aspect of Allah's call to us. But not everyone responds—and of those who do, not everyone responds in a timely manner. I can sit in my living room and my daughter will be calling me, "Daddy, Daddy!" I hear the first "Daddy," but it fades from my consciousness. Maybe after the third "Daddy!" I say, "Just a minute...I'll be right there...I'm busy..." Finally, I pull my attention away from whatever it's on and say, "Yes?" She's already called me ten times.

"Just a minute—I'll be right there—I'm busy" equals a lifetime. "I'm ready!" "Sorry, you're too late. Your legs have been taken away from you; you can't walk. Your mind is gone; you forgot I was calling. You're dead, and this part of the journey had to be done while you were alive. You were too distracted. You wanted to be over here, and not over there. I was calling you from the ocean, but you wanted to be on the mountain."

The *mureed* on the spiritual journey is a person who is uniquely able to hear Allah's call. He or she has a special quality of *jadhb* (attraction) which enables the development of *nisbah*, a relationship with Allah

(Subhaanahu wa ta'aalaa). Allah *(Subhaanahu wa ta'aalaa)* pursues the possibility of the *muraad* inside a person. The moment the person responds, he or she becomes a *mureed* or *mureeda* and begins the spiritual journey. His or her desire toward Allah *(Subhaanahu wa ta'aalaa)* has been awakened; by definition, that person is now a *mureed.* If and when that person in that *jadhb*, in that *nisbah*, achieves *ihsaan*, that person is again *muraad:* the one for whom Allah *(Subhaanahu wa ta'aalaa)* wished.

The Prophet Muhammad *(salla-Llaahu ʿalayhi wa sallam)* is the model for being both *mureed* and *muraad.* He retreated to the cave on Mount Hira, calling out to God. He called out to Allah *(Subhaanahu wa ta'aalaa)*; the shock was that in response, God called out to him! The Prophet *(salla-Llaahu ʿalayhi wa sallam)* not only desired Allah, but was desired by Allah *(Subhaanahu wa ta'aalaa)*.

Just as Allah *(Subhaanahu wa ta'aalaa)* called the Prophet Muhammad *(salla-Llaahu ʿalayhi wa sallam)* to Him, Allah speaks to the undisclosed aspect within each individual. Typically, the spiritual path is described as a progression from being a *mureed* to being a *muraad.* But it is really a journey from potential *muraad* to *mureed* to *muraad.* When Allah *(Subhaanahu wa ta'aalaa)* states in the Qur'an,

> ***Yaa ayyatuha-n-nafsu-l-mutma'innah irjiʿee ilaa Rabbiki raadiyatam-mardiyyah. Fa-dkhulee fee ʿibaadee wa-dkhulee Jannatee.*** **But ah, you soul at peace!**
>
> **Return to your Lord content in His good pleasure. Enter you among My worshippers. Enter you My Garden.** (89:27-30)

Allah is addressing the *muraad.* Allah *(Subhaanahu wa ta'aalaa)* is saying to the soul, "Return to Me, content in My good pleasure, My desire."

When we respond to God's call, we take the role of the seeker.

When we respond to God's call—not thinking that we chose, or constructed the situation, but instead realizing that God has called us, and we are simply responding—then we become *mureeds* or *mureedas*, and God becomes the sought, the *muraad*.

The catch in this process is that owing to our ego, we think we are seeking God. We think that it is our idea to seek Allah *(Subhaanahu wa ta'aalaa)*, and consequently, we believe the journey originates in our initiative. In fact, the desire to find Allah is planted in us by Allah *(Subhaanahu wa ta'aalaa)*. We had nothing to do with it. Our only role is to respond: to become conscious that we are being called, and to either resist or acquiesce.

Of course, being human, we like to think we are the ones doing the choosing. We become experts in resistance just to prove that we are in control. We try to change our lives, only to find ourselves repeating the same mistakes and encountering the same situations again and again. Why? Perhaps because Allah *(Subhaanahu wa ta'aalaa)* is trying to tell us, "Stop insisting on being in charge. Submit. Live *fee sabeeli-Llaah* (for the sake of Allah)."

But resistance to guidance and the need to "control" are, for the most part, gross responses, not befitting the human potential or possibility, not befitting a believer, a Sufi, a *mureed/muraad*. The inheritance of the Sufi is the subtlety of the expression of love and mercy in the life of the sincere human being. On the one hand, the Sufis avoid the extreme of denying the satisfaction that can come from performing religious and spiritual practices. For there is a unique and special contentment and *hikmah* that comes from such acts of submission. On the other hand, they also reject the extremism of so-called "fundamentalists" who insist on forcing these religious practices on people without explaining in positive terms their benefits, or who do them as a proof of their piety, as opposed to from their hearts' purpose and desire—those people who, with a stick or whip, with their hand or their harshness, create fear, and then call it belief or piety.

There is a difference between being religious and praying and doing what one is coerced or threatened to do, and realizing that each of us has a unique purpose in life that Allah *(Subhaanahu wa ta'aalaa)* wants to reveal to us, and that that purpose is revealed through the religious practices, through the teachings and guidance we receive from our *shuyukh*, through the practices of *Tasawwuf*, and through the inner guidance that those practices reveal. Following the example of the Prophet *(salla-Llaahu 'alayhi wa sallam)*, the Sufis perform religious and spiritual practices out of love and glorification of Allah *(Subhaanahu wa ta'aalaa)*, Who is near and present at all times.

In order to hear or respond to anything, we must pay attention to it. In the practices of the Naqshbandi Order, we recite *"main mutawwajuh...* (I pay attention...)." Otherwise, Allah *(Subhaanahu wa ta'aalaa)* may be knocking on our door, but we will not reply. Remember the *sunnah* of the Prophet *(salla-Llaahu 'alayhi wa sallam)*, where he relates:

> **Allah will ask on the Day of Awakening, "O child of Adam, I fell ill and you did not visit Me." He will reply, "O my Lord! How could I have visited You, when You are the Lord of all the worlds?" Allah will say, "Did you not know that so-and-so among My servants was sick, but you did not visit him? And did you not know that if you had visited him, you would surely have found Me with him?"**
>
> **Again, Allah will say, "O child of Adam, I asked for food from you, but you did not give Me food." He will reply, "O my Lord! How could I have fed You, when You are the Lord of all the worlds?" Allah will say, "Did you not know that so-and-so of My servants asked you for food, but you**

> **did not feed him? Did you not know, that if you had fed him, you would surely have found Me with him?"**
>
> **Again, Allah will say, "O child of Adam, I asked you to give Me to drink, but you gave Me not to drink." He will say: "O Lord, how could I give You to drink, when You are the Lord of all the worlds?" Allah will say, "My servant so-and-so asked you to give him to drink and you gave him not to drink. Had you given him to drink, you would surely have found Me with him"** (Abu Hurayra/Muslim).

Small groups of devoted, dedicated people can alter the course of history: for good or for evil. If we aspire to be *mureeduun*–those who desire God—and *muraad*—those whom God wishes to draw near to Him—then we have a responsibility to define the middle way, the way of moderation as exemplified by the Prophet *(salla-Llaahu ʿalayhi wa sallam)* in terms and on issues that are manifest in today's world. We face an immediate imperative to distinguish, by action, philosophy, and theology, the extremist members of our communities from those who are firmly committed to the essentials of Islam as based in moderation and inclusivity: essentials such as *tarbiyah* (education), *muhaasabah* (self-examination), *ʿadl* (justice), *salaam* and *sulh* (peace and reconciliation), and others which today parallel democratic mainstays like freedom of opinion, decision-making by consensus, freedom of speech, citizens' duties to the community. This in turn necessitates a defined spectrum of moderate opinion so that the different voices and visions of moderation may be heard. A self-critical, constructive, and honest approach will go a long way toward creating trust within and outside of the community.

In addition, there must be both a theological and a social/ethical basis for dialogue among people of faith, allowing opportunities for difference of perspective yet making evident our unity in the common human/Divine values at the core of the hearts of all faithful people. The once mainstream Christian community in the United States has been similarly marginalized by fundamentalist, evangelical elements. The founding Christian principles of the American Republic, which derived from Calvinist, Quaker, Deist, Methodist, and even Catholic thought, have been subsumed by non-ecumenical extremism under the banner of evangelism. Growing numbers of right-wing Christians have co-opted the symbols (and, in some cases, the realities) of American pluralistic democracy: the flag, the concept of patriotism, and the principle of separation of church and state.

A pall of silence has fallen upon moderate institutions in both the secular political and the religious mainstream spheres. Silenced by the din of rhetoric—by strong elements of neo-conservatism in government, the waves of patriotism associated with September 11 and the war in Iraq, and what some perceive to be rising tides of anti-Semitism, Islamophobia, and techniques of dehumanization and humiliation formerly seen in other countries—people of the center, of moderation, of deep conviction, need to find a voice. Moderate members of the Muslim community, along with their counterparts in the Christian and Jewish faiths, need to regain their position as spokespersons. They need to re-take the spiritual high-ground that represents the Abrahamic impulse that unites and should direct our respective communities.

The Prophet *(ṣalla-Llaahu ʿalayhi wa sallam)* prayed:

> **O Allah! Grant me love of You, and to love those who love You, and to love whatever brings me nearer to You. O Allah, make Your love more precious to me than cool water is for the thirsty** (Abu Darda'a/Tirmidhi).

* * *

Wa-Llaahu lahu-l-haqqu wa huwa yahdis-sabeel.
Hasbuna-Llaahu wahdahu wa ni^cma-l-wakeel.
Wa salli ^calaa Sayyidinaa Muhammadin wa ahlihi wa sahbihi ajma^ceen
Wa-l-hamdu li-Llaahi Rabbi-l-^caalameen.

Truth belongs to Allah; it is He who shows the way.
Allah, alone, suffices us, and what a fine guardian is He!
Blessings upon our Master Muhammad
and his family and companions altogether
and praise is due to Allah, Lord of the Worlds.

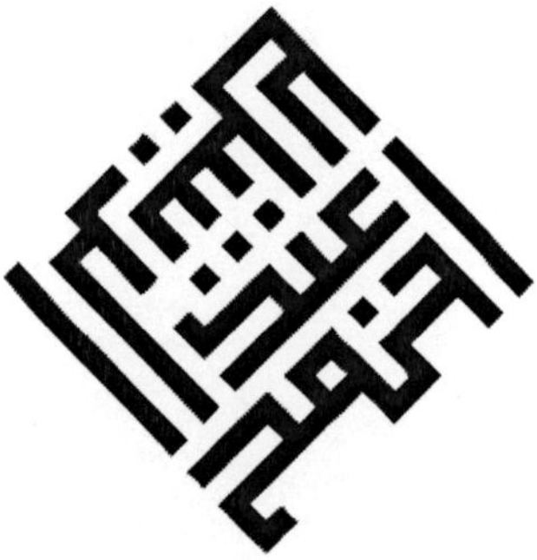

بسم الله الرحمن الرحيم

Remembering How to Remember Allah

Part I: Remembrance of Allah: The Way to Peace and Fulfillment

Bismi-Llaah, Alẖamduli-Llaah
Allaahumma s̲alli wa sallim ʿalaa Sayyidinaa Muẖammadin,
wa ʿalaa aalihi wa saẖbih

The Ease and Dis-Eases of Forgetting

Dhikru-Llaah, or the remembrance of Allah *(Subẖaanahu wa taʿaalaa)*, is often associated with specific practices and recitations. It may refer to a group gathering for the purpose of recollecting and supplicating to Allah *(Subẖaanahu wa taʿaalaa)* and praising the Prophet Muhammad *(s̲alla-Llaahu ʿalayhi wa sallam)* aloud. It may also encompass the time an individual sets aside to reflect on Allah in silent prayer and meditation. Much has been written about the benefits and formats of such practices, both collective and private, aloud and silent.

But beyond gatherings, ceremonies, and recitations, what does *dhikru-Llaah* really mean? What are the full implications of mentioning or remembering Allah *(Subẖaanahu wa taʿaalaa)*, as we are enjoined to do by the Qur'an and the *sunnah*?

Dhikru-Llaah is the very purpose of our being. It is the goal which Allah *(Subẖaanahu wa taʿaalaa)* created us to fulfill. It is that which brings us nearer to Allah *(Subẖaanahu wa taʿaalaa)*, for Allah *(Subẖaanahu wa taʿaalaa)* assures us in the Qur'an:

Fa-dhkuruunee adhkurkum...

Remember Me, and I shall remember you... (2:152).

In a *hadith qudsi*, Allah *(Subhaanahu wa ta'aalaa)* made known to the Prophet Muhammad *(salla-Llaahu 'alayhi wa sallam)*:

> **I am as My servant thinks I am. I am with him if he remembers Me. If he remembers Me to himself, I remember him to Myself. If he remembers Me in an assembly, I remember him in an assembly better than it. If he draws near to Me a hand span, I draw near to him an arm's length. If he draws near to Me an arm's length, I draw near to him a fathom's length. And if he comes to Me walking, I go to him running** (Bukhari, Muslim).

As remembrance draws us closer to God, it also instills in us a sense of inner peace.

> ***...inna-Llaaha yudillu mañy-yashaaa'u wa yahdee ilayhi man anaab, al-ladheena aamanuu wa tatma'innu quluubuhum-bi-dhikri-Llaah; alaa bi-dhikri-Llaahi tatma'innu-l-quluub.***

> **...Allah sends whom He will astray, and guides to Himself all who turn [to Him], who have believed and whose hearts have rest in the remembrance of Allah. Verily, in the remembrance of Allah do hearts find rest!** (Qur'an 13:27-28).

The root of the Arabic word for "rest," *tam'ana*, implies not just repose, but a sense of calmness, tranquility, and security; a feeling of being reassured; a confidence, certainty, and equanimity born of trust.

Awareness of our Creator sows these qualities within us. It permeates and makes meaningful every aspect of our existence—from our roles at home to our actions in the community, from our day-to-day decisions to our highest aspirations.

Yet, for all the benefits derived from remembering Allah *(Subhaanahu wa ta'aalaa)*, we remain experts in forgetting. We think of remembrance as a special act, an exceptional state of awareness that requires effort and focus. We wonder, "How can I remember Allah more?" In contrast, we never think about forgetfulness as a special act, because forgetfulness comes naturally! We seem to have an inbred disposition to forget. Our ego slips in like the whisperer, Shaytan, spreading magic dust over our remembrance and putting our consciousness to sleep, even while our bodies go on about the business of daily life.

To cultivate remembrance, we must examine the tendency to forget and how to overcome it. Shaykh Ahmed Farooqi Sirhindi *(rahmatu-Llaahi 'alayhi)* said, "*Dhikr* means to avoid forgetting Allah in any way possible" (Ansari 232). In our homes and offices, we employ many tools to avoid forgetting responsibilities. We have calendar software on our computers, notes on our refrigerators, daily planners in our pockets. We exchange reminders with those around us: making sure our children take their lunches to school, confirming that someone in the family will get the car inspected, relying on a co-worker to alert us to upcoming deadlines, counting on the dentist's office to call before our next appointment. Forms of reminding and remembering pervade our lives—and all these forms are linked to something material.

Allah *(Subhaanahu wa ta'aalaa)*, on the other hand, is intangible. This raises a question for contemplation. Do we have difficulty remembering Allah *(Subhaanahu wa ta'aalaa)* because the Divine Presence is not material? Or does the difficulty arise because we treat Allah *(Subhaanahu wa ta'aalaa)* as material, yet fail to devise means of reminding ourselves of His significance?

Whatever our reasons for forgetting, we have little excuse, for material reminders of the Creator surround us. God puts everything we need to remember Him before our very eyes: our homes, our families, our friendships, the food we eat, the technologies we use, the bounties of nature, the animals and plants, the beauties of this universe. So numerous are the blessings bestowed by Allah *(Subhaanahu wa ta'aalaa)* that

> ***Wa iñ ta'udduu ni'mata-Llaahi laa tuh-suuhaa....***
>
> **If you were to count the favors of Allah, you would never be able to number them...** (Qur'an 16:18).

Allah *(Subhaanahu ta'aalaa)* further reveals,

> ***Sanureehim aayaatinaa fi-l-'aafaaqi wa fee añfusihim hattaa yatabayyana lahum annahu-l-haqq....***
>
> **We shall show them Our signs on the horizons and within themselves until it will be manifest to them that it is the Truth...** (Qur'an 41:53).

All of the signs of Allah *(Subhaanahu wa ta'aalaa)* are perfect, and we witness Allah's artistry in them all: in the rain that descends from the sky, in the crops that Allah *(Subhaanahu wa ta'aalaa)* grows for us through the efforts of our hands and feet, in the canopy of the heavens arching above us. These reminders have material forms—but, unlike computer calendars or refrigerator notes, they also point us toward that which transcends the physical. In *Suuratu-n-Nahl* we read:

> ***Wa sakh-khara lakumu-l-layla wa-n-nahaara wa-sh-shamsa wa-l-qamar; wa-n-nujuumu***

> ***musakh-kharaatum-bi-amrih; inna fee dhaalika la-aayaatil-li-qawmiñy-ya*ᶜ*qiluun.***
>
> **[Allah] has subjected to your service the night and the day, the sun and the moon, and likewise the stars also serve you by His command: surely there are signs in this for people who use their common sense** (16:12).

When evening comes upon us, do we think of sleep, or do we think of the One Who created the night and enabled us to find in it rest and rejuvenation? When dawn breaks, do we think of the tasks we must accomplish that day, or do we think of the One Who created the sun and set the planets in motion, of the One Who allowed us to witness another morning, to rise and work and make use of our capabilities?

As a boy growing up in Pittsburgh, I dreamed of someday living near the beach. I would imagine getting up each day, walking down to the edge of the sand, gazing out across the ocean's expanse. Finally, in my early thirties, I moved to Virginia Beach. At last, I had a home within walking distance of the shore! It fulfilled all my expectations—for about two months. Then I stopped seeing the ocean. Oh, I would glance at it every once in a while; but I no longer noticed it. My feelings of awe and wonderment passed. I got out of the habit of finding my way to the beach each morning, of meditating to the rhythm of the sea.

Too often, we become like the people whom Allah *(Subhaanahu wa ta*ᶜ*aalaa)* describes as having **"hearts that do not understand, and eyes that do not see, and ears that do not hear...** ***(lahum quluubul-laa yafqahuuna bihaa, wa lahum a*ᶜ*yunul-laa yubsiruuna bihaa, wa lahum aadhaanul-laa yasma*ᶜ*uuna bihaa...)"*** (Qur'an 7:179).

We forget Allah *(Subhaanahu wa ta'aalaa)*, because we are busy reacting instead of acting, being unconscious instead of attentive. We get caught up in playing the games of this world, trying to look good in others' eyes while forgetting that all that really matters is how we look in the eyes of Allah *(Subhaanahu wa ta'aalaa)*. We focus on fulfilling our material responsibilities—not striving to make our work a form of *'ibaadah* (worship), but rather solely for worldly ends. We forget that the Qur'anic enjoinder to **"seek of Allah's bounty *(wa-b-taghuu miñ fadli-Llaahi)*"** is followed immediately by the instruction to **"remember Allah much, that you may be successful *(wa-dh-kuru-Llaaha katheeral-la'allakum tuflihuu)*"** (62:10).

This is why the Qur'an and the *sunnah* of the Prophet Muhammad *(salla-Llaahu 'alayhi wa sallam)*, as well as the teachings of the great masters, do not dwell exclusively on issues of *dunyaa* (the material world), but rather turn our attention again and again toward our hearts, toward Allah *(Subhaanahu wa ta'aalaa)*, toward the One Truth that transcends the limitations of physical life, toward the One Reality to which all aspects of created reality continuously point. How we approach Allah *(Subhaanahu wa ta'aalaa)* this minute is much more important than anything else we deem important. Either we approach this moment in remembrance, or we forget. The contrast between the two states is dramatic, as the Prophet *(salla-Llaahu 'alayhi wa sallam)* made clear when he said, **"The likeness of one who remembers the Lord and one who does not is like that of a living person to one who is dead"** (Bukhari). My Shaykh, Hazrat Azad Rasool, has observed, "The person who remembers God finds happiness; the person who forgets finds only desolation. Forgetfulness is the petrifying force that turns a tree to stone" (Rasool 135-6).

Hazrat goes on to tell the story of two travelers who were on their way to meet a famous Shaykh when they passed some cats in conversation. To their surprise, they could understand the cats' words; and as they listened, they heard one cat remark that the Shaykh whom they hoped to meet had died. Greatly saddened by this news, the travelers debated whether to proceed or to return home. At last they decided that out of respect for the Shaykh, they would continue on their journey, find his tomb, and offer *du'aas* for him there.

When they arrived in the Shaykh's town, they asked where he was buried. The villagers replied, "We can't direct you to his tomb, because he's still alive!"

Puzzled, the travelers sought out the Shaykh and told him of their experiences. He asked, "When exactly did you hear that I was dead?" They recalled the day and time. He replied, "At that particular moment, I had forgotten Allah; so, in the higher realms, it was announced that I had died" (Rasool 60).

Allah informs us in the Qur'an:

> ***Wa man a'rada 'añ dhikree fa'inna lahuu ma'eeshatañ dañkañw-wa nahshuruhuu yawma-l-qiyaamati a'maa.***
>
> **The one who turns away from remembering Me shall live a meager life, and We shall raise that one up blind on the Day of Resurrection** (20:124).

The word translated here as meager—*dank*—means not only impoverished, but cramped or confined in circumstances; weak and exhausted; in distress or hardship.

The results of forgetting Allah *(Subhaanahu wa ta'aalaa)* make themselves readily apparent in our lives. They come in the guise of the problems that we encounter every day, the issues that confront us time and time again, the struggles within ourselves. The scope of our lives narrows with every mistake we make, every oversight we commit, every moment we forget our purpose. Hardships arise as we overlook the needs around us, as we fail to acknowledge our responsibilities towards our communities, as we succumb to doubt, fear, or misjudgment. Where do these failings and difficulties come from? Whether major or minor, they all emerge at times when we are heedless of Allah *(Subhaanahu wa ta'aalaa)*.

Dhikru-Llaah: More than a Practice

The solution is to pay attention. In *Suuratu Aal ʿImraan*, Allah *(Subhaanahu wa ta'aalaa)* describes people of understanding as **"those who remember Allah standing, sitting, and reclining... *(alladheena yadhkuruuna-Llaaha qiyaamañw-wa quʿuudañw-wa ʿalaa junuubihim...)*"** (3:191). We need to remember Allah *(Subhaanahu wa ta'aalaa)* in all positions, at all times, day and night, seizing every opportunity for recollection.

> The Prophet *(salla-Llaahu ʿalayhi wa sallam)* said to his companions (*sahaabah*), **"Shall I tell you about the best of deeds, the most pure in the sight of your Lord, about the ones that are of the highest order, and far better for you than spending gold and silver, even better for you than meeting your enemies on the battlefields, when you strike at their necks and they at yours?"** The *sahaabah* replied, "Yes, O Messenger of Allah!" The Prophet *(salla-Llaahu ʿalayhi wa sallam)* said, **"Remembrance of Allah"** (Tirmidhi, Ahmad, al-Hakim).

Such a high level of remembrance is not solely a matter of reading Qur'an or repeating *"Laa ilaaha illa-Llaah"* (There is no god but Allah). Certainly, reading Qur'an and affirming the existence and unity of Allah *(Subhaanahu wa ta'aalaa)* bring many benefits. On the other hand, throughout history, there have been individuals who have done both, yet also committed acts of injustice, oppression, and violence that belie genuine awareness of the Divine.

To be born a Muslim or to embrace Islam is only the first step on the road to becoming conscious of Allah *(Subhaanahu wa ta'aalaa)*. We each must make our Islam alive. We each must strive to be a *mu'min* (believer) and *shaheed* (witness) of Allah *(Subhaanahu wa ta'aalaa)*. To believe and witness means living sincerely, humbly, and in accordance with the standards established by Allah *(Subhaanahu wa ta'aalaa)*—and, when we fail to do so, seeking the forgiveness of Allah *(Subhaanahu wa ta'aalaa)*. In *Suuratu-r-Ruum*, Allah *(Subhaanahu wa ta'aalaa)* guides us:

> ***Fa-aqim wajhaka li-d-deeni hanifaa; fitrata-Llaahi-l-latee fatara-n-naasa ʿalayhaa; laa tabdeela li-khalqi-Llaah; dhaalika-d-deenu-l-qayyimu wa laakinna akthara-n-naasi laa yaʿlamuun.***
>
> **Therefore, stand firm in your devotion to the upright faith—the nature made by Allah, the one on which humanity is created—and the laws of nature ordained by Allah cannot be changed. That is the standard of true faith, but most among humanity do not know** (30:30).

We are born with an innate sense of how to act correctly. Now, we must remember that standard of faith again.

A relationship exists between our *adab*— our manners, refinement, and courtesy; our cultural and social affect—and our remembrance of Allah *(Subhaanahu wa ta'aalaa)*. The means of standing firm in faith, the means of overcoming forgetfulness, the means of seeing the signs of the Divine Presence in the material world, the means of using our senses and experiencing our emotions in ways that facilitate rather than impede remembrance of Allah *(Subḫaanahu wa ta'aalaa)*, all depend on having a certain level of *adab.* Phrased another way: through *adab*, we can construct an environment for remembering.

Dhikr both builds and requires *adab.* How can it do both? An analogy may be made to parents raising a child to be well-mannered. The parents encourage the child to live up to a certain standard of politeness: to be considerate towards his or her peers, for example. As the child practices applying this standard with friends and classmates, his or her *adab* grows. A refinement of character takes place. At the same time, as the child matures and develops *adab*, he or she gains new understandings of how best to act considerately.

Four facets of the *adab* that *dhikru-Llaah* both depends upon and reinforces are as follows:

1. Reflection and Repentance
2. Firm Belief
3. The Expression of Higher Qualities
4. Remembrance of Allah for Allah's Sake

THE ADAB OF DHIKRU-LLAAH

Facet #1: Reflection and Repentance

To make *dhikru-Llaah,* we must be willing to face ourselves, to submit to Allah *(Subḫaanahu wa ta'aalaa)*, to talk to Allah *(Subḫaanahu wa ta'aalaa)* and learn how to listen to His response.

A person came to the Prophet *(ṣalla-Llaahu 'alayhi wa sallam)* and asked him what to do in a certain matter. The Prophet *(ṣalla-Llaahu 'alayhi wa sallam)* said, **"Consult your heart."** Consulting the heart can be difficult, for the heart is the seat of our human, material desires. We must convert those desires, linking them to the desire for Truth and for Allah *(Subḥaanahu wa ta'aalaa)*, to ensure that the responses received lead us in the right way rather than astray.

Converting our desires requires that we examine our character flaws; and examining our flaws is integral to engaging in *dhikr.* Indeed, unless the thought of Allah *(Subḥaanahu wa ta'aalaa)* leads to self-reflection, we have not begun to appreciate the full depths of *dhikru-Llaah.* If we say, *Yaa Ghafuur* (O All-Forgiving) or *Astaghfiru-Llaah* (I ask Allah's forgiveness) without considering our own need for forgiveness, then we have not yet perfected *dhikr.* If we recite *Yaa Raḥmaan, Yaa Raḥeem* (O Merciful, O Compassionate) or *al-Ḥayy, al-Qayyuum* (the Living, the Everlasting) without reflecting on some element of those attributes in our own lives and experiences, then we still need to strengthen our remembrance.

When we contemplate how great Allah *(Subḥaanahu wa ta'aalaa)* is, we must contemplate also how small we are—how forgiving He is, and how blaming we are; how creative and expansive He is, and how literal and narrow-minded we are. Yet, human beings tend to put a great deal of energy into *not* seeing themselves, into denying their flaws and trying to conceal their weaknesses. *Dhikru-Llaah* entails doing exactly the opposite. To truly remember Allah, we must put our energy into looking honestly in the mirror of the self, the mirror that will allow us to repent to Allah *(Subḥaanahu wa ta'aalaa.*

Repentance is the most basic form of *dhikr.* Think about it. If you reach the point where you know you have done something wrong and you repent, are you not remembering Allah *(Subḥaanahu wa ta'aalaa)*? It starts at the most base level of our existence, when we have shame, guilt, or simply knowledge of an error we have made. What supposedly is a very low state is in fact our first encounter with Allah *(Subḥaanahu wa ta'aalaa)* in remembrance. From another angle, we might say that one way of remembering Allah *(Subḥaanahu wa ta'aalaa)* is to feel that we are forgetting Him. I cannot stress this perspective enough, for it disallows self-indulgence.

The beginning of *dhikru-Llaah* lies in *muhaasabatu-n-nafs*: accounting for ourselves, facing ourselves consciously, and repenting. Abu Bakr *(radiya-Llaahu ʿanhu)* narrated that the Prophet *(salla-Llaahu ʿalayhi wa sallam)* said, **"No man will commit a sin, then get up and purify himself, then pray, then ask Allah's forgiveness without Allah forgiving him"** (Tirmidhi). Then he recited,

> ***Wa-l-ladheena idhaa fa-ᶜaluu faahishatan aw dhalamuu añfusahum dhakaru-Llaaha fa-s-taghfaruu li-dhunuubihim: wa mañy-yaghfiru-dh-dhunuuba illaa-Llaah: wa lam yusirruu ᶜalaa maa fa-ᶜaluu wa hum yaᶜlamuun, ulaaa'ika jazaaa'uhum-maghfiratum-mir-Rabbihim....***
>
> **And those who, when they do something to be ashamed of or wrong themselves, remember Allah and ask forgiveness for their sins—and who can forgive sins except Allah?—and are never obstinate in persisting knowingly in [the wrong] they have done, the reward of such will be forgiveness from their Lord...** (Qur'an 3:135-6).

We should have no question that Allah *(Subhaanahu wa taʿaalaa)* will forgive us. But we also should not treat the mercy of Allah *(Subhaanahu wa taʿaalaa)* as a guarantee that we can continue to sin without repercussions. Instead, we should strive to be conscious in every moment. Every time we stand to pray, or walk into the masjid, each of us should ask himself or herself, "What have I done to earn the right to pray?" Of course, *salah* (prayer) is prescribed for us—it is *fard* (obligatory)—but it is not prescribed for us to do as an unconscious act; and it is not, therefore, an unconscious right. It is a privilege to pray to Allah *(Subhaanahu wa taʿaalaa)*. Every time we sit or stand to offer *duʿaa* (supplication) or *dhikr*, we should ask ourselves, "Have I earned the right to be doing this?" If the answer is no, we should pray to Allah *(Subhaanahu wa ta'aalaa)* for forgiveness and seek His permission. Before reading the Qur'an, we should pause and ask, "Do I have the right to touch this, let alone open it, let alone read it?" In studying the *hadith* and *seerah* (life of the Prophet *[salla-Llaahu 'alayhi wa sallam]*), in offering advice based on the teachings, in striving to educate others, and in all the other aspects of our practices and faith, we should ask, "Have I qualified to do this?" In this way, we keep our *muhaasabah* going. Perhaps we say to ourselves, "No, I don't have the right to do this at the moment. Such-and-such an event happened, or such-and-such a thought arose. O Allah *(Subhaanahu wa ta'aalaa)*, forgive me for that action or thought." Then immediately, we are forgiven, and we can go on with the practice we had intended to undertake—consciously, now, with mindfulness of Allah *(Subhaanahu wa ta'aalaa)*.

We have all made mistakes, and will make more in the future. But *dhikr* is not about bemoaning our mistakes; it is a process through which we refine our *adab*. Ultimately, it is the way we protect our character and save spiritual face. When we remember Allah *(Subhaanahu wa ta'aalaa)* with an attitude of reflection and repentance, we create an environment where we will grow spiritually, and where everyone around us will also have the opportunity to grow.

Facet #2: Firm Belief

The second facet of *adab* that *dhikr* both reinforces and requires is certainty of belief.

According to as-Samarqandi, the Prophet *(salla-Llaahu 'alayhi wa sallam)* is reported to have said, **"Remembrance of God is certain knowledge of one's belief (*'ilm al-imaan*), immunity from hypocrisy, a fortress against Shaytan, and a guarded refuge from the fire"** (al-Safuri).

Through remembrance, we build not only a strong spiritual foundation, but a staircase to further levels of understanding. As Muslims, we all affirm that the Prophet Muhammad *(salla-Llaahu 'alayhi wa sallam)* is the final prophet; that Paradise and hell exist; that on the Day of Judgment, we will be called to account for our intentions and actions; that Allah is **"as near as [our] jugular vein[s] *(nahnu aqrabu ilayhi min habli-l-wareed)*"** (Qur'an 50:16).

But it is one thing to accept these teachings based on habit or custom, or because the physical signs of their truth are obvious; and it is another to make them conscious, relevant, and active beliefs which we affirm without doubt or question. For example, we can easily believe that Allah looks after our needs: as I have said, we see the beauties of nature, the alternation of day and night, the food spread before us. Who among us can make it rain? We may plant gardens; but who among us can cause the plants to grow? We see these miracles in the material world, and we readily believe that Allah *(Subhaanahu wa ta'aalaa)* provides for us.

But other teachings of Islam are harder to grasp. We are told that if we commit *shirk* now, we will be punished in the life to come. But having never experienced the Day of Judgment or the *akhirah* (Hereafter), we struggle to understand fully what this means.

Allah asks us to believe not only in the signs that are right before us, not only in that which is supported by proofs within creation, but in realities that we have not experienced. By recollecting and remembering Allah, we become able to use our reason, our capacity to perceive interrelationships, and our experiences in this world as stepping stones to deeper faith in the unseen. We become attuned to the truths that we have not heard with our ears, but hear with our hearts; to the realities that we do not see with our eyes, but perceive through our insight; to the knowledge that we cannot acquire through rational inquiry, but know in the core of our souls. *Dhikr* promotes the experience of Allah *(Subhaanahu wa ta'aalaa)* in ways that extend our faith far beyond the confines of *dunyaa*, enabling us to become fully certain in all aspects of our belief.

Facet #3: The Expression of Higher Qualities

The firmer our faith, the better we can fulfill the third facet of the *adab* of *dhikr*: to express the attributes of Allah in our day-to-day lives.

While Islam teaches harmony, open-mindedness, equity, and tolerance, there remain disparities between what Muslims affirm and what they do. We see too much conflict in the homes, too much narrow-mindedness in the presentation of the *deen* (religion), too much inequity in the community, too much prejudice among sects or nationalities, too much enmity toward other people, including our fellow *ahl al-kitaab* (people of the Book, meaning the adherents of revealed religion such as Christians and Jews).

Dhikru-Llaah aligns our outer behavior with the will of God. One author wrote, "*Dhikr* polishes the heart and is the source of the Divine Breath that revives the dead spirits by filling them with the Blessings of Allah, decorating them with His Attributes, and bringing them from a state of heedlessness to the state of complete wakefulness" (Naqshbandi-Haqqani).

What is meant by "...decorating the spirits with Allah's Attributes…"?

As we focus more and more on Allah *(Subhaanahu wa ta'aalaa)*, we focus our lives around *al-Asmaa' al-Husnaa* (the Ninety-Nine Beautiful Names). We ourselves begin to manifest the qualities of the Divine Attributes: *ar-Rahmaan* (the Compassionate), *ar-Raheem* (the Merciful), *al-Ghaffar* (the Forgiver), *al-Hafeedh* (the Protector), *al-Kareem* (the Generous), *as-Sabuur* (the Patient). We begin to do what Allah *(Subhaanahu wa ta'aalaa)* guides us to do, whether we find it easy or difficult: to be honest and just in our dealings, to be patient in the face of tests and trials, to persevere, to be generous and loving. As we act with those Attributes, we become reminders of the Divine Presence. We personally become signs *(aayaat)*. Every person, every believer, every *mu'min*, can be one of the *aayaat* of Allah *(Subhaanahu wa ta'aalaa)*.

> The Prophet Muhammad *(salla-Llaahu 'alayhi wa sallam)* once asked his companions, **"Shall I not tell you about those who are the best among you?"** They replied, "Yes, by all means!" The Prophet *(salla-Llaahu 'alayhi wa sallam)* said, **"Most superior among you are those who remind you of Allah as soon as you look at them."**

Who among us would not wish to be of those people? This is what we were born to be. This is the potential we fulfill through *dhikru-Llaah*.

Facet #4: Remembrance of Allah for Allah's Sake

A fourth aspect of the *adab* of *dhikr* is to remember Allah *(Subhaanahu wa ta'aalaa)* on Allah's terms, not on our terms. We need to engage in *dhikru-Llaah* not for selfish reasons, but as the key to fulfilling the spiritual journey that Allah *(Subhaanahu wa ta'aalaa)* created us to undertake and has commanded us to pursue.

We remember Allah because doing so is *fard*. It is not the key to avoiding pain or to gaining material success, name, or fame. Those rewards may come; but the outer, worldly outcomes of our remembrance are determined by Allah *(Subhaanahu wa ta'aalaa)*, not by us. Inwardly, however, remembrance is the key to spiritual success, for it brings us to a state of consciousness, peacefulness, tranquility, security, and safety in the presence of the Divine that endures no matter what else may transpire in our lives.

Are we making *dhikr* for our sake, or for the sake of Allah *(Subhaanahu wa ta'aalaa)*? Are we doing good works because we desire Paradise, or do we trust in the process, knowing that Paradise is granted as the result of sincere efforts? Are we remembering Allah *(Subhaanahu wa ta'aalaa)* because it "feels good," or because Allah *(Subhaanahu wa ta'aalaa)* instructs us to remember Him, and we humbly endeavor to fulfill His instruction? Do we turn to Allah *(Subhaanahu wa ta'aalaa)* only when we want something—or do we turn to Allah *(Subhaanahu wa ta'aalaa)* all the time, because we understand the purpose for which we were born?

Dhikru-Llaah is cumulative. We may perform it initially for selfish reasons; but as we continue to do it, we become less selfish. We gain knowledge (*ma'rifah*). As we gain *ma'rifah*, truth (*haqeeqah*) becomes clear. As *haqeeqah* becomes clear, we understand exactly why we have been given this physical existence. We understand it for flashes, then for moments, then for periods, then for longer periods, in a dimensional, developmental process. If we do not undertake and persevere in the process, we have no chance of experiencing its benefits. If we do undertake the process, then inevitably, we will remember more and more.

I sometimes reflect on what has motivated me to remember Allah *(Subhaanahu wa ta'aalaa)* over the years. Necessity, sometimes. Fear, sometimes. Love, sometimes. Guilt, sometimes. Doubt, sometimes. I run through a long list of reasons. Then I ask, how many times have I turned to Allah *(Subhaanahu wa ta'aalaa)* with ease? The answer I come to is, "Not often enough." Allah *(Subhaanahu wa ta'aalaa)* tells us in the Qur'an:

> ***Wa idhaa saalaka 'ibaadee 'annee fa-'innee qareeb: ujeebu da'wata-d-daa'i idhaa da'aanee fa-l-yastajeebuu lee wa-l-yu'minuu bee la'allahum yarshuduun.***

> **When My servants question you about Me, tell them that I am near. I answer the call of the supplicant when he [or she] calls to Me. Therefore, let them answer Me and put their trust in Me that they may be rightly guided** (2:186).

How deaf and blind we must be, if Allah *(Subhaanahu wa ta'aalaa)* is that close to us, and still we do not see! To the extent that we succumb to human arrogance, we even allow ourselves to think, "Maybe God doesn't exist," simply because we ourselves do not perceive the nearness of Allah *(Subhaanahu wa ta'aalaa)*. Our arrogance convinces us that our eyes alone can prove or disprove the existence of Allah *(Subhaanahu wa ta'aalaa)*. Yet, how many times has each of us read a book, and missed the author's point? How many times has each of us heard a statement and replied to it, only to be told, "No, no, you don't understand what I mean"? How, then, can we ever think that our seeing or not seeing, our feeling or not feeling, is any proof of the existence of Allah *(Subhaanahu wa ta'aalaa)*?

Alhamduli-Llaah, Allah *(Subhaanahu wa ta'aalaa)* has given us models of humility and trust in the form of the prophets. Imam al-Ghazali *(rahmatu-Llaahi 'alayhi)*, writing in his *Ihya*, recounted that the Prophet Musa *('alayhi-s-salaam)* said, "O my Lord! Are You near, so that I may speak to You intimately, or are You far, so that I may call out to You?" God inspired to him, "I am sitting next to the one who remembers Me" (al-Safuri).

When our heart is turned to Allah *(Subhaanahu wa ta'aalaa)*, when we fully concentrate on Allah *(Subhaanahu wa ta'aalaa)*, when we make any request or plea to Allah *(Subhaanahu wa ta'aalaa)*, then we establish a relationship with Allah *(Subhaanahu wa ta'aalaa)*. We whisper to Allah *(Subhaanahu wa ta'aalaa)*, pouring out our hearts, and Allah *(Subhaanahu wa ta'aalaa)* turns and answers our call. When this *munaasabah* (congenial relationship) is established, we are imbued with a special kind of peace. Our eyes fill with tears of joy. Our breath is filled with the blessings of Allah *(Subhaanahu wa ta'aalaa)* as they roll off our tongues. Our ears hear Him reply to us, as He replies to us in our own language, in our own voices, and His words inspire our hearts. This is the experience that comes from having the *adab* to remember Allah *(Subhaanahu wa ta'aalaa)* for the sake of Allah *(Subhaanahu wa ta'aalaa)*. In short, it is to fulfill the hadith of the Prophet *(salla-Llaahu 'alayhi wa sallam)*: **"One who remembers God much is loved by God"** (al-Safuri).

I have touched on four aspects of the *adab* of *dhikr*. Now, let me briefly comment on methods of *dhikru-Llaah*.

TECHNIQUES OF DHIKRU-LLAAH

Dhikr has been called "the intoxicant of lovers" (al-Safuri). Remembering Allah *(Subhaanahu wa ta'aalaa)* is not only an act of worship, but an act of love.

We all know that at times, the lover wants to shout his or her love from the mountaintop. But as the lover and beloved mature in their relationship, they deepen their love and discover subtle ways of communicating it. The maturity of love hears the whispers; notices the smile; knows the significance of the raised eyebrow, the curl of the hair. In mature love, subtleties predominate over declarations from mountaintops.

The goal of doing *dhikr* with *adab* is to capture the subtlety of our love for Allah and of Allah's love for us. The Qur'an and the *sunnah* give guidance in the means of doing that: both by doing *dhikr jalee* (aloud) and by doing *dhikr khafee* (silently).

As for doing *dhikr* aloud, the Prophet *(salla-Llaahu 'alayhi wa sallam)* said, **"...remember God to such an extent that people call you mad"** (Ahmad).

Ibn Abbas *(radiya-Llaahu 'anhu)* said that "they used to say the *dhikr* loudly during the lifetime of the Prophet *(Salla-Llaahu 'alayhi wa sallam)* after they had completed the obligatory prayers" (Bukhari). In the Qur'an, Allah *(Subhaanahu wa ta'aalaa)* tells the believers,

> ***Fa-'idhaa qadaytum-manaasikakum fa-dh-kuru-Llaaha ka-dhikrikum aabaaa'akum aw ashadda dhikrañ....***
>
> **And when you have completed your devotions, then remember Allah as you remember your fathers, or with a more lively remembrance...** (Qur'an 2:200).

But the Prophet *(salla-Llaahu 'alayhi wa sallam)* also suggested that doing *dhikr* aloud does not mean that one must do it loudly. He said, "**You are not addressing a deaf and an absent being, but you call unto a Being who is All-Hearing, All-Seeing**" (Bukhari).

The Qur'an makes clear that *dhikr* may be done in a low voice, or even silently (*khafee*).

> ***Wa-dh-kur-Rabbaka fee nafsika tadarru'añw-wa kheefatañw-wa duuna-l-jahri mina-l-qawli bi-l-ghuduwwi wa-l-'aasaali wa laa takum-mina-l-ghaafileen.***
>
> **And perform the *dhikr* of your Lord in your very soul, with humility and without loudness in words, in the mornings and evenings, and be not of those who are heedless** (7:205).

Finally, doing *dhikr* silently is supported in the following *hadith*, reported by Aisha *(radiya-Llaahu 'anhaa):*

> ***Dhikr khafee*, which is not heard by angels, is rewarded seventy times over. When, on the Day of Resurrection, Allah will summon all the creation for reckoning, the recording angels will bring the recorded accounts of all the people, and Allah will ask them to verify if there are any more good deeds to the credit of a certain individual. They will submit that they have not omitted anything from his or her recorded account. Allah will then say, "There is yet one good deed to this person's credit, which is not known to the angels: doing *dhikr* in silence"** (Baihaqi).

I am not here to make a judgment as to whether *dhikr khafee* or *dhikr jalee* is better. Either method offers benefits. (I come from a line of *shuyukh* that performs *dhikr* both ways, although most often we do it silently.)

One of the Sufis' quietest yet most refined forms of *dhikru-Llaah* is through *muraaqabah* and *tawajjuh:* techniques of silent remembrance in which the practicant turns his or her attention toward Allah *(Subhaanahu wa ta'aalaa)* through the *lataa'if* (subtle centers of perception). In addition to such silent techniques, Sufi guides also employ *dhikr jalee* in the training of students, for it can heighten receptivity and strengthen the *nisbah* (the relationship and affinity) and the *jadhb* (attraction) of the seeker to Allah through the guidance of the shaykh or teacher.

Whichever modes of *dhikr* a shaykh prescribes for students, they are tailored to students' spiritual needs. They are not dictated by seekers' emotions, but rather chosen for the purpose of assisting seekers in coming ever-closer to Allah *(Subhaanahu wa ta'aalaa)* and in deepening their understanding of the Qur'an, the *sunnah,* and the *seerah* of Nebi Muhammad *(salla-Llaahu 'alayhi wa sallam).*

There are dimensions and levels of *dhikru-Llaah*. *Dhikr* in the form of continual remembrance of Allah *(Subhaanahu wa ta'aalaa)* throughout our daily lives can be practiced by everyone. If a person inclines to undertake specific methods of *dhikr* in addition, then he or she should be aware that many elements are involved. Such factors as breathing, movement, intensity, and time all play a profound role. The Sufic techniques are carefully structured to refine each of these dimensions; therefore, in applying these techniques, it is best to be guided, humble, and consistent in and committed to the practices.

For example, consider the refinement of something as apparently simple as breathing. Students may periodically attain the proper rhythm of breath spontaneously, particularly if they are in a *hadrah* (Sufi circle) where the power of other people's breathing regulates their own. But there is a difference between occasionally conforming to a rhythm of breathing, and learning specific methods of breath that then can be used for developing insight or intuition. For day-to-day purification (*tazkiyah*), a student needs the education of the *dhikru-Llaah*.

Because the students' breath and attention are being trained and focused for specific purposes, seekers will benefit most fully if they do the assigned practices without adding practices which have not been assigned or which may not be done for the correct reasons or to completion. *Shuyukh* also advise new students not to randomly attend *dhikrs* and *hadrahs* of other Orders.

The practices of meditation (*muraaqabah*) and transmission (*tawajjuh*) lead to deeper and deeper states of awareness. As a seeker progresses, the practices also demand greater maturity, more profound understanding of *adab*, and increased responsibility. Through either a moment of direct contact or through performing the practices regularly over a period of time, one's heart is affected. When one sits with sincerity and openness, especially with a well-trained, authorized guide, one receives transmission and embarks on processes of transformation, awakening, and fulfillment in awareness of the Divine Presence.

Some seekers find that they must undergo a process of emptying before they can experience the process of being filled. They have to learn how to learn; then they can learn. Other people come to the spiritual path more empty, and the filling takes place rapidly. *Dhikr* plays a pivotal role in both the emptying and the filling.

Students on the path of *Taṣawwuf* often question how one can know if one is making spiritual progress. The question is difficult to answer in the abstract, particularly if the questioner is not actually doing the practices. But for the seeker who performs the assigned practices regularly, progress becomes clear, first subtly, then obviously. The character of one's life changes; the direction of one's thoughts changes; the way people relate to one changes; one exudes a different kind of light. When one opens the Qur'an, one discovers new levels of meaning. One's prayers seem to have a kind of power. One's presence seems to calm others at times of distress, need, or grief. Such are the fruits of *dhikru-Llaah*.

An Invitation

Readers who wish to experience *dhikr* may find benefit in the following method.

Set aside fifteen to thirty minutes to sit quietly in a place free of distractions. Recite *Astaghfiru-Llaah* (I ask Allah's forgiveness), trying to imbue your recitation with heartfelt sincerity. Then, perform *muḥaasabatu-n-nafs* (accounting for the self), beginning with the recitation:

> ***Qaala Rasuulu-Llaah (salawaatu-Llaahi wa salaamuhu ʿalayh), "Haasibu anfusakum qabla an tuhaasibu, wa zinu aʿmalakum qabla an tuzanu ʿalaykum."***
>
> **The Messenger of Allah *(salawaatu-Llaahi wa salaamuhu ʿalayh)* said, "Account for yourself before you are accounted; weigh your actions before your actions become a weight upon you."** [1]

Keeping this teaching in mind, reflect on your day. Review its events, from the time you awoke this morning to the present moment. Contemplate how well your actions and decisions reflected the purpose of your life. Ask yourself, "What could I have done more in accordance with the will of Allah *(Subhaanahu wa taʿaalaa)*? How could I have changed my (responses, words, thoughts, actions) to be more in harmony with the guidance of Allah *(Subhaanahu wa taʿaalaa)*?"

Finally, after spending time in self-reflection, you may deepen your remembrance by reciting short *suurahs* (passages of Qur'an) or *duʿaas* (supplications).

This is just one technique of *dhikr*. Other techniques are available to students who undertake formal instruction with a shaykh.

Affirming Remembrance Amidst Forgetfulness

Having touched on techniques, let me conclude by stressing that *dhikru-Llaah* encompasses far more than techniques. To emphasize this point, my Shaykh recounts that once Shaykh Muhammad Saʿeed Khan *(rahmatu-Llaahi ʿalayhi)* asked his Shaykh, Hazrat Hamid Hasan ʿAlawi *(rahmatu-Llaahi ʿalayhi)*, to explain *dhikr katheer* ("remembering [Allah] much," a practice enjoined in the Qur'an). He expected his teacher to specify some number of recitations to be done. Instead, the Shaykh replied that "remembering Allah much" is not a matter of quantity: it is a matter of forgetting everything other than Allah *(Subhaanahu wa ta'aalaa)* (Rasool 133).

Dhikr is the character of all that we do. It is the basis of the reason for our existence. It is the *adab*, the attention, the consciousness. It is how we treat people, how we think, how we act, how we shape and pursue our expectations, how we approach Allah *(Subhaanahu wa ta'aalaa)* in our prayers.

The Prophet *(salla-Llaahu 'alayhi wa sallam)* said,

> **The one who remembers Allah among those who forget Him is like a warrior behind those who run away. The one who remembers Allah among those who forget Him is like a green tree in the midst of dry ones. The one who remembers Allah among those who forget Him is like a light in a dark house. The one who remembers Allah among those who forget Him is shown by Allah his seat in Paradise while he is still alive. One who remembers Allah among those who forget Him is forgiven as many sins as the number of eloquent and non-eloquent speakers** [that is, the number of animals and human beings] (Razin).

Where are we? *Inshaa'a-Llaah*, we are remembering Allah *(Subhaanahu wa ta'aalaa)* among those who forget Him.

* * *

O Allah *(Subhaanahu wa ta'aalaa)*, may we turn to You continually in remembrance, properly, humbly, longingly, and with *adab*.
O Allah *(Subhaanahu wa ta'aalaa)*, reduce our hearts' attachments to all that is transient in this world,
and increase our attachment to that which is Eternal.

O Allah *(Subhaanahu wa ta'aalaa)*, make forgetting difficult for us and remembering easy for us.
O Allah *(Subhaanahu wa ta'aalaa)*, make each of us one **"who remembers God in seclusion and whose eyes become flooded with tears,"** so that we might be among the seven people **"shaded by Allah on the day when there will be no shade except Allah's"** (Bukhari).
O Allah *(Subhaanahu wa ta'aalaa)*, keep us conscious of our misdeeds and of our need to repent; grateful for Your forgiveness; mindful of the gifts You have bestowed upon us; and humble before the bounties of Existence.

O Allah *(Subhaanahu wa ta'aalaa)*, help us so that we may pray and worship You in the correct way, as the Prophet *(salla-Llaahu 'alayhi wa sallam)* guided, so that our worship may be accepted, especially our supplications for those who are in need and who are suffering.

Wa Llaahu lahu-l-haqqu wa huwa yahdis-sabeel.
Hasbuna-Llaahu wahdahu wa ni'ma-l-wakeel.
Wa salli 'alaa Sayyidinaa Muhammadin wa aaalihi wa sahbihi ajma'een
Wa-l-hamdu li-Llaahi Rabbi-l-'aalameen.

Truth belongs to Allah; it is He who shows the way.
Allah, alone, suffices us, and what a fine guardian is He!
Blessings upon our Master Muhammad
and his family and Companions altogether
and praise is due to Allah, Lord of the Worlds.

Part II: The Spirit of *Dhikru-Llaah*

Remembering in the heart means reflecting on the realities of Allah's Existence and on the Unity of His Being and creation—that is, on Allah's Names and Attributes as reflected in the physical universe. It means meditating on His commands, His promises, and His warnings; contemplating the design and order of life; and attempting to grasp inner dimensions of the mystery hidden behind the veil of *dunyaa* (the material world) by plumbing the depths of His Divine science through spiritual efforts and practices.

By taking the time to turn one's attention outwardly to the beauty of creation, one's understanding, remembrance, and ability to attend to Allah *(Subhaanahu wa ta'aalaa)* inwardly is enhanced. To penetrate the mystery of existence—including one's own existence—means to try to listen and attend to the depth and breadth of the pulse of this created universe. It means listening to the breath of life, looking into the rhythms of the heart, submitting to the continuum of experiences emanating from the unseen world. The poetry of life and of the yearnings of the inner heart (*quwwata-l-baatin*) speaks clearly to the Beauty, Grace, and Majesty of the Divine. One hour in that awareness is equal to a lifetime without it.

When we recite Qur'an, when we recite *dhikr* or sit in *muraaqabah* (meditation) with such attention, the reward comes in the way of awareness of the Divine Truth and Presence, with unprecedented feelings of joy and depths of peace. Even a few seconds spent in this state of consciousness brings profound happiness.

By attending sincerely and properly to the obligations of *sharee'ah* as well as engaging in frequent and constant recitation, taking a position of humility and refuge, one makes progress in one's pursuit of recognition of the nearness of Allah *(Subhaanahu wa ta'aalaa)*. Allah *(Subhaanahu wa ta'aalaa)* protects and uplifts the one who calls upon and remembers Him while performing his or her daily duties. Allah *(Subḥaanahu wa taʿaalaa)* is the Friend of the one in need of friendship. If one remembers Allah *(Subḥaanahu wa taʿaalaa)* with happiness, Allah *(Subḥaanahu wa taʿaalaa)* brings happiness; and if one is in pain, the Mercy of Allah *(Subḥaanahu wa taʿaalaa)* reaches out to one. One who speaks of His name with love will find peace in this world and in the next.

In *Suuratu-l-Baqara*, Allah *(Subḥaanahu wa taʿaalaa)* says,

> ***Fa-dhkuruunee adhkurkum wa-sh-kuruu lee wa laa takfuruun.***
>
> **So remember Me, and I will remember you; be grateful to Me and deny [Me] not** (2:152).

This *aayat* indicates a cycle of recitation and gratitude and thankfulness. The real practice of Islam is characterized by this cycle of goodness: remembrance, worship, and action, remembrance, worship, and action, all based on an intention to do good for the sake of Allah *(Subḥaanahu wa taʿaalaa)*.

The basis and essence of all worship lies in recitation, which is itself remembrance. How important is it? According to the Prophet *(ṣalla-Llaahu ʿalayhi wa sallam)*, **"The total destruction of the universe will take place when there exist almost no people to proclaim Allah's Name"** (Muslim).

The mere act of placing the name of Allah *(Subḥaanahu wa taʿaalaa)* on the tongue strengthens one's consciousness and deepens one's belief. It is a dimensional journey toward the Divine which enables and ennobles those who seek the Truth **"...Those who remember Allah standing, sitting, and lying down (...*yadhkuruuna-Llaaha qiyaamańw-wa quʿuudańw-wa ʿalaa junuubihim)*"** (Qurʾan 3:191).

From the first admonition in Qur'an, to the *ahaadith* of the Prophet *(salla-Llaahu 'alayhi wa sallam)*, through the teachings of the scholars and the *shuyukh*, *dhikru-Llaah* is the practice most recommended after prayer. Whether one knows Allah *(Subhaanahu wa ta'aalaa)* in one's heart and mind, through sensing a Presence, or in finding refuge in the Divine, the more constant the remembrance in one's sincere heart, in one's conscience, and in one's life and actions, the more peace and fulfillment will be attained.

The following short *suurahs* (chapters of Qur'an) and *du'aas* (supplications) are frequently recited as part of the practice of *dhikr khafee,* or silent remembrance of Allah *(Subhaanahu wa ta'aalaa):*

Suuratu-l-Faatihah (1)
Bismi-Llaahi-r-Rahmaani-r-Raheem
Alhamdu-li-Llaahi Rabbi-l-'aalameen,
Ar-Rahmaani-r-Raheem.
Maaliki yawmi-d-deen.
Iyyaaka na'budu wa'iyyaaka nasta'een.
Ihdina-s-siraata-l-mustaqeem,
Siraata-lladheena an'amta 'alayhim, ghayri-l-maghduubi 'alayhim, wa la-d-daaalleen.

Suurah 1: The Opening
In the Name of Allah, the Universally Merciful, the Singularly Compassionate
Praise be to Allah, the Lord of All the Worlds—
the Universally Merciful, the Singularly Compassionate—
Master of the Day of Judgment.
You alone we worship, and You alone we ask for help.
Guide us [to] the straight way,
The way of those whom You have blessed, not [the way of] those on whom is [Your] anger, nor those who are astray.

Suuratu-l-Iñshirah (94)

Bismi-Llaahi-r-Rahmaani-r-Raheem
Alam nashrah laka sadrak
Wa wadaʿnaa ʿañka wizrak
Al-ladhee añqada dhahrak
Wa rafaʿnaa laka dhikrak
Fa-inna maʿa-l-ʿusri yusraa
Inna maʿa-l-ʿusri yusraa.
Fa-idhaa faraghta fa-ñ-sab,
Wa'ilaa Rabbika fa-r-ghab

Suurah 94: The Expanding

In the Name of Allah, the Universally Merciful, the
Singularly Compassionate
Did We not open wide your heart?
And lift your heavy load from you—
that waas breaking your back—
and [have] We [not] exalted your remembrance?
So truly with difficulty—ease;
truly with difficulty—ease.
So when the load is lifted—then rise up [and go on]—
and to your Lord —strive.

Suuratu-l-ʿAsr (103)

Bismi-Llaahi-r-Rahmaani-r-Raheem
Wa-l-ʿasr.
Inna-l-'iñsaana lafee khusr,
Illaa-lladheena aamanuu wa ʿamilu-s-saalihaati, wa tawaasaw bi-l-haqqi, wa tawaasaw bi-s-sabr.

Suurah 103: The Late Afternoon

In the Name of Allah, the Universally Merciful, the
Singularly Compassionate
[I swear] by what remains of time—

that surely the human being is at a loss—
except for those who faithfully believe, and perform good deeds, and counsel one another to the truth and counsel one another to steadfast patience.

Durood Shareef

Allaahumma s̲alli ʿaala Sayyidinaa Muh̲ammadin, waseelatee ilayka, wa aaalihi, wa sallim.

O Allah, send blessings upon our master Muhammad, my means to You, and upon his family, and preserve him and protect him from harm.

Allaahumma s̲alli ʿaala Sayyidinaa Muh̲ammadin, as-siraaji-l-muneeri, wa aaalihi, wa sallim.

O Allah, send blessing upon our master Muhammad, the illuminating lamp, and upon his family, and preserve him and protect him from harm.

Allaahumma s̲alli ʿaala Sayyidinaa Muh̲ammadin wa ʿaala aaali Sayyidinaa Muh̲ammadin wa baarik wa sallim.

O God, send blessing upon our master Muhammad and upon the family of our master Muhammad and bless and preserve him and protect him from harm.

S̲alla-Llaahu ʿalayk, yaa Muh̲ammad.

May Allah send His blessings upon you, O Muhammad.

Notes

1 The statement which begins "Account for yourselves before you are taken into account…" is usually attributed to the companion of the Prophet *(ṣalla-Llaahu 'alayhi wa sallam)* and later imam Umar Ibn Khattab *(raḏiya-Llaahu 'anhu)*, as Imam Ghazali indicates in his book Ihya 'Ulum ad-Din. Although it lacks a clear chain or transmission, by tradition many Sufis and scholars have attributed the saying and/or the wisdom behind it to the Prophet *(ṣalla-Llaahu 'alayhi wa sallam)*.

References

Ansari, Muhammad Abdul Haq. *Sufism and Shari'ah: A Study of Shaykh Ahmad Sirhindi's Effort to Reform Sufism.* Leicester, UK: The Islamic Foundation, 1986.

Godlas, Alan. Sufism's Many Paths. Online. Available at http://www.arches.uga.edu/~godlas/Sufism.html. Accessed January 2001.

Islamic Dawah: Adh-Dhikr. Online. Available at http://www.islamicdawah.mobilixnet.dk/islam/adhdhikr.htm. Accessed January 2001.

Naqshbandi-Haqqani Sufi Order. Dhikr: Remembrance of God. Online. Available at http://www.naqshbandi.org/topics/dhikr.htm. Accessed January 2001.

Rasool, Hazrat Azad. *Turning Toward the Heart: Awakening to the Sufi Way.* Loiusville, KY: Fons Vitae, 2002.

Rumaysah, Abu. Some General Guidelines for Performing Dhikr. Online. Available at http://www.islaam.net/ilm/ibaadah/dhikrprinciples.html. Accessed January 2001.

al-Safuri al-Shafi'i, 'Abd ar-Rahman. Dhikr (Remembrance of God). Translated excerpt from *Nuzhat al-Majalis.* Online. Available at http://naqshbandi.net/haqqani/Sufi/zikr.html. Accessed January 2001.

Zakariyya, Shaykhul Hadith Maulana Muhammad. Virtues of Dhikr. *Fazail-e-A'mal*, Vol. I. Translated by Abdul Rashid Arshad. New Delhi: Idara Asha'at-e-Diniyat, 1990.

بسم الله الرحمن الرحيم

Healing and Meditation

Bismi-Llaah, Alhamduli-Llaah.
Allaahumma salli wa sallim ʿalaa Sayyidinaa Muhammadin,
wa ʿalaa aalihi wa sahbih

In medical terms, the key to healing lies in re-activating the immune system's ability to respond appropriately. Our natural state is to resist disease and destructive forces. Most bodies have cancer cells within them at one point or another; and most of the time, the immune system destroys those cells before they do any damage.

So, too, as long as we live, we will have temptations, we will have battles, we will encounter physical, mental, and emotional difficulties. Just as Allah *(Subhaanahu wa taʿaalaa)* has equipped us with built-in physiological systems to counteract diseased cells, we have been equipped with all that we need to remain spiritually healthy. We have been created with a good and upright nature—our *fitrah.* We are created in a balanced, healthy state. According to the Qur'an,

> ***Thumma sawwaahu wa nafakha feehi mir-ruuhihi wa jaʿala lakumu-s-samʿa wa-l-'absaara wa-l-'af'idah; qaleelam-maa tashkuruun.***
>
> **...Then [Allah] fashioned [the human being] in due proportion and breathed into [the human being] of His spirit. He gave you ears, and eyes, and hearts, yet you are seldom thankful** (32:9).

How often do we upset our own innate proportion? How often do we become imbalanced, so that the negative tendencies within us multiply, growing out of control, taking over, threatening to destroy us?

At every step in a disease's progression, Allah *(Subḥaanahu wa taʿaalaa)* grants us the power to reverse its course, to rein our lesser tendencies back into manageable proportions—as medical researchers hope one day to render cancer "a chronic but manageable illness" (Lemonick). The fulcrum of our capacity to preserve a healthy balance is what the Prophet Muhammad *(ṣalla-Llaahu ʿalayhi wa sallam)* described as a "special organ" placed within us by Allah *(Subḥaanahu wa taʿaalaa)*. This organ can fight disease, stimulate the immune system, ward off attacks of grief, misery, sorrow, complaining, fear, doubt, anger, and sadness. It is, of course, our heart *(qalb)*. If the heart is healthy, the body is healthy. If the heart is diseased, then the body is diseased.

Physically, the heart is a distribution point for life's energy via oxygenated blood. Spiritually, it is the gathering point for the essence. Allah *(Subḥaanahu wa taʿaalaa)* placed this—the most important of our organs—in the center of our body, protected by a cage of ribs. The heart not only serves the most prominent functional role in maintaining our lives, but it also has its own mind or consciousness.

Our outer illnesses are indications of weaknesses or diseases of our hearts. These dis-eases manifest in symptoms such as ignorance, possessiveness, hatred, inhumane acts, blame, thinking that the solutions to our problems lie in changing our circumstances, not ourselves. Our heart condition depends upon the degree of our faith and trust in God, our ability to turn toward Allah *(Subḥaanahu wa taʿaalaa)*, the One, the True, the Healer *(ash-Shaafee)*, the Compassionate, versus our tendency to rely solely upon our self. Denial of the presence and ultimate authority of God casts us into a whirlpool of contradictions and confusion. We become disconnected from reality. Our hearts grow weak; we suffer and fall ill.

The cure is to turn toward God. In the Qur'an, we read:

> ***...bi-dhikri-Llaahi taṯma'innu-l-quluub.***
>
> **It is the remembrance of Allah that provides tranquillity to the heart** (13:28).

The root of the Arabic word for tranquillity *(ṯam'ana)* also means to be secure. In the remembrance of Allah *(Subḫaanahu wa ta'aalaa)*, we find security, satisfaction, and rest.

One of the most focused means of remembering Allah is through meditation *(muraaqabah)*. The healing benefits of meditation are widely recognized today. One study found that "[a] mind-body intervention including...meditation techniques" helped relieve symptoms of fibromyalgia (Singh). At the U.S. Army War College, anger-management programs that included training in meditation were shown to improve the cardiovascular health of military officers (Barko). Prison inmates who have been given courses in meditation are "less prone to depression [and] hostility," are "less likely to smoke," and have lower incidences of drug and alcohol addiction (Prisoners). Transcendental meditation has been shown to lower blood pressure by helping to keep blood vessels open (Meditation).

Such studies have helped popularize spiritual paths like yoga in recent decades. Often, individuals turn to meditation more as a means for outer health and mental stability than as a means for spiritual growth and fulfillment. Yet from a Sufic Islamic point of view, the purpose of meditation is not to engender feelings of well-being. The aim is to develop a progressively more comprehensive awareness of the Presence of the Divine in all aspects of life—to sense that there is a relatedness *(nisbah)* between all aspects of creation, all thoughts and all human experiences. This becomes the inner and outer goal: to come near to Allah *(Subḫaanahu wa ta'aalaa)* and be conscious of Allah's Presence.

The Prophet Muhammad *(salla-Llaahu ʿalayhi wa sallam)* described this goal in terms of *iḥsaan*, which he said is **"to worship Allah as though you are seeing Him, and while you see Him not yet truly He sees you"** (Abu Musa/Bukhari). *Iḥsaan* is a sustainable, living consciousness of the presence of God in our lives—a consciousness so strong, so vivid, that when we attain it, we feel as if we were actually seeing God.

It is true that as we go deeper in meditation, our stress levels go down, our physical symptoms diminish, cholesterol levels drop. Even chronically ill people may be cured. But for spiritual seekers, all this should be incidental, not the goal. In the Qur'an, Allah *(Subḥaanahu wa taʿaalaa)* reveals:

> ***...lahum quluubul-laa yafqahuuna bihaa, wa lahum aʿyunul-laa yubṣiruuna bihaa, wa lahum aadhaanul-laa yasmaʿuuna bihaa...***

> **...they have hearts that do not understand, and eyes that do not see, and ears that do not hear...** (7:179).

Only when the physical senses are aligned with the *laṭaa'if* (the subtle organs of perception) can we truly see. When we visit an optometrist, he or she places different lenses in front of our eyes to determine which ones can most improve our vision. Meditation engages us in a similar process of alignment, clarifying internally and externally that which is perceived.

If we are to progress in meditation, we need to establish some peace of mind before we sit to meditate. That may seem contradictory; after all, isn't meditation a means to achieve equanimity? Again, the student of Sufism should not be meditating for peace of mind (nor, for that matter, for the sake of the ego or to attain paradise). We should be doing this for the sake of God—*fee sabeeli-Llaah.*

We are not checking into a mystical out-patient clinic when we sit to meditate. On the contrary, we must enter meditation with a mature personal peacefulness, based on understanding the reasons for undertaking these practices. The Sufi is not seeking enlightenment. The Sufi is the servant of Allah *(Subhaanahu wa ta'aalaa)*. The Sufi is striving to be aware of the Presence of God within and around all life and its experiences. Why? Because we must. For what purpose? Because we are drawn by our hearts to worship and glorify our Creator. Allah *(Subhaanahu wa ta'aalaa)* reveals:

> ***Wa maa khalaqtu-l-jinna wa-l-'iñsa illaa li-ya'buduun.***
>
> **I created the jinn and humankind only that they might worship Me** (Qur'an 51:56).

One Sufi master wrote:

> When the heart becomes pure, serene, and sound... it will draw near to [God] so that its life will mean nearness to Him, and its death will mean remoteness from Him. [The heart's] satisfaction will lie in having private conversation with Him. [The seeker] will become totally content to the exclusion of anything else, and will not care if this world turned its back to him [or her]; nor...care about hunger, thirst, nakedness, and disease.

The Divine energy is all around us. God's gifts are always flowing toward us. God's forgiveness, mercy, and love are always flowing toward us. God's healing is always upon us.

> ***Wa li-Llaahi mulku-s-samaawaati wa-l-'ard, wa-Llaahu 'alaa kulli shay'iñ qadeer.***

> **All the dominions of the heavens and the earth belong to Allah, Who has power over everything** (Qur'an 3:189).

God's healing power is not contingent upon a specific event. If I fall and injure myself, it is not as if a signal instantly reaches Allah *(Subhaanahu wa ta'aalaa)*—"Abdur Rashid bruised his knee!"—and Allah *(Subhaanahu wa ta'aalaa)* sends a bolt of compassion to my knee. Rather, the student of Sufism strives progressively to remember Allah *(Subhaanahu wa ta'aalaa)* moment-to-moment. He or she progressively develops a personal and congenial relationship with the friends of Allah and then with Allah *(Subhaanahu wa ta'aalaa)*, awakening to the realization that the Divine attributes are continually present. When we are in misery, relief is there— when we suffer loss, prosperity is there—if we can recognize relief and prosperity in ways that may not fit our expectations.

We see circumstances as we choose to see them. Allah's Presence is always penetrating us, always holding us—but do we allow ourselves to accept this? Or do we swim through life obliviously, like the young fish who asked its grandfather to explain the concept of water? We are busy making money, paying bills, raising children, pursuing careers, changing our minds and then changing our minds again. God has said we should contemplate the signs of the Divine Presence throughout creation, but we are too smart. We want answers: answers that we can affirm intellectually and empirically.

One of the greatest mistakes made by human beings is to think that our minds and physical senses are adequate for understanding the truth of this world. In reality, our minds, intellects, and senses cannot decode aspects of events and phenomena that are right in front of us. To understand more fully, we must learn to see through more subtle organs of perception: the *lataa'if.*

Bahaudin Naqshband *(radiya-Llaahu ʿanhu)* described meditation (more specifically, *muraaqabah*) as waiting for the *lataa'if* to attract the Divine energy. We sit, and we wait. Khwaja Khurud *(radiya-Llaahu ʿanhu)* said:

> *Muraaqabah* is leaving behind one's power and strength. It is... waiting in expectation of the encounter while longing for its beauty and being immersed in its desire and love.

As we direct attention toward the *lataa'if*, we are tuning to the Divine energy, in much the same way that we might adjust the dials on a short-wave radio to receive a broadcast. First, we turn the knob in large motions, then we refine the tuning, one kilohertz at a time.

What happens when we become receptive to the Divine energy? There is a story that once a companion of the Prophet *(salla-Llaahu ʿalayhi wa sallam)*

> ...climbed onto the roof of his house during a full moon to contemplate the grandeur of the heavens and the earth. However, he became so engaged in his meditation, looking at the sky and weeping, that he fell down into his neighbor's house. The neighbor jumped out of bed with his sword in his hand, thinking a thief had come in. When he saw that the intruder was his neighbor, he put down his sword and asked him who had pushed him off his own roof. The companion said, "By God, I was never aware of that!"

We meditate to be aware of the Presence of God within and around us. The deeper our meditation, the more we move from the cold state of intellectual knowledge to the warmth of feeling the Presence of Allah *(Subhaanahu wa ta'aalaa)* or God or truth in our lives. We come to a place of submission and trust, where our reality is always related to God.

When meditation is regarded as a way to heal oneself, it is often reduced to a technique. But it is not a technique. There may be certain techniques involved in specific types of meditation, but meditation is inherently part of our *fitrah* (essential nature). Analogously, music is not a technique, although one's approach to music might reflect technique. So too love and love-making are not the same, although certainly the latter may be an important part of a loving relationship. So then in another sense, the idea of "healing yourself" is *a priori* problematic. One is healed by Allah *(Subhaanahu wa ta'aalaa)*, although personal effort and intention are elements in the process of becoming receptive to Allah's Mercy.

Man ʿarafa nafsahu, faqad ʿarafa Rabbahu.

One who knows oneself knows one's Lord. [1]

If you know your self, you know your Lord. It is not "I" who is healing; it is Allah *(Subhaanahu wa ta'aalaa)* Who is the Healing, the Healer, and the Healed. The disease that is being cured arose from separation from or lack of awareness of Allah's Presence. Overcoming this separation or lack is the ultimate and only lasting healing. All else passes.

Spiritual knowledge of oneself and of the Divine is the foundation for wisdom. In Arabic, the word for wisdom (*hikmah*) comes from the same root as the word for doctor *(hakeem)*. Among the Sufis, the shaykh is frequently referred to as a *hakeem*. The shaykh prescribes for the student, thinking carefully about the qualities and tendencies of that individual, seeing him or her by the light of *kashf* (inner sight), which is the light of faith, wisdom, and experience.

Let me touch briefly on several of the types of meditative techniques that a shaykh may prescribe.

Awareness of Breath

To be healthy, we need to be aware, conscious beings in harmony with reality. Taking time to observe the breath is a way to be more reflective and present with Allah's attributes. Making the effort to breathe correctly helps us to be fully present each moment. We have probably all had the experience of being distracted inwardly, while outwardly we may be talking to associates, seeing clients, greeting friends, putting the children to bed. The problem with operating from distraction is that we assume we understand aspects of the world around us (and that those around us share our understandings), even when these "understandings" have little bearing on reality. The farther removed we are from reality, the farther removed we are from harmony. The farther we move from harmony, the more disbalanced we are. The more disbalanced we are, the more dis-eased we are.

Time Pause

Shaykhs may also prescribe the practice of time pause, in which the student periodically pauses to reflect, at any given moment, under any circumstance. Bahaudin Naqshband *(raḏiya-Llaahu ʿanhu)* described time pause as the agent that smoothes the way for the seeker. Through time pause, we become aware of our states and of where we stand in relationship to Allah *(Subḥaanahu wa taʿaalaa)*. It is as if we are standing on top of a mountain and surveying the land before us, determining how we will proceed. Are we in a state of gratitude, or getting involved in our *nafs*? If there is chaos in our household or workplace, how are we dealing with it? Are we operating from the realm of the attributes of Allah *(Subhaanahu wa ta'aalaa)*, or just reacting?

MUHAASABAH

Muhaasabah literally means to reckon, to reconcile, or to take account of (as in balancing an organization's financial records). The Prophet Muhammad *(salla-Llaahu 'alayhi wa sallam)* is sometimes reported to have said:

> ***Haasibuu anfusakum qabla an tuhaasabuu, wa zinuu a'maalakum qabla an tuzana 'alaykum.***
>
> **Account for yourselves before you are accounted; weigh your actions before your actions become a weight upon you.** [2]

In *muhaasabah*, we become better able to see what we have done well, and we thank Allah *(Subhaanahu wa ta'aalaa)* for it. We also recognize the limitations or weaknesses of our efforts and ask Allah *(Subhaanahu wa ta'aalaa)* for forgiveness.

Every day we are called upon to restructure our priorities. One of the priorities that we should move up on our "to do" list is meditation. Meditation is a vehicle that helps us to travel from our present perspective to a new paradigm. If we fit it into our schedule only after we have addressed all the other aspects of daily life, then we will not be able to bring its benefits to those other needs. We should focus first on being at peace spiritually; then our outer as well as our inner state will improve.

Some spiritual teachings portray materiality as the enemy of spiritual health and advocate withdrawal from the world. But the material world is not an enemy. Rather, we are endangered by our choices in that world. We choose to become so absorbed in our work and responsibilities that we segment our lives into "practical" and "spiritual" components. We begin to live two lives, ignoring the threads of the inner that help to support the outer, and the threads of the outer that contain the inner.

What is the alternative? To make our inner and outer lives seamless: to treat our outer activities as part of our worship, and our inner pursuits as part of our job.

Allah *(Subhaanahu wa ta'aalaa)* tells us,

> ***Nahnu aqrabu ilayhi min habli-l-wareed.***
>
> **We are nearer to a person than the jugular vein** (Qur'an 50:16).

There is no outside of us except in the material world (*dunyaa*). *Laa illaaha illa-Llaah*: there is only Allah *(Subhaanahu wa ta'aalaa)*. We have never been anywhere else. We exist only to discover that we do not.

Meditation assists in this discovery. When we sit, we practice opening and closing the door. Ultimately, we practice removing the doorway altogether. We enter a realm of peace and unity, linked through the *lataa'if* to what Naqshbandis call "the golden chain." When a person relaxes and allows the Divine light to enter each of the *lataa'if*, he or she gains strength in two ways. First, in the collective sense of seeing all humanity as part of the same chain; and second, independently, as the light of wisdom now illumines the world in which we live. A light is extended in the physical world, and in consciousness here and beyond.

By identifying with the *lataa'if* in meditation, we extend our awareness of the Presence of the Divine *(ihsaan)* and our normal perceptions beyond the physical world. We realize that life encompasses more than physical existence. As long as we think of health as being only something of the body and mind, we will be limited to defining health in physical, emotional, and psychological terms. When we overcome this limited view, we experience healthfulness in its true sense.

Allah *(Subhaanahu wa ta'aalaa)* says in a *hadith qudsi*, **"I am as My servant thinks of Me."** If we strive to deepen and affirm our faith, we will come to conceive of God in increasingly profound and loving ways. If our aim is simply to make our lives free of strain, problems, and illness, these aims will likewise determine our relationship with God, arousing within us guilt without meaning or questions without answers. "What have I done to deserve this punishment?" "Why has God put such a hardship on me?" There are people in this world who have never considered such questions. Those of us raised in Western intellectual climates may find it difficult to understand how some individuals who are impoverished can smile and seemingly accept their state (which is not to say that, given the opportunity, they would not develop more of their potential). It is indeed possible to reach a level where one sees God's wisdom, God's healing, God's love in everything.

Health is a promise extended to us by Allah *(Subhaanahu wa ta'aalaa)*. All we must do is go toward it with open hands and open minds, instead of complaining. You can have a broken foot and not complain. You can have a congenital heart condition and be happy. Exposure to pollution may give you cancer or cause your kidneys to fail, and you become either a victim or an environmental advocate working for other people's well-being. A Sufi and a Muslim should be positive, with good intentions, good words, and goodness exuding through their actions. If we have the right attitude, Allah *(Subhaanahu wa ta'aalaa)* provides.

For every struggle we face, we can go deeper and become better. Even if our body is failing, we can be in a process of becoming more healed, not less healed. We are not worse off because we have those experiences; we are better off because Allah *(Subhaanahu wa taᶜaalaa)* has given us tests and trials.

How do we attain contentment? Through surrender. When we have surrendered, God will cover us with His love, heal our wounds, and attach Himself to our souls. Why should we wait for the death bed to force our surrender? Healing is available as soon as we are no longer afraid to attach ourselves to truth and to God as the Truth, with full confidence that we are being asked by God to serve Him—not to get some reward, not because we are "supposed to," but because we have arrived at a stage where concern for oneself has been supplanted by concern from oneself. Know yourself and you know your Lord. As the famous saying states, "Physician, heal thyself." It does not state, "Physician, heal thy body."

* * *

Wa Llaahu lahu-l-haqqu wa huwa yahdis-sabeel.
Hasbuna-Llaahu wahdahu wa niᶜma-l-wakeel.
Wa salli ᶜalaa Sayyidinaa Muhammadin wa aaalihi wa sahbihi ajmaᶜeen
Wa-l-hamdu li-Llaahi Rabbi-l-ᶜaalameen.

Truth belongs to Allah; it is He who shows the way.
Allah, alone, suffices us, and what a fine guardian is He!
Blessings upon our Master Muhammad
and his family and Companions altogether
and praise is due to Allah, Lord of the Worlds.

Notes

1 There is considerable controversy about the origin of the widely quoted statement, "one who knows oneself knows his Lord." Some believe it was a statement of the Prophet, although it does not appear in *ḫadith* literature. Some attribute it to a close companion, Imam Ali *(raḏiya-Llaahu 'anhu)*. The respected scholar and Sufi Ibn Arabi said "This *ḫadith*, although it is not proved by way of narration, is proved to us by way of *kashf* (inner vision)," while other scholars reject Arabi's method of verification as extremely dangerous. Imam Suyuti wrote a beautiful essay about it, demonstrating that even if it can not be traced back directly to the Prophet *(ṣalla-Llaahu 'alayhi wa sallam)*, its meaning is still true. In keeping with Sufic literature, the statement is respectfully included here.

2 The statement which begins "Account for yourselves before you are taken into account…" is usually attributed to the companion of the Prophet *(ṣalla-Llaahu 'alayhi wa sallam)* and later imam Umar Ibn Khattab *(raḏiya-Llaahu 'anhu)*, as Imam Ghazali indicates in his book Ihya 'Ulum ad-Din. Although it lacks a clear chain or transmission, by tradition many Sufis and scholars have attributed the saying and/or the wisdom behind it to the Prophet *(ṣalla-Llaahu 'alayhi wa sallam)*.

References

Barko, William F. and Mark A. Vaitkus, editors. *The U.S. Army War College Guide To Executive Health and Fitness.* Online at http://www.cdc.gov/nccdphp/dnpa/usphs/ pdfs/army.pdf.

Lemonick, Michael D. and Alice Park. "New Hope for Cancer." *Time* magazine, May 28, 2001, 62-69.

"Meditation lowers blood pressure." BBC News, 2 August 1999. Online at http://news.bbc.co.uk/1/low/health/410003.stm.

"Prisoners benefit from meditation." BBC News Online, 10 July 2001. Online at http://news.bbc.co.uk/1/low/health/1430311.stm.

Singh, B.B., B.M. Berman, V.A. Hadhazy, and P. Creamer. "A pilot study of cognitive behavioral therapy in fibromyalgia." *Alternative Therapies in Health and Medicine* 1998 Mar 4(2):67-70. University of Maryland School of Medicine, Baltimore. Precis posted online at http://home.tampabay.rr.com/lymecfs/abstract98.htm.

بسم الله الرحمن الرحيم

Washing One's Heart With the Tears of Shame

Bismi-Llaahi-r-Rah̲maani-r-Rah̲eem

Bismi-Llaah, Alh̲amduli-Llaah.
Allaahumma s̲alli wa sallim ʿalaa Sayyidinaa Muh̲ammadin,
wa ʿalaa aalihi wa sah̲bih

Al-h̲amdu-li-Llaahi-l-ladhee baʿthaa-r-rusuul wa-r-risaalat
wa atummahum bi Sayyidinaa Muh̲ammad
li yuteema makarim al-akhlaq.
Al-h̲amdu-li-Llaahi-lladhee lahu-l-asmaa'u-l-h̲usnaa,
wa-lladhee baʿthaa-n-Nabi Muh̲ammad
li-yaftah̲ bihi maa ughliq.

All praise to Allah Who sent messages to the messengers
and sealed them with Sayyidina Muhammad (peace be upon him)
[who brought] the most complete and the best of ethics.
All praise to Allah Who has the most beautiful names,
and [Who sent to us] the Prophet Muhammad (peace be upon him)
to open what had been closed.

Opening Ourselves to Faith Through Shame

In this *duʿaa*, we remember the spiritual refinement of the Prophet *(s̲alla-Llaahu ʿalayhi wa sallam)* as one who "open[ed] what had been closed." The concepts of opening and closing here may be understood in many possible ways, but this afternoon I would like to focus on just one implication. I would like to suggest that to accept the Prophet Muhammad *(s̲alla-Llaahu ʿalayhi wa sallam)* as one who opens that which is closed means to recognize that *shame* is a gift of Allah *(Subhaanahu wa ta'aalaa)* and situations of personal shame, as difficult as they are to accept and bear, in fact are doorways to faith and healing.

> **Abul Hasan ᶜAbdan reported that he went to see Aisha *(radiya-Llaahu ᶜanhaa)*, and said, "Tell me the most wonderful thing you ever saw from the Messenger of Allah *(salla-Llaahu ᶜalayhi wa sallam)*." She wept, and she said, "What affair of his was not wonderful? One night, he came to me and he crawled in under the blanket. His skin touched mine, and then he said, 'O daughter of Abu Bakr, let me worship my Lord.' 'I love your being close,' said I. Then he got up and went over to the waterskin and made his ablution, pouring a great deal of water. Then he stood and prayed and wept until tears flowed upon his chest. Then he bowed and he wept, and then he made prostration and he wept, and then he raised his head and he wept. Then he made prostration again and he continued like this until Bilal came to give him the announcement of the *fajr* prayer. And I said to him, 'O Messenger of Allah! What made you weep? God has forgiven your sins, whether they came before or might come later.' And he said, 'Shall I not be a grateful servant? Why should I not do this when God has sent down upon me this verse: "In the creation of the heavens and the earth are signs for people who reflect." ' "**

The Prophet's repentance was an affirmation of his faith. He himself illustrated the relationship between wrongdoing and shame and repentance and faith. He had nothing of which to be ashamed, yet he repented. In contrast, *we* all have things of which to be ashamed—but we are ashamed to admit our shame to ourselves, let alone to repent to Allah *(Subhaanahu wa ta'aalaa)*.

Pushing the Boundaries of Shame

People of every age struggle with the seductive nature of today's society. We are all affected (or shall I say infected) by the polluting effect of the environment. The youth of each generation (and I believe especially of the current generation) have a particularly difficult struggle. Advertisements, the media, and peer pressure call us to taste the forbidden fruit—the fruit of seduction, not of values. Now these enticements are reinforced by borderless and anonymous Internet chat groups and spam, offering opportunities to expand one's experiences under new and apparently secret identities. This encourages personality crises and disorder as well as subverting individual integrity and culture.

How many detours we open to ourselves, without regard for the caution revealed by Allah *(Subhaanahu wa ta'aalaa)*:

> ***Wa ʿala-Llaahi qasdu-s-sabeeli wa minhaa jaa'ir.***
>
> **Allah's is the direction of the way, from it, some deviate** (Qur'an 16:9).

Powerful agents of social change are pushing back the boundaries at which we feel shame. Consequently they are undermining our values and changing our sense of reality.

We can see these processes at work from our own childhood to today. When I was growing up, teenage boys would feel ashamed if an adult saw them holding hands with a girl. Today the criteria by which an average teen measures shame are too graphic for me to describe (though you can read about "hooking up" in a recent article in *Time* or *Newsweek*). The boundaries may have needed to be extended, but now they are virtually absent. Worse yet is that the idea of shame has been "shamed." One dare not mention shame or even repentance in modern Western or Westernized society; it offends too many people. So, not only have the ways we define shame been stretched to new boundaries, the concept itself has been vilified.

The Qur'an speaks to the idea of *qareen*, sometimes translated as the lower nature of each human being, in recounting the story of Qarun.

> ***Inna Qaaruuna kaana miñ qawmi Muusaa fa-baghaa ᶜalayhim; wa aataynaahu mina-l-kunuuzi maaa inna mafaatiḫahuu la-tanuu'u bi-l-ᶜuṣbati uli-l-quwwah: idh qaala lahuu qawmuhuu laa tafraḫ inna-Llaaha laa yuḫibbu-l-fariḫeen.***
>
> ***Wa-b-taghi feemaaa aataaka-Llaahu-d-daara-l-'aakhirata wa laa tañsa naṣeebaka mina-d-dunyaaa wa aḫsiñ kamaa aḫsana-Llaahu ilayka wa laa tabghi-l-fasaada fi-l-'arḏ; inna-Llaaha laa yuḫibbu-l-mufsideen.***
>
> ***Qaala innamaaa uuteetuhuu ᶜalaa ᶜilmin ᶜiñdee; awa lam yaᶜlam anna-Llaaha qad ahlaka miñ qablihee mina-l-quruuni man huwa ashaddu minhu quwwatañw-wa aktharu jamᶜaa? Wa laa yus'alu ᶜañ dhunuubihimu-l-mujrimuun.***

Fa-kharaja ᶜalaa qawmihee fee zeenatih; qaala-l-ladheena yureeduuna-l-hayaata-d-dunyaaa yaa- layta lanaa mithla maaa uutiya Qaaruunu innahu ladhuu hadh-dhin ᶜadheem.

Wa qaala-l-ladheena uutu-l-ᶜilma waylakum thawaabu-Llaahi khayrul-li-man aamana wa ᶜamila saalihaa: wa laa yulaqqaahaaa illa-s-saabiruun.

Fa-khasafnaa bihee wa bidaarihi-l-'ard; fa-maa kaana lahuu miñ fi'atiñy-yañsuruunahuu miñ duuni-Llaahi wa maa kaana mina-l-muñtasireen.

Indeed Qarun was from the people of Musa, but he tyrannized them. We had given him a trove of treasure chests whose keys would have been a burden for a whole host of strong men. His own people said to him, "Do not exult [in your wealth]. For surely Allah does not love those who exult [in what soon passes].

But instead seek, through that which Allah has given you, the Final Abode, [while at the same time] not forgetting your portion in the world, and be kind, even as Allah has been kind to you, and do not seek [to cause] corruption on the earth, for surely Allah does not love the corrupters."

He said, "I have been given [this wealth] on account of my knowledge." Did he not know that before him Allah had destroyed generations

> **of those who were more powerful than him in strength and accumulated [wealth]? But evil-doers will not be asked about their faults [because Allah already knows them].**
>
> **So he went out to his people in his adornment. Those who desired the life of the world said, "Ah! If only we had the like of what has been given to Qarun! Indeed he is a man of mighty fortune."**
>
> **But those who had been given knowledge [of the Truth] said, "Agony is yours! The reward of Allah for the one who believes and does righteous deeds is better, and only the patiently steadfast will attain it."**
>
> **So We caused the earth to swallow him and his dwelling. And then he had no one and nothing to aid him other than Allah, nor was he of those who were able to defend themselves** (28:76-81).

This story shows the give and take between the attractions of the world, and our innate remembrance of Allah's guidance to be generous, faithful, and steadfast. Some people say that there is a *shayṯan* within us, and that is *qareen,* as found in such *ayats* as:

> ***Qaala qareenuhuu Rabbanaa maaa aṯghay-tuhuu wa laakiñ kaana fee ḏalaalim ba'eed.***
>
> **[The person's] other self *(qareen)* will say: "O our Sustainer! It was not I that led him into evil, but it had gone far astray [of its own accord]!"** (Qur'an 50:27).

Let us remember that the heart of even the Prophet *(salla-Llaahu ʿalayhi wa sallam)* had to be washed before the *Isra* and *Miʿraaj*. Today, the forces that undermine our *fitrah*—the forces that encourage *fitnah*—are subtle and all-pervasive. They are as widely accepted as a daily dose of fluoride in one's toothpaste or chemicals in one's food. We imagine that we can resist them, or we dismiss them with the age-old refrain: "I'm not addicted, I'm in control, I know where the line is." This is the kind of delusion to which Allah *(Subhaanahu wa taʿaalaa)* refers in the Qur'an:

> ***…bal zuyyina li-l-ladheena kafaruu makruhum wa sudduu ʿani-s-sabeel; wa mañy-yudlili-Llaahu fa-maa lahuu min haad.***
>
> **…Nay, their contrivance is made seeming fair for those who disbelieve and they are kept from the right road. He whom Allah sends astray, for him there is no guide** (13:33).

Examples of shamelessness abound in the media. The trailer for a new television sitcom called *Complete Savages* shows a boy pushing his little brother's head under his sweaty, smelly armpit. Sexual content is part of almost every program. Reality programs focus on human weakness, fantasy, and public crude behavior and embarrassment. The news channels and Internet make accessible videos of people being slaughtered. Politicians twist the truth or blatantly lie without qualms, placing political ideology above truth, all for the sake of winning elections or extending power. Whether through disreputable behavior, dishonesty, decisions which cost thousand of lives, or their choice to turn a blind eye to genocide, starvation, or poverty, the politicians earn the mistrust of thinking people, but unfortunately sometimes dupe the majority through mere constant repetition and slogans. These shameless individuals present themselves as people of faith: as Jews, Christians, Muslims, or adherents of other religions.

How distorted this has become is evident. In place of shame and the consequent opportunity to truly deepen one's humility and faith, we find blatant stretching of the boundaries of social norms coupled with a fascination with exposès that feign indignation at the ways in which the boundaries have been stretched.

HIDING THE FAULTS OF OTHERS AND OF OURSELVES

It seems evident that few news or media editors, let alone politicians or popular icons, have reflected upon the injunctions regarding covering the faults of others, such as this from the Qur'an:

Yaaa-ayyuhaa-l-ladheena aamanuu laa yaskhar qawmum-miñ qawmin ʿasaaa añy-yakuunuu khayram-minhum wa laa nisaaa'um-min-nisaaa'in ʿasaaa añy-yakunna khayram-minhunn: wa laa talmizuu añfusakum wa laa tanaabazuu bi-l-'alqaab; bi'sa-l-'ismu-l-fusuuqu baʿda-l-'eemaan: wa mal-lam yatub fa-ulaaa'ika humu-<u>dh</u>-<u>dh</u>aalimuun. Yaaa ayyuhaa-l-ladheena aamanu-j-tanibuu katheeram-mina-<u>dh</u>-<u>dh</u>ann: inna baʿda-<u>dh</u>-<u>dh</u>anni ithmuñw-wa laa tajassasuu wa laa yaghtab-baʿdukum baʿdaa; ayu<u>h</u>ibbu a<u>h</u>adukum añy-ya'kula la<u>h</u>ma akheehi maytañ fa-karihtumuuh? wa-t-taqu-Llaah; inna-Llaaha tawwaabur-Ra<u>h</u>eem.

O believers! Let no men laugh at other men who may perhaps be better than themselves; and let no woman laugh at another woman, who may perhaps be better than herself. Do not defame

> **one another through sarcastic remarks, nor call one another by offensive nicknames. It is an evil thing to be called by a bad name after being a believer, and those who do not repent are the ones who are the wrongdoers. O believers! Avoid immoderate suspicion, for in some cases suspicion is a sin. Do not spy on one another, nor backbite one another. Would any of you like to eat the flesh of his dead brother? Surely you would abhor it. Fear Allah; for Allah is the Accepter of repentance, Merciful** (49:11-12).

The Prophet *(salla-Llaahu 'alayhi wa sallam)* recognized that the door of repentance is open to everyone. He therefore concealed the faults of others while simultaneously he assisted them in refining their vision and understanding. In order to make humility and faith our most valued character traits, specific and simple admonitions were given, such as the following passage of the Qur'an:

> ***Qul li-l-mu'mineena yaghudduu min absaarihim wa yahfadhuu furuujahum; dhaalika azkaa lahum; inna-Llaaha Khabeerum-bimaa yasna'uun. Wa qul li-l-mu'minaati yaghdudna min absaarihinna wa yahfadhna furuujahunna wa laa yubdeena zeenatahunna illaa maa dhahara minhaa wa-l-yadribna bi-khumurihinna 'alaa juyuubihinna...***
>
> **Tell the believing men to lower their gaze and be modest. That is purer for them. Lo! Allah is Aware of what they do. And tell the believing women to lower their gaze and be modest, and to display of their adornment only that which is apparent, and to draw their veils over their bosoms...** (24:30-31).

Whether we are male or female, we are to veil our shame from *others'* view, but not from our*selves.* We are to be silent about it outwardly, but inwardly reflecting and repenting. It is the process of embracing that shame, feeling that shame, but in a context of determination to correct one's errors, return to one's values, understand the principles of contentment and peace in one's life and how to manifest them with a permanence and sincerity. Then the shame naturally and spontaneously becomes a powerful catalyst for turning toward Allah and deepening one's *imaan* (faith).

Everything points to Allah when we have begun to understand who we are—when we realize that we are sent here to awaken and to find ourselves. As the masters of *Tasawwuf* have said:

Man ʿarafa nafsahu, faqad ʿarafa Rabbahu.

One who knows oneself, knows one's Lord.

Rasuulu-Llaah (salla-Llaahu ʿalayhi wa sallam), like the prophets Isa and Ibrahim before him *(ʿalayhumma-s-salaam)*, had that personality of *imaan*, that manifestation of faith based upon knowing oneself. Every one of those individuals had fear, doubt, grief and loss. Each was ashamed or confused at times. Think of Sidna Ibrahim *(ʿalayhi-s-salaam)* facing the sacrifice of his beloved son. Think of Jesus *(ʿalayhi-s-salaam)* on the mountain, trembling alone in prayer while his companions slept. Think of the prophet Muhammad *(salla-Llaahu ʿalayhi wa sallam)* at the time of the first revelation and in the dark of the night as he prostrated in repentance.

The Antiquation of Repentance

In contrast, to the extent that we do not feel shame—to the extent that our decisions and actions are outside of the context of shame—we do not think to repent. We gloss over the bounties that are promised to us in the Qur'an.

> ***Thumma inna Rabbaka li-l-ladheena ʿamilu-s-suuu'a bi-jahaalatiñ thumma taabuu mim-baʿdi dhaalika wa aslahuuu inna Rabbaka mim-baʿdihaa la-Ghafuurur-Raheem.***
>
> **Lo, your Lord is forgiving and merciful towards those who do something wrong through ignorance, but later repent and mend their ways** (16:119).

To be among those who seek forgiveness, we must be cognizant that there are situations and acts of which to repent. What happens when repentance joins shame as an outcast, antiquated idea? Fewer and fewer people experience Allah's mercy, while more and more people find themselves addicted to drugs, alcohol, or fantasy relationships. They find their lives playing out as Allah describes:

> ***Al-haakumu-t-takaathur hattaa zurtumu-l-maqaabir.***
>
> **You are obsessed by greed for more and more until you go down to your graves** (Qur'an 102:1-2).

Yet, despite the rationalizations that we ourselves use to justify extended and false boundaries, if we are honest, we will find the concept of shame still present in society and in ourselves. *Alhamduli-Llaah*, for the repentance that comes from allowing ourselves to feel shame is such a powerful and transforming force for the good that to cast it off would be like denying the effect of the polio vaccine.

Creating a Private, Personal Relationship with Allah

There is a necessity to create a private and personal relationship with Allah *(Subhaanahu wa ta'aalaa)*. In the Qur'an we are told that each of Allah's creatures **"will come to Him individually on the Day of Resurrection *(aateehi yawma-l-qiyaamati fardaa)*"** (19:95). According to the *hadith qudsi*: **"The heavens and the earth contain Me not, but the heart of My servant contains Me."**

To develop a personal, heart-based relationship with Allah, we must create and sustain a personal relationship with our *selves.*

If you go to the store and you want to buy something that will last, you buy a quality product. You are willing to pay more for the item because of its quality. If instead you settle for cheap goods that keep breaking, you eventually lose your taste and sense of quality. Similarly, if we do not have *taqwah*, if we do not have piety before God, if we do not make ourselves tremble by our own state, if we do not concern ourselves, if we are not worried by our doubts, by our shame, by our suffering, by our negative qualities, then we are **"...truly of the lost."** In contrast, if we feel concern within ourselves stemming from our piety and *taqwah*, then we become sensitive to the Divine presence. Our faith deepens automatically and we are living our life in *ihsaan.*

Shame's Positive Role

The fact that people cringe at the word "shame," preferring to think of it as "modesty" or "humility," obscures and diverts us from recognizing the *blessing* that it offers.

When people are ashamed, they try to put a veil of secrecy over their actions. This tendency is correct and good; Islam tells us to protect people's secrets from the sight of others, from the gossip of others, from the judgments of others. But the individual must lift the veil of secrecy from his or her *own* sight, reflect *privately* on oneself in one's own heart, and center attention on one's shame which will then force one at some point to turn toward God and rend the veil. So, the secrecy and humiliation is between oneself and others. But the veil is taken *off* between oneself and Allah.

When *our* attention alone is on our shame, we turn toward God. When instead we find *others* focusing on our shame, we become defensive, humiliated, or embarrassed. Our mind turns outward rather than inward. When shame and repentance are preserved inwardly and privately, one naturally turns toward God. One's faith is increased because one feels the Presence of the Divine in one's private life. But when it is turned outward and made public, people's natural inclination is to flee or to turn away. Their attention goes to the preservation of themselves or their *nafs*.

So, Aisha is sleeping in the dead of the night. She awakens and looks for the Prophet. Reaching out, she touches his feet as he is in *sajda*, silent, immersed in the ocean of his *imaan*, repenting to Allah. He himself is the open doorway, veiled by the darkness of the night, while the light of Allah shines in his heart.

It is in humble acceptance of our state that we can ascend inwardly to that place near the Throne. It is by placing ourselves in physical, mental and emotional prostration that we find the doorway to *imaan*. Turning our shame into faith is turning our *qareen* into a believer. It is the way to inoculate oneself, once and for all, from the pollution and the seduction of this world and find the protection and upliftment in the Presence of Allah *(Subhaanahu wa ta'aalaa)* and the Prophet *(salla-Llaahu 'alayhi wa sallam)*.

Let me share with you an excerpt from a traditional prayer known as *Du'aa Kumayl*.

> *Allaahumma mawlaaya kam min qabeeh'in satartahoo wa kam min faadih'im minal balaa-i aqaltahoo wa kam min i'thaarin waqaytahoo wa kam mim makroohin daf'-tahoo wa kam min thanaa-in jameelil lastu ahlal lahoo nashartahoo. Allaahumma a'z'uma balaa-ee wa afrat'a bee soo-u h'aalee wa qas'urat bee a'-maalee wa qa-a'dat bee aghlaalee wa h'abasanee a'n naf-e'e bu'du aamaalee wa khada-a'tnid dunyaaa bighuroorihaa wa nafsee bikhiyaanatihihaa wa mit'aalee. …Yaa ilaahee, ba'-da taqs'eeree wa israafee a'laa nafsee, mu'-tad'iran naadiman munkasiran, mustaqeelan, mustaghfiran, muneeban, muqirran, mud'-i'nan, mu'-tarifan.*
>
> O Allah, my Master, many a fault You have overlooked. Many a hardship You have mitigated. Many an error You have prevented. Many an ordeal You have averted, and my beautiful praise, [which] I did not deserve, You have made known. O Allah, worst is my distress; intense is my discomfort; few are my virtues; chains pull me down. My far-fetched desires keep me from my gains. I have been deceived by the wily world and by my dishonest, unwary self. ...O my God, guilty of acts of omission and commission against my own self, I have come to You, and I stand before You, apologetic, repentant, humble and debased, asking mercy, confessing my sins, confiding in You, disclosing my faults.

How can we not see the simplicity and sweetness, the purity and faith in such a supplication?

As people have turned away from religion and toward a self-referencing, self-aggrandizing, and psychologically-oriented lifestyle, they have lost understanding of the positivity of acknowledging one's faults and imploring forgiveness. How does one get beyond one's reactions, and, in so doing, allow oneself to experience the beneficence and generosity of the Creator, the Compassionate, the Merciful? One must recognize the pollutants and seductiveness of the world around us; acknowledge one's conditioning, limited definitions, prejudices, and developmental handicaps; and see the need to constantly cleanse oneself.

Contemplate the power of repentance as embodied in this *duʿaa.* The repentance expressed here is more than saying "I'm sorry" because one is expected to say it, or repenting out of a momentary bout of remorse. It involves a heartfelt evaluation of self. Such repentance brings one to a level of honesty that guarantees protection and security.

Allah *(Subḇaanahu wa taʿaalaa)* reveals in the Qur'an:

> ***Yaaa-ayyuha-l-ladheena aamanuu tuubuuu ilaa-Llaahi tawbatan-naṣuuḇaa; ʿasaa Rabbukum añy-yukaffira ʿañkum sayyi'aatikum wa yudkhilakum jannaatiñ tajree miñ taḇtiha-l-'anhaaru yawma laa yukhzi-Llaahu-n-nabiyya wa-l-ladheena aamanuu maʿah: nuuruhum yasʿaa bayna aydeehim wa bi-'aymaanihim yaquuluuna Rabbanaa atmim lanaa nuuranaa wa-gh-fir-lanaa: innaka ʿalaa kulli shay'iñ qadeer.***
>
> **O believers! Turn to Allah in sincere repentance. It may well be that your *Rabb* (Lord) will remove from you your sins and admit you to gardens beneath which rivers flow. On that Day Allah will not humiliate the Prophet and those who believe with him. Their light will shine in front of them and on their right, and they will say: "Our *Rabb* (Lord)! Perfect our light for us and grant us forgiveness, for You have power over all things"** (66:8).

A well-operating, self-reproaching, self-controlled value system based on a deep love and affection for Islam, for Truth, for our Prophet *(salla-Llaahu 'alayhi wa sallam)* and for one's own integrity provides the only protection against the ills of our society. Islam (and specifically Sufism) encourages integration, inclusivity, and the balancing and molding of different aspects of our character into one healthy, conscious and spiritually motivated individual. It also advises us that under the guidance of Qur'an, *Hadith*, and the expert vision and experience of a guide we can privately and internally transition away from the external verification of our existence and worth, to the internal and peaceful experience of our essential being. We can live from, make decisions from, and find confidence, skill, and success in the unified character and person that was intended and created by Allah *(Subhaanahu wa ta'aalaa)*, as described in the Qur'an:

> ***Laqada khalaqana-l-insaana fee ahsani taqaweem, thumma radadanaahu asfala saafileen; illa-l-ladheena aamanuu wa 'amilu-s-saalihaat....***
>
> **We created the human being of the best stature, then We reduced him [or her] to the lowest of the low, save those who believe and do good works...** (95:4-6).

In sum, repentance born of admitting one's shame privately to oneself and to Allah *(Subhaanahu wa ta'aalaa)* opens the door to the inner chamber where we can speak freely with Allah *(Subhaanahu wa ta'aalaa)* and His Prophet *(salla-Llaahu 'alayhi wa sallam)* about our most intimate feelings and needs, where we see and hear their responses and can change our lives.

That which we strive for, struggle for, fight for is the transformation of our life experiences into something good and beneficial. Allah *(subhaanahu wa ta'aalaa)* reminds us in the Qur'an:

... yaaa-ayyuha-n-naasu innamaa baghyukum ᶜalaaaañfusikum-mataaᶜa-l-ḫayaati-d-dunyaaa thumma ilaynaa marjiᶜukum fa-nunabbi'ukum-bi-maa kuñtum taᶜmaluun.

O humanity! Your rebellion is against your own souls – [you may] enjoy the transitory pleasure of this world – [but] in the end you have to return to Us. Then We shall inform you of what you have done (10:23).

As we prepare for that return, we need to cover our suffering, our shame, our fears, and our doubts with love, faith, trust, self-confidence, and self-esteem. We need to integrate all of our experiences into something that is so sweet, so tasty and appealing that we could not imagine wandering astray from it. Recognizing with gratitude the Mercy of Allah and the blessings of admission of shame with sincere repentance, we regain the strength to overcome our addictions, our wanderings, our destructive desires, and to affirm our presence in the Presence of the Truth, Mercy, Compassion, and Love that are Allah *(Subḫaanahu wa taᶜaalaa)*.

* * *

Wa Llaahu lahu ul-ḫaqqi wa huwa yahdis-sabeel.
Ḫasbuna Llaahu waḫdahu wa niᶜmal-wakeel.
Wa salli ᶜalaa Sayyidinaa Muḫammadin wa ahli wa saḫbihi ajmaᶜeen
Wa-l-ḫamdu li-Llaahi Rabbi-l-ᶜalameen.

Truth belongs to Allah; it is He who shows the way.
Allah alone suffices us, and what a fine guardian is He!
Blessings upon our Master Muhammad
and his family and companions altogether.
And praise is due to Allah, Lord of the Worlds.

بسم الله الرحمن الرحيم

Drinking the Well Water: Reflections on Family Life in Islam

Bismillaahi-r-Rahmaani-r-Raheem

Al-hamdu-li-Llaahi, muqaaliba-l-quluubi wa-l-absaar.
Allaahumma thabit quluubana ʿalaa siraatika-l-qaweem,
Wa-jʿalnaa li-wajhika muttajiheen,
Wa salli ʿala-sh-shafeeʿi-l-habeeb,
Rahmatil-ʿaalameen,
Wa manaari-l-najiyeen, wa marsaa-l-ʿaarifeen

Praise be to Allah, the turner of the hearts and sight.
O Allah, fix our hearts on the best of Your ways,
and make us face You in our way,
and bestow blessings on the beloved intercessor,
the mercy of all the worlds,
the lighthouse of the survivors, the harbor of the knowers.

Bismi-Llaah, Al-hamdu-li-Llaah
Allaahumma salli wa sallim ʿalaa sayyidinaa Muhammadin,
wa ʿalaa aaalihi wa sahbih

What's Wrong with the Well Water?

Families today are assailed by many forces, as evident in statistics like the following:

- Each year in the United States, one out of every ten teenage women (ages 15-19) gets pregnant (National Vital Statistics Report).

- a study of elder abuse in the years 1992-1997 found that on average, about 36,000 senior citizens were injured by a relative, intimate, or close acquaintance each year. Five hundred were killed (NCVC, Elder Abuse).
- Women between the ages of 15 and 44 suffer more injuries from domestic violence than from any other cause (Lord and Edwards).
- In a 1999 survey, approximately one out of every 16 parents surveyed had hit his or her child with an object. One in 50 had kicked, bitten, or punched his or her child (NCVC, Child Abuse).
- On an average day, roughly 107,000 youths are imprisoned in the United States (Austin).
- In the mid-1990s, a study comparing the United States to 25 other industrialized nations found that the average annual suicide rate among children ages 5-14 in the U.S. was twice the combined rate for the other nations. The homicide rate among children in the United States was five times higher that the average for the other countries studied (1999 National Report Series).

Numerous factors underlie these figures, including:
- racist policies in the law enforcement system
- two career families
- the onslaught of the media
- aberrant definitions of success, beauty, and popularity
- materialism, individualism and self-centeredness
- the belief that children differ so drastically from their parents that they are justified in rejecting their parents' values
- the perception that looking after the elderly is a burden
- large economic and educational disparities between the "haves" and "have-nots"

These factors combine into a self-perpetuating spiral that magnifies their effects. The more we consume, the more we feel compelled to consume. The larger our debts, the more debt we accumulate. The more self-centered we become, the more we believe that's the only way to be. We become less and less able to help others, to give charity or service. Ultimately, these forces undermine the fabric of society, because they challenge the natural inclinations of our *fitrah*—our essential goodness, our ability to refine ourselves and to choose what is right.

You may have heard the story of the well that drove people crazy. Khidr once appeared to a pious man and said, "Because you are so devout, I have come to warn you that a catastrophe is about to befall your village. The well is going to dry up for a period of time. When the water comes back, whoever drinks it will go insane." The man told everyone in the village, but no one believed him. So, he filled up many large urns with water, and moved to the mountain.

The catastrophe transpired as Khidr had predicted. The well dried up, but after some time, its waters were restored, and people began to drink from it. Throughout this time, the man stayed up on the mountain. Finally, he ventured down to the valley one day. He saw that the people had taken leave of their senses: they were harming each other, acting paranoid, mismanaging their affairs, neglecting their farms. When he tried to talk to them, to point out what they were doing and explain the problem with the water, they accused *him* of being crazy. The more belligerent villagers even threatened him. Discouraged, he retreated to the mountain.

The man had stored up enough water to last for many years. But as time passed, he grew lonely. Weeks went by. His isolation became increasingly difficult to bear, and he decided to go back down the mountain and try speaking with the villagers again. He talked to everyone he could find, in groups and individually, to old friends and people he had never known, hoping that someone would listen. He invited them to join him on the mountain, to drink the pure water and regain their reason. But not a single person heeded him. No one accepted his invitation, and he returned to his mountain alone.

Months went by, and his loneliness deepened. Finally, he could stand it no longer. He threw his water away, strode down to the village well, and drank. Soon he, too, became crazy.

Often we are "forced" to make choices that we would prefer not to make; and, having made such choices, we acclimate and adjust to them, even to the point of believing that they were correct. Given this adaptability, how are we to maintain the Qur'anic command to choose good over evil? The story suggests that simply knowing the difference between the two is not enough. Also essential is a supportive environment—a community wherein we can maintain clear values; find encouragement in operating *fee sabeeli-Llaah*; keep our hearts from becoming filled with greed, lust, or desire for people, money, power, or status; lead balanced lives; and put before our children the example of harmonious family life. Such a community was all the pious man needed to resist drinking from the well. But establishing community is no easy matter, as he discovered.

Looking to the Community of Saẖaabah for Inspiration

Muslims have faced the challenge of creating and sustaining values-based communities from the start. Think about the difficulties that confronted the Prophet Muhammad *(ṣalla-Llaahu 'alayhi wa sallam)* and the *ṣaẖaabah.* Their own families took up arms against them simply because they affirmed One God. Many were beaten, tied to stakes, hunted down in the middle of the night. They came from different backgrounds—some from rival clans—yet they had to forge a community that could work together, come to consensus on critical issues, and share limited resources. Inside themselves, they had to wrestle with previous prejudices, customs, and, in some cases, their own polytheistic upbringing. Externally, they were on the front lines of defending a way of life that they themselves were just learning how to live—a way of life that was, in fact, still developing, as practices and guidelines continued to be revealed.

Despite these pressures, the Prophet Muhammad *(s̲alla-Llaahu ʿalayhi wa sallam)* and the *s̲ah̲aabah* did not drink the well water. They drank the nectar of Truth.

The community of the Prophet *(s̲alla-Llaahu ʿalayhi wa sallam)* and his companions existed historically in a particular time and place. Its difficulties and aspirations, however, have been shared by human beings throughout the ages. The struggle *(jih̲aad)* of choosing between ignorance *(jaahiliyah)* and guidance, between good and evil, is an inevitable part of human existence. As long as we are living in *dunyaa*, we will have temptations; we will have battles; we will have physical, mental, and emotional difficulties to face. At the most basic cellular level within us, constructive and destructive forces wage a constant tug-of-war: our bodies naturally generate cancer cells, but healthy bodies in healthy environments usually slough off these cells.

Just as Allah *(Subh̲aanahu wa taʿaalaa)* has equipped us with built-in physiological systems to counteract diseased cells, He has equipped us with all that we need to remain spiritually healthy. Allah *(Subh̲aanahu wa taʿaalaa)* has created us with an essentially good and upright nature—our *fit̲rah*—and has revealed to us through His prophets guidance in using the physical bounties of this world to achieve the *h̲ayaat-i-t̲ayyibah*. But in an environment of materialism, greed, and desire, the physical and worldly aspects of our lives start to mutate—to become dominant—to cease to fulfill the purposes for which Allah *(Subh̲aanahu wa taʿaalaa)* created them. They grow out of control, taking us over, threatening to destroy us. As Allah *(Subh̲aanahu wa taʿaalaa)* tells us in the Qur'an:

Al-haakumu-t-takaathur hattaa zurtumu-l-maqaabir.

You are obsessed by greed for more and more until you go down to your graves (102:1-2).

At every step in our disease's progression, Allah *(Subhaanahu wa ta'aalaa)* grants us the power to reverse its course, to rein our lesser tendencies back into manageable proportions, as medical researchers hope one day to render cancer "a chronic but manageable illness" (Lemonick 64). Even in a debilitating environment, we can choose to live consciously, Islamically, and in so doing, gain the ability to live with the diseases around and within us, even if we cannot cure them.

The rejuvenating power of the message of Allah *(Subhaanahu wa ta'aalaa)* has been evident historically in the communities to which Islam has spread. Like the latest cancer treatments, which boost the immune system's defenses, Islam has boosted the health of communities and nations from the time of the Prophet *(salla-Llaahu 'alayhi wa sallam)* to the present.

The society of *jaahiliyah* Arabia had developed an acute case of materialism, acquisitiveness, and competitiveness. So steeped was Mecca in human weaknesses that the Prophet *(salla-Llaahu 'alayhi wa sallam)* and his companions ultimately were compelled to flee the city altogether. In Medina, they found enough security to be able to establish a community of faith. From there, they reclaimed Mecca, and together Medina and Mecca became centers from which Muslims could go out to the rest of the world. They traveled outward in diverse roles—as traders, educators, and civil servants; as soldiers and missionaries; as craftspeople and farmers—yet each among them carried the weight of the trust, the *amaanaat*, as he or she set forth from the center of the wheel.

The Spread of Islam: A Healing Infusion

Wherever Islam spread, individuals' paradigms were re-defined. Newcomers to Islam came from particular families and tribes, but they became Muslims first and foremost. The Malaysian remained Malaysian, but the overriding framework of his or her life became Islam. The person from the *Bani Isra'eel* was still of that heritage, but embraced the world view of Islam. Persian society remained distinctively Persian, but it also became Islamic. Indeed, the Persians adopted an Arab and his family—the Prophet Muhammad *(ṣalla-Llaahu 'alayhi wa sallam)*, Imam Ali *(raḏiya-Llaahu 'anhu)*, Fatima *(raḏiya-Llaahu 'anhaa)*, Hassan and Hussain *(raḏiya-Llaahu 'anhumma)*—as if they were Persians.

Wherever Islam replicated itself, it reflected the local cultural norms while simultaneously transforming society. Its effects extended beyond cultural customs to shape the very core of how people responded to the age-old need to balance self-interest and communal interests, material desires and spiritual development, worldly necessities and one's relationship with the Higher Power.

Now the United States is receiving the largest injection of Islam in its history, as the ranks of American Muslims grow. With Muslims moving into communities across the nation, we need to ask ourselves: How are we to maintain our Islam? How can we best facilitate its healing action? How will we ensure that our values and faith ameliorate rather than succumb to the illnesses of materialism?

Guidelines for Muslim Families in the United States

Muslim families have a critical role to play in fortifying individuals against the toxins in this environment, and in improving the overall health of American society. Recognizing families' importance, let me suggest a number of guidelines for Islamic family life in the contemporary United States.

1. **Beware of saying "those are diseases of the *kaafiruun*; they don't affect us"; instead, honestly acknowledge the issues that we (and even more so, our children) face.**

We can no longer stand off to the side, pretending that Muslims are immune to trends in the United States. "Yes, of course there are drug problems among average Americans; but not among *us*." "Of course there are teenage pregnancies among those girls, but *our* girls don't have that problem." "Domestic violence is a very serious issue; but it doesn't happen in *our* homes."

Allah *(Subhaanahu wa ta'aalaa)* cautions against such smugness in the Qur'an:

> ***Ahasiba-n-naasu añy-yutrakuu añy-yaquuluuu aamannaa wa hum laa yuftanuun?***
>
> **Do people imagine that they will be left [at ease] because they say, "We believe," and will not be tested with affliction?** (29:2).

Just as Muslims are coming to grips with their own historical misinterpretations of the Islamic perspective on women, so, too, we must come to grips with our other blind spots. Certainly, many good qualities distinguish real Muslims and *mu'minuun* from the mainstream population. But we face issues of our own, as evident in messages posted on Islamic web sites. A wife seeks advice because an otherwise good husband and father recently started physically abusing her. An English revert wonders how to address "difficulties in relations with Arab sisters." A young man wrestles with choosing between marrying the woman he loves, or a "good Muslim girl" that his parents will pick. Another man confides that his rage towards Muslims who commit sins has gotten him in trouble. An American who recently embraced Islam says, "I'm trying hard to adapt to an Islamic lifestyle, because I used to love being outgoing and loud." Another asks, succinctly: "How can I enjoy life after reverting?" (IslamOnline).

Parents need to look honestly at issues, and to recognize what our children already know: that Muslim young people, not their elders, will bear the brunt of dealing with these challenges. Today's high school and college students will play the leading role in integrating Islam with the demands of the twenty-first century. They will confront issues that humanity has never before encountered: the implications of the Internet; the impacts of globalization; the ethical dilemmas posed by medical advances and bio-technologies that promise virtual immortality.

In sum, we must stop ignoring the present and future issues of our *ummah*, and start preparing our children to bring forth from Islam solutions that have yet to be found elsewhere.

2. **In facing materialism, beware of both inaction and overreaction; instead, be the *ummata wasaṯa*, working constructively "in the world, but not of the world."**

Few cancer victims sit back and simply allow the disease to run its course. But in coping with the effects of materialism, Muslims all too often succumb passively, letting their families be absorbed into the secular, self-centered model. They watch their values deteriorate, saying nothing can be done to save them, while moaning and groaning, "Why did this happen to my kids?" In many cases, their children work hard, earn good grades, succeed in their careers—but something is missing. They treat Islam as an add-on, not an expression of the heart. Parents and children alike sense that a valuable dimension of life is slipping through their fingers, but they become less and less conscious of what that dimension is, for they themselves have drunk the water. No longer do they measure the quality of their lives by *adab*, *rahmat*, and the feeling of nearness to Allah *(Subhaanahu wa ta'aalaa)*. Instead, they measure their lives by the number of cars in their garages, the size of their houses, and the prestige of their professions.

Passively drifting into secular and material models poses one kind of danger to our *ummah*. A second kind of danger takes the form of overreacting to secular society. Determined not to be infected by the water, some Muslim communities try to cut themselves off entirely from the rest of the world. They "ghettoize" themselves in the name of an original, ideologically pure Islam as they define it. They become obsessed with "religious correctness," disregarding the roots of Islam in compassion and patience. Ultimately, they undermine the very faith they claim to defend, for by clinging to outmoded perspectives, they collide head-on with powerful local forces for change.

Given that neither inaction nor overreaction can preserve Islamic families in the long run, we need to look for the middle ground, for the way to fulfill the *ayat:*

> ***Wa kadhaalika ja'alnaakum ummatañw-wasatal-li-takuunuu shuhadaaa'a 'alaa-n-naasi wa yakuuna-r-Rasuulu 'alaykum shaheedaa.***
>
> **Thus We made you a community of the middle way, that you might be a witness to the people, and the Messenger, a witness to you** (Qur'an 2:143).

Our "community of the middle" walks a narrow path. On the one hand, as the *khalifahs* of Allah *(Subhaanahu wa ta'aalaa)* and as followers of the Prophet Muhammad *(salla-Llaahu 'alayhi wa sallam)* (who was sent as a **"mercy to all the worlds"**) we have a responsibility to serve society. On the other hand, we must retain some distance from society if we wish to stay sensitive to the Eternal Essence that runs through our moment-to-moment lives. We need to stay on the margins of the mainstream if we are to catch the current of the experience of the Divine.

Unfortunately, many Muslims who were blessed to grow up with life styles that kept them close to the spiritual current now are gravitating toward mainstream society. Their conditioning tells them that to settle for less would mean giving up some part of the dream for which their families strove. Perhaps their parents came from a poor village and struggled just to get a basic education. Perhaps their grandparents came from a ghetto and strived their entire lives to make it into the middle class. Perhaps they themselves escaped from Bosnia or Kosovo; or perhaps they spent everything they had on a chance to come to the United States, to find greater economic opportunities, to make enough money to send to relatives back home.

Given this heritage, many Muslims feel (understandably) that it would be a sacrifice to choose not to embrace aspects of American society. Excuses rise to the surface, such as, "We were subjugated under colonialism. Our people were exploited. Our resources were taken. Now it's our turn for a better life!"

No one can deny the wrongs of the past, but using them to justify joining the mainstream in the present is like demanding a chance to drink from the well. It takes us so far from the truth that we start to agree that it is Americans' God-given right to burn all the fossil fuels we want. We begin to believe that we are entitled to our cars—even if our cars get only eight miles to the gallon and have 360 horsepower in V8 engines.

Islam does not tell us we cannot have things. It tells us that our things should not have *us*. Abu Hurayra *(raḏiya-Llaahu ʿanhu)* narrated that the Prophet *(ṣalla-Llaahu ʿalayhi wa sallam)* said:

> **Allah looks not to your figures nor to your wealth, but He looks to your hearts and your deeds** (Muslim).

If we can choose to be of the *ummata wasaṯa* consciously, then we can wear our clothes with humility and drive our cars with humility. We can accept where Allah has put us, striving to be the best we can be while considering ourselves least. We can accept what Allah *(Subẖaanahu wa ta'aalaa)* has given us, and use however much or little we have to help create a more healthy environment. We can establish successful businesses in the West, based on Islamic management principles. We can practice medicine, while maintaining clear values regarding medical ethics. We can enjoy friendships at school and college, yet know our boundaries. Whatever our worldly obligations may be, we can seek our peace and find our safety in Islam. We can stop for prayer, read Qur'an, fast during Ramadan. We can build up our immune systems with *niyyah*, *muraaqabah*, and *dhikr*; by putting a higher value on family relations and time than on business relations and time; by being examples for all to see.

"Being an example" may or may not mean making our Islam known. The point is not to stand out as a label, as a *muẖajjab*, as a *topi*-and-*gellabia*-wearer. Whether or not we wear beards or head scarves, whether we wear native costumes or Western clothes, whether we tell people we are Muslims or keep our faith private is relevant only when we are striving in the way of Islam for balance, as tolerant, compassionate people. This is the real meaning of being an example. We must contribute positively to our society, as Allah *(Subẖaanahu wa ta'aalaa)* enjoins in *Suuratu-l-Baqarah:*

> ***Laysa-l-birra añ tuwalluu wujuuhakum qibala-l-mashriqi wa-l-maghribi wa laakinna-l-birra man aamana bi-Llaahi wa-l-yawmi-l-'aakhiri wa-l-malaaa'ikati wa-l-kitaabi wa-n-nabiyyeen:***

> ***wa aata-l-maala ᶜalaa hubbihee dhawi-l-qurbaa wa-l-yataamaa wa-l-masaakeena wa-b-na-s-sabeeli wa-s-saaa'ileena wa fi-r-riqaab.***
>
> **True piety does not consist in turning your faces towards the East or the West, but truly pious is the one who believes in God, and the Last Day, and the angels, and revelation, and the prophets; and spends his substance—however much he himself may cherish it—upon his near of kin, and the orphans, and the needy, and the wayfarer, and the beggars, and for the freeing of human beings from bondage** (Qur'an 2:177).

We exemplify Islam when we create practical, up-to-date models that address the needs of our society using Islamic concepts. For example, principles such as *sadaqah* and *zakat* could do much to ameliorate issues of poverty and inequity in the United States. Formats and guidelines related to *ijmaaᶜ*, *shuuraa*, and *majlis* could be melded with forms of local governance or corporate management to yield new ways of encouraging citizen and employee involvement.

If we reach out in the right way, we will find that the United States provides rich soil for putting Islamic principles into action. Its culture readily absorbs ideas and customs, thriving on the sparks that fly off various traditions. A spark of Mevlana Jelalladin Rumi flies off the Sufic tradition, and Americans catch it. Omar Khayyam caught on in the fifties and sixties. *Qawwali* became popular in the past twenty years. One can find Middle Eastern foods and cultural programs in any major U.S. city. National grocery store chains offer pita bread and hummus in a dozen varieties.

Of course, associating Islam with hummus, Indian or Middle Eastern music, and English-language versions of Mevlana's poetry is like defining Italian culture by pizza. The association has little bearing on reality—but we can nevertheless appreciate Americans' willingness to try new things. Their openness means that while Muslims are being shaped by American culture, American culture has the potential to be shaped, too—why not by Islamic values?

I acknowledge: enthusiasm for falafel (a Middle Eastern dish) is a far cry from willingness to embrace Islamic approaches to helping those in need, conducting local politics, or managing companies. Although many people in the United States are becoming more familiar with Muslims' customs and cuisine, with Islamic symbols, and even with some of the principles of Islam, too few read the Qur'an and seek its assistance, and fewer yet associate Islam with their own values.

While the gap between Islam and mainstream American culture is serious, it can be bridged, for it stems from poor communication rather than fundamental incompatibility. The ideals of the United States closely parallel Islamic concepts such as *tarbiyah*, *adab*, *khidmah*, and *ṣadaqah*. Americans, for the most part, are service-oriented and philanthropic. We value heroicism and qualities of chivalry that are reminiscent of *futuwwah*. We admire the person who works hard to overcome negative circumstances, then helps others do the same. We love gaining knowledge: not just in classrooms, but through experience, climbing mountains and going down rivers, sailing the oceans and charting the skies. We pursue self-refinement; we are curious and willing to experiment with different approaches.

Some Americans (I among them) have been drawn to Islam in part because the espoused values of the United States reflect the values that a Muslim is encouraged to exemplify. Islamic alternatives should appeal strongly to people in the United States—*if* they are presented in ways that non-Muslims can understand and relate to, with a sincere intention to translate our values into healing for all members of this society. The key lies in understanding how best to engage with this society. The best way to present the insights of the Qur'an, the *sharee'ah* and the *sunnah* is through Sufism. I do not refer to popularized offshoots of Sufism, but to real Sufism: to the mystical path that leads to a personal experience of Islam, into a personal relationship with the Prophet Muhammad *(salla-Llaahu 'alayhi wa sallam)*, as exemplified by the *awliyaa'*. One does not come to know these exemplars through rigidity. One knows them through *Tasawwuf*.

Sufism reflects core values and experiences that resonate with individuals of all faiths and backgrounds. Americans today are especially drawn to Sufism, because they have become sensitive to the differences between superficial forms of expression and deeper forms. They yearn for essence: an essence available through *Tasawwuf*.

3. Beware of emphasizing the forms of Islam to the exclusion of Islam's essence; instead, nurture spirituality.

If we wish to keep our children and our families whole, then we must view Islam holistically. We must cherish the values of Islam, for only when Islam lives in our hearts and souls will its outer aspects have meaning and relevance to our lives.

The forms of Islam—the guidelines for *salah*, *wuduu'*, dress, diet, marriage, justice, and so on—are essential. They provide clarity and direction. They ensure consistency. They establish a unique identification of Islam, distinct from other religions. For these and other reasons, forms are important. But we must remember: Islam originates not in form, but in the personal and direct experience of the Presence of Allah *(Subhaanahu wa ta'aalaa)*. Its root lies in the heart of the Prophet *(salla-Llaahu 'alayhi wa sallam)*.

We tend to live in the myth that a monolithic reality called "Islam" existed in totality the moment the Prophet Muhammad *(salla-Llaahu 'alayhi wa sallam)* came down from Mount Hira and told Khadija *(radiya-Llaahu anhaa)* about the first revelation. Did the Prophet *(salla-Llaahu 'alayhi wa sallam)* immediately start offering *salah* as we do now? No. The specific movements of prayer were taught somewhat later; and related guidelines, including the method of summoning worshippers and the final direction of the *qiblah*, were not revealed until after the *hijrah*. Most of the specific guidelines for daily activities also came after the *hijrah*. Some directives were revealed in stages; for example, Allah *(Subhaanahu wa ta'aalaa)* in the Qur'an first prohibited intoxicants in the context of doing prayer (4:43); a later *ayat* cautioned against intoxicants more generally (2:219); but not until the third revelation on the subject did Allah *(Subhaanahu wa ta'aalaa)* unequivocally command believers to "shun intoxicants" (5:90-91). Suuratu-t-Tawba, which gives guidelines for treaties, was one of the last *suurahs* to be revealed, yet the Prophet *(salla-Llaahu 'alayhi wa sallam)* had been making treaties for years before its revelation.

The community of the Prophet *(salla-Llaahu 'alayhi wa sallam)* and his companions did not revolve around a predefined set of forms. The companions of the Prophet *(salla-Llaahu 'alayhi wa sallam)*, like those of Musa *('alayhi salaam)* and Isa *('alayhi salaam)*, were brought together by a message—the message of what life is all about. They gathered around the teaching that human beings exist to gain knowledge in the service of Allah *(Subhaanahu wa ta'aalaa)*, in the service of Allah's creation, for the purpose of coming nearer to His Presence.

Quite honestly, as I look around at Muslim families, at Muslim communities, and at the Islamic world today, it seems that what people lack (and what will hold people to any path) is personal contact with the Divine. Studying Qur'an and hadith, learning *fiqh*, dressing modestly, knowing how to pray correctly—these practices are all beneficial; but if we embrace the dress, names, and structures, yet give up the yearning for personal experience, we reduce Islam to an empty shell. If, for example, we commit to *fiqh* but lack understanding of *ijtihaad*—one of the dynamic forces behind the *fiqh*—then *fiqh* becomes nothing more than a set of rules. It has no life to it.

Real Islam is the synergy of the essence of orthodox Islam and the mysticism, creativity, spirituality, and experience of the Sufi. Real understanding is form with essence, which reveals the Divine Presence and discloses the true self. Sufism is the means to understand not just Islam, but oneself, one's purpose, from the heart, not just the mind.

I can only speak from what I know, and what I know is how I was taught: to look at Islam through the eyes of *Tasawwuf*. This means through *adab*, social responsibility, care and concern for other human beings, striving always to gain more knowledge, both about prayer, *'uluum*, *kalaam*, and other Islamic disciplines, and about our personal relationship with Allah *(Subhaanahu wa ta'aalaa)*. Allah *(Subhaanahu wa ta'aalaa)* is not only the *Rabbi-l-'aalameen* (Lord of the Universes), but also our personal Lord.

Nearness to Allah cannot be experienced if we submit to a materialistic world view. Materialism constantly fragments our lives, and eclipses the *non*-material aspects of our existence. It discourages reflection and contemplation—what Naqshbandis call "time pauses"—amidst a busy day. It causes us to de-value remembrance, supplication, and prayer: in part because the environment blocks us from doing them properly; and in part because we are conditioned to want immediate, obvious feedback, whereas the feedback from spiritual practices is subtle. The effects of these practices register upon the heart, and our hearts have been desensitized by the cacophony around us. So, we start to relegate prayer, *du'aa'*, *dhikr*, *fikr* to special times and places, segregating them from moment-to-moment life to keep them from disturbing our pursuit of money, our work, our ability to pay the bills.

To counteract this desensitization, we must encourage time pauses in our homes. We must nurture each family member's capacity to experience Allah's Presence in day-to-day life. The most valuable gift we can pass on to others is the key to the door of *Tasawwuf.* When we share a mystical poem that moves us, or when we invite family members to join us in meditation, we welcome them into the company of the *fuqaraa'*, of those who are blessed by Allah *(Subhaanahu wa ta'aalaa)*.

We cannot be so myopic as to think that educating our children to Islam means having them memorize Qur'an, *Hadith*, and history without understanding *adab,* without *taqwah*, and without *futuwwah*. As families, we cannot claim success if our children just wear *hijaab* or adopt other symbols without the essence. We have not succeeded if our young people *look* like Muslims, but act with arrogance, jealousy, and envy and do not know how to imbue their lives with Islam.

Tarbiyah, the Arabic word for education, means much more than academic discipline or knowledge. It refers to upbringing and breeding. Its root, *rabaa*, means to increase, to grow, to grow up, to exceed, and to raise. *Murabban*, a derivative, means well-mannered. When we think about educating our children, we need to think about the purpose of life, about the purpose for which Allah *(Subhaanahu wa ta'aalaa)* created our children and caused them to grow. We need to ensure that we are bringing up young people to continually expand in knowledge and refinement. We need to raise up our children to be well-bred, to be mature, to excel as human beings. In sum, we must provide an education that is evolutionary, supporting intellectual development, but at the same time, providing a deeply spiritual basis for life and for decision making.

4. Beware of presenting Islam to young people in ways that are boring, dogmatic, or irrelevant; instead, listen to their experiences, share with them the dynamism of Islam, and prepare them to make their own decisions.

Between sixty and eighty percent of Muslim young people in the United States leave Islam for some period of time. Clearly, the methods and modes used to convey Islam to the next generation are failing.

The United States is a long way from Fez, Cairo, and Delhi—from places where Friday's revolve around attending *khuṯbah*, where the *adhaan* echoes from minaret to minaret five times a day, where contemporary apartments house traditional extended families. Muslim American youths are surrounded not by reminders of their faith, but by the lures of the media, malls, and material images of success, all telling them, "The world is here for *you*!" As one thirteen-year-old wrote in *The Message:* "...The culture of this nation has come together to crush the identity of young Muslims...." Suggesting antidotes, he observed: "When children come home [from school], they should know they're in an Islamic environment. They should get the feeling that their parents care about Islam and about them" (Mughol 40).

Note that this young man links caring about Islam with caring about our children. Part of caring for our children is to avoid enjoining obedience or forcing practice without explanation. Another part is to avoid painting society as the "enemy," while turning a blind eye and deaf ear to our young people's real-life experiences in that society.

If we want our children to value Islam, we must help them discover its relevance to the issues they face. Islam is a vibrant way of life, with the potential to adapt and contribute to the Internet age as it did to civilizations in the past, able to adapt to and benefit people of every time and place. But are we awakening youths to Islam's dynamism? Or are we boring them with dogma? Are we recognizing that they are creative, sensitive, aware, and enthusiastic young members of the *ummah*, ripe with ideas and seeking a vision and a way to contribute to the world? "Hey, kids, I found this great site on the Internet. It's a social, moral, ethical, Islamic site. Doesn't that sound exciting? You can do all kinds of wonderful things like take a quiz about who was the most ethical of the *ṣaḫaabah*. You can even have an online chat about that, with prizes for the best chatters. You might win a signed copy of the last book by the site's founder! A few lucky girls will get $10 gift certificates to the online *ḫijaab* mall, too."

Such approaches do little to prepare young people to apply Islam to the world as they know it. Instead, we need to inspire progressive thinking and provide concrete skills. Every parent and elder family member must ask, "Am I teaching the children about the model of the Prophet *(ṣalla-Llaahu ʿalayhi wa sallam)*?" Even more importantly, ask, "*How* am I doing so?" Consider, for example, the suggestion of the Prophet *(ṣalla-Llaahu ʿalayhi wa sallam)* that individuals divide their days into three equal portions, devoting one portion to worship, one to work, and one to family (Lings 210). We could present that guidance simply as one more principle to be memorized. Or, we could work with our children to dive into it, to discover in it clues for leading a fulfilling life. We can bring in real-world examples, like Silicon Valley programmers who earn huge salaries—but are working 14 to 16 hour days, burning themselves out, ruining their bodies, finding that they have no time for families. We can pose the question: "If the lifestyles of dot.com entrepreneurs are not necessarily models of success, what other models could we aspire to in this society?" Practical, timely examples and open-ended questions give young people the chance to express their concerns, to ask questions and clarify answers. They enable youths to practice thinking through ways in which Islamic guidance applies to their daily concerns—practice that is essential if youths are to be prepared to find meaningful answers within Islam in adulthood.

If our children initiate conversations on sensitive topics, we again must weigh our methods of responding. Attempts to resolve their dilemmas with simplistic answers may fail to address deeper questions. For example, beneath immediate concerns (such as attraction to the opposite sex or participation in social events) lie broader issues. How can one know if one is motivated by selfish interests, or genuine concern for another person? How can one deal with the urge to follow the crowd, especially when it seems much stronger than the urge towards self-development? How can one be an individual, and also maintain the spiritual identity of the *ummah*? How does pursuing self-gratification really compare to pursuing the study of *sharee'ah* and the personal experience of Allah *(Subhaanahu wa ta'aalaa)*?

A straightforward, yes or no answer may be crucial to guiding a young person in the moment. Lasting understanding, however, depends on teaching youths to think through who they are, what they need, and what they value. We should engage our sons and daughters in exploring the questions behind their questions as mature, thinking young adults. We may help them by sharing the answers that *we* have come to; but we offer much more when, in addition, we encourage them to "seek out knowledge from cradle to grave" for *themselves*.

> **It is said that when the Prophet Muhammad *(salla-Llaahu 'alayhi wa sallam)* enjoined the seeking of knowledge, someone asked him, "Do you not fear that people will be aversely affected by this pursuit?" He replied, "No, it will strengthen their faith."**

To foster strong faith, we must allow our young people to expand their horizons. We must allow for evolution in our definitions of "Islamic identity."

Recognition of the importance of such evolution is being heard even from conservative Muslims overseas. A *Washington Post* article published in June 2001 quoted Mohammad Javad Larijani, a theoretician of right wing Islam in Iran, as saying that there is "A 'practical urgency' for conservatives to modernize their thoughts 'so educated, young, devoted Muslims know how to be devoted and faithful Muslims at the beginning of the 21st century. These are not things to be ordered. We should discuss it; we should acquire it.' For example, he said, 'Young Iranians....want to be independent, listen to their own music, chat and write and talk to their friends. This is not bad; it's a new way of thinking about life. It's not against Islam. But the older generation feels unsafe, because they're not ready to accept new ideas. But [new ways of thinking] are good, and we should provoke and participate and enrich that rather than being afraid of it' " (Anderson).

Dr. Larijani echoes the wisdom voiced by Imam Jaᶜfar as-Saadiq *(radiya-Llaahu ᶜanhu)* more than twelve centuries ago: **"Do not expect your children to do what you did, because they belong to a different generation"** (Haeri).

The difference between generations is most evident among children of immigrants. As first or second generation Americans, they embody the conflict between old and new. They feel that they should uphold their families' traditions, teachings, and expectations; but they are being drawn into another model. The parental guidance that they receive often focuses on convincing them to stay near their families and choose specific careers. There is nothing wrong with such guidance, but guidance cannot stop there. Parents need to go beyond stating *what* makes a pious Muslim, and offer realistic guidance on *how* to be a pious Muslim.

Our children's generation is facing more difficult issues at earlier ages than we did. There is no way we can provide a rule for every situation they will encounter. We can, however, help them understand that the capacity for choice is a gift of Allah *(Subhaanahu wa ta'aalaa)*, to be used wisely and within certain parameters which sustain the infrastructure of society. We can help them recognize that freedom does not equal "doing whatever we want," an attitude that in fact enslaves us to our *nafs*. We can guide them to discover the true freedom that comes from choosing to live according to the way pointed out by Allah *(Subhaanahu wa ta'aalaa)* and His prophets—to realize that by curbing the lower self, we allow the higher self to discover true emotional, mental, and physical fulfillment.

Allah *(Subhaanahu wa ta'aalaa)* states in the Qur'an:

> ***...wa laakinna-Llaaha habbaba ilaykumu-l-'eemaana wa zayyanahuu fee quluubikum wa karraha ilaykumu-l-kufra wa-l-fusuuqa wa-l-ᶜisyaan.***
>
> **...but Allah has endeared the faith to you and has made it beautiful in your hearts, and He has made hateful to you unbelief, iniquity, and rebellion [against what is good]** (49:7).

This *ayat* contains the secret of preventing our children from joining the sixty to eighty percent who leave Islam. The secret lies in empowering youths to make wise choices, based on the faith that Allah *(Subhaanahu wa ta'aalaa)* has made beautiful in their hearts.

5. **Beware of equating the Islamic family with Western concepts of extended family; instead, affirm the communal family model of the Prophet *(salla-Llaahu ʿalayhi wa sallam)* and the *sahaabah.***

When we speak about family life in Islam, we have already bought into Western models of family. We are thinking about groups related by blood or marriage. We have abandoned the model of the Prophet Muhammad *(salla-Llaahu ʿalayhi wa sallam)*, within which family life is analogous to community.

The message of the Prophet *(salla-Llaahu ʿalayhi wa sallam)* unified people of many tribes. The nuclear and extended family remained important; but Muslims also came to recognize a broader family, bound not by blood but by faith. Allah *(Subhaanahu wa taʿaalaa)* revealed:

> ***...wa-dhkuruu niʿmata-Llaahi ʿalaykum idh kuntum aʿdaaa'añ fa-allafa bayna quluubikum fa-asbahtum-bi-niʿmatihee ikhwaanaa...***
>
> **...and remember with gratitude God's favor on you, for you were enemies and He joined your hearts in love, so that by His Grace you became brothers...** (Qur'an 3:103).

Elsewhere in the Qur'an, Allah *(Subhaanahu wa taʿaalaa)* states:

> ***Innaa khalaqnaakum-miñ dhakariñw-wa 'uñthaa wa jaʿalnaakum shuʿuubañw-wa qabaaa'ila li-taʿaarafuu...***
>
> **We have created you all out of a male and a female, and We have made you into nations and tribes, so that you might come to know one another...** (49:13).

The understanding of family that the Prophet Muhammad introduced (or, more accurately, re-awakened) included all those who loved Allah *(Subhaanahu wa ta'aalaa)* and His prophets, who were willing to sacrifice and be sacrificed for each other. The Prophet *(salla-Llaahu 'alayhi wa sallam)* reached out to everyone: Christians from Abyssinia, Romans of the Byzantine Empire, the Jewish tribes of Arabia, slaves of all backgrounds, leaders of nations and empires. All were welcomed to the family—a family that was not only the *ummah* of Muhammad *(salla-Llaahu 'alayhi wa sallam)*, but the *ummah* of Allah *(Subhaanahu wa ta'aalaa)*.

This welcoming, inclusive family is the model we should aspire to today. We can talk all we want about *adab*, brotherhood and sisterhood, and concern for others; but we need to build bridges between saying and doing. What message are we sending our children if we pay lip service to tolerance, but have attitudes of cultural elitism? What is the message sent by retreating into ethnic or racial enclaves: into the Yemeni masjid, the Ethiopian masjid, the "this-ethnicity" or "that-language-group" masjid? What is the message if, when we see a fellow Muslim from the Indian subcontinent, we eagerly engage in conversation—but when we meet an Iranian Shi'i, we move away (or vice versa)? What do "family values" mean, if we who preach them are judging others by the scent of their perfume, or the way they wear their scarves, or whether they move their heads from side to side or up and down when they talk? What do our lessons in care and compassion mean if, as soon as a person fails to meet our standards linguistically, economically, socially, or in terms of beauty or status, we become insensitive to his or her plight? Judgmentalness and exclusivity are not Islam. They are not what Muslim family life is about. They are not attitudes that will endear Islam to our children.

Like Americans in general, our young people value openness. They disdain prejudice and stereotypes. Indeed, the United States has inculcated such tolerance in younger generations that we find here a rare opportunity to revivify the *ummah* across boundaries of ethnicity and sect. We can forge communities where Muslims of differing viewpoints respectfully acknowledge their differences, while focusing on commonalities. Parents and elders can model acceptance by presenting differences openly and honestly; by saying, for example, "There's no point debating whether the Shiᶜi or Sunni history texts are 'correct'; they're irreconcilable. But Shiᶜis and Sunnis agree fully on the five pillars, and this is ample foundation for getting along."

As the next generation grows to adulthood, our hope must be that just as we strive to do our best for them, they in turn will do their best for us—not just the "us" of their immediate families, but the "us" of all humanity. Selflessness and generosity distinguished the *s̱aẖaabah* from their contemporaries fourteen centuries ago. Selflessness and generosity can distinguish us, as well, as we strive to live as real Muslims, real *mu'mins*, real *mujaaẖids*.

How can we translate the communal family model into today's world? In Virginia, we have tried to do so by bringing people together on a shared property. For thirty years, our community has attracted individuals of diverse backgrounds, as did the community of the Prophet *(s̱alla-Llaahu ʿalayhi wa sallam)*. We have had the opportunity to learn from many of the same issues that the early *ummah* faced: hostility from outsiders, our own habits, laziness, and fear; differences in temperaments; the struggle to practice non-violence, forgiveness, and recognition of our own mistakes. *Alẖamduli-Llaah*, our struggles have helped us reflect on the example of family and communities put forth by the Prophet Muhammad *(s̱alla-Llaahu ʿalayhi wa sallam)* and his companions.

Living on a shared property is one approach to forging Muslim communities today. Another approach to forging community is evident in places like Bluefield, West Virginia and other urban and suburban areas where Muslims attend the same masjid, develop close friendships, cooperate in organizing Islamic programs, and raise their children as brothers and sisters to one another.

The Bedford, Virginia and the Bluefield models help families connect to a larger circle of Muslims, building interdependency. Both counter the West's fixation with independence and personal rights, and bring to the forefront concepts of mutual support, duty, and responsibility.

Effort is needed if we are to reverse the trend towards individualism in Muslim communities, many of which have become communities in name only. The members may gather on Friday and during Sunday school—they may have a few friends among themselves, like residents of other suburban communities—but their bonds are not strong enough to serve as a support network for Muslim families.

The degree to which we communalize is the degree to which we will experience firsthand the example of the Prophet Muhammad *(salla-Llaahu 'alayhi wa sallam)*. Only when we take part in community will we see in the mirror of self-reflection and in the mirrors of those around us how well we are living up to the example of the *sahaabah*. If we engage only with selected Muslims, we limit our opportunities for refinement. We must engage broadly—not necessarily with every Muslim, but with Muslims of like mind—creating activities and relationships that cultivate co-dependencies. Together we must ensure that as our children mature, they, too, are exposed to examples of community.

In conclusion, let me return to our man on the mountain, to the village of crazy people below, and to the water in the well. Muslim family life provides the foundation and strength we need to refrain from drinking the water. But its benefits need not stop there. Quietly, gradually, our families can help to create an overriding environment where the message, the ideals, and the models that we operate from can spread. If we can present Islam in the proper way, truthfully and without ethnic biases, then we can help others to find "more healthful waters." By affirming a value system that is spiritually nourishing, we can start to shift the paradigm away from the self-centered, materialistic, secularly-oriented world view. We can help to replace money-oriented definitions of success with more holistic definitions which recognize that human well-being depends on a balance between inner piety and outer security.

If we as Muslims in the United States strive to understand and assist the society of which we are a part, then *inshaa'a-Llaah*, a day may come when we need not fear that our children will feel compelled to drink the tainted water. *Inshaa'a-Llaah*, a day may come when we can live with confidence that the next generation, drawing strength from the *ummah*, will steadfastly drink from the waters towards which Allah *(Subhaanahu wa ta'aalaa)* directs us and will generously share their bounties. *Inshaa'a-Llaah*, a day may come when our children will succeed where the man in the story failed: succeed not only in remaining on the straight path, but in revitalizing their communities for the benefit of all.

* * *

Wa-Llaahu lahu-l-haqqu wa huwa yahdi-s-sabeel.
Hasbuna-Llaahu wahdahu wa ni'mal-wakil.
Wa salli 'alaa Sayyidina Muhammadin
wa aaalihi wa sahbihi ajma'een
wa-l-hamdu li-Llaahi Rabbi-l-'aalameen.

Truth belongs to Allah; it is He who shows the way.
Allah, alone, suffices us, and what a fine guardian is He!
Blessings upon our Master Muhammad
and his family and companions altogether
and praise is due to Allah, Lord of the Worlds.

Jazaakum Allah khayran. As-salaam alaykum.

References

1999 National Report Series, Juvenile Justice Bulletin: Kids and Guns. U.S. child homicide and suicide rates exceed rates for other industrialized countries. March 2000. Online. Available at http://www.ncjrs.org/html/ojjdp/jjbul2000_03_2/kid6.html. Accessed 10 June 2001.

Anderson, John Ward. Iran's Conservatives Face a Growing Split: Extremist Clerics Blamed for Rise of Secularism. *Washington Post*. 2 June 2001: A13.

Austin, James, Kelly Dedel Johnson, Maria Gregoriou. Juveniles in Adult Prisons and Jails: A National Assessment. Published October 2000. Online. Available at http://www.ncjrs.org/txtfiles1/bja/182503.txt. Accessed 10 June 2001.

Haeri, Fadhlalla. *Sufism*. Rockport, MA: Element Books, 1990.

IslamOnline.net. Cyber Counselor. Online. Available at http://www.islamonline.net/QuestionApplication/English/Browse.asp. Accessed 15 June 2001.

Lemonick, Michael D. and Alice Park. New Hope for Cancer. *Time* magazine, May 28, 2001, 62-69.

Lings, Martin. *Muhammad: his life based on the earliest sources*. Kuala Lumper: A.S. Noordeen, 1983.

Lords and Edwards Enterprises. The Courage of a Woman. Online. Available at http://biz.arkansas.net/lordandedw/absestat.html. Accessed 10 June 2001.

Mughol, Haroon. We Weep for Ourselves. *The Message*, August 1997, 40-41.

Murad, Abdul Hakim. The Fall of the Family. Courtesy of Belfast Masjid. Downloaded from the Internet in May 2001.

National Vital Statistics Report, Vol. 47, No. 12. Teen Births. National Vital Statistics Report 1997. Online. Available at http://www.cdc.gov/nchs/fastats/fastats.htm. Accessed 2 February 2000.

NCVC (National Center for Victims of Crime, Arlington, VA). Elder Abuse Statistics. Online. Available at http://www.ncvc.org/stats/ea.htm. Accessed 10 June 2001.

NCVC (National Center for Victims of Crime, Arlington, VA). Child Abuse and Child Sexual Abuse Statistics. Online. Available at http://www.ncvc.org/stats/ca_csa.htm. Accessed 10 June 2001.

بسم الله الرحمن الرحيم

The Failings of the Western Ethic

Evolutionary Ethics—An Invitation to a New/Old Perspective

Bismi-Llaah, Alh̲amduli-Llaah,
Allaahumma s̲alli wa sallim ʿalaa sayyidinaa Muh̲ammadin,
wa ʿalaa aalihi wa sah̲bih

Introduction: Signs of the Failure of the Western Ethic

Allah *(Subh̲aanahu wa taᶜaalaa)* guides us in the Holy Qur'an:

> ***Wa-l-takum-miñkum ummatuñy-yadᶜuuna ila-l-khayri wa ya'muruuna bi-l-maᶜruufi wa-yanhawna ʿani-l-muñkar; wa ulaaa'ika humu-l-muflih̲uun.***
>
> **Let there be of you an *ummah* to call to the good, to enjoin virtue and forbid vice. Those who do so are the felicitous** (3:104).

How are we to "call to the good"? Where can we begin, in a country where poverty crushes the dreams of inner city youths; where prejudice preys upon minorities and immigrants; and where unrestrained sexuality encroaches further and further upon childhood, preparing youths for lives of passion, not compassion?

Our situation may be likened to a crisis that once faced the Khalifah Umar *(rad̲iya-Llaahu ʿanhu)*. A fire broke out in Medina and spread rapidly, until half the city was burning. People threw waterskin after waterskin of vinegar and water on the flames, but they continued, unabated.

Someone ran to Hazrat Umar *(radiya-Llaahu 'anhu)* exclaiming, "The water won't put the fire out!"

Umar *(radiya-Llaahu 'anhu)* replied, "That fire is a sign from Allah. It is the multiple flames of your wrong actions and laziness. Forget the water and distribute bread. Abandon greed, if you are of the people of Islam."

The people protested that they already gave freely in charity. Hazrat Umar *(radiya-Llaahu 'anhu)* said, "You give bread from habit. You do not open your hands for the sake of Allah. You give not out of gratitude, but out of greed for recognition."

This story offers a metaphor for the state of ethics in much of the Westernized world today. Outer affirmations of ethics, inner greed, unconscious habits, bewilderment: these are the messages of modern-day headlines. Americans talk about morality, but what does our society really promote? Individualism, self-centeredness, hedonism, cosmetic beauty over inner contentment, information over wisdom. Now there are signs of growing racism and the threat of fascism and anarchy.

There *are* people in our society who strive to uphold ethical standards. Unfortunately, in keeping with structuralist world views, some reduce ethics to black and white terms, unresponsive to our changing culture or times. The Christian Right rails against iniquity, yet supports a witch hunt mentality that fosters prejudice, if not violence. Conservative Americans emphasize the sanctity of the family, while backing prosecutors' decisions to call mothers to testify against their children. Lawyer/client privilege is abrogated and the accused are guilty until proven innocent, at least in the court of public opinion.

In about the year 9 A.H., the Prophet Muhammad *(salla-Llaahu ᶜalayhi wa sallam)* received a revelation warning him as follows:

> ***...Wa mimman hawlakum-mina-l-aᶜraabi munaa-fiquun. Wa min ahli-l-Madeenati maraduu ᶜala-n-nifaaq...***
>
> **...And among the Arabs who dwell around you there are hypocrites (*munaafiquun*); and among the people of Medina, also, there are such as have grown insolent in hypocrisy...** (Qur'an 9:101).

We, too, live in a time of *munaafiquun.* Where does civilization end up in a world of self-serving politicians, religious extremists of all faiths, corporate monopolists, and unethical school teachers? Where else could we find ourselves? What does a genuinely ethical society lead to?

Ethics, or *akhlaaq* (to use the Islamic term), has long been a favorite topic of Muslim scholars. But it is not centuries of scholarship that make *akhlaaq* important today: it is the pressing needs of our times, needs that we as Muslims and as students of the Way have a responsibility to address.

We have not only a responsibility, but the strongest foundation from which to address these needs. It is to this foundation that I would like to turn my attention next.

Foundations for "Evolutionary Ethics": Qur'an and Sunnah

Sufism provides an experiential introduction to qualities such as compassion, patience, and tolerance as tools for adjusting personal and collective patterns of behavior. It enables individuals and groups to manifest their deepest and most sublime human character in the service of Allah *(Subhaanahu wa ta'aalaa)* and of Allah's creation.

At the core of this transformative process lies the Divine revelation and the teachings and examples of the Prophet Muhammad *(ṣalla-Llaahu ʿalayhi wa sallam)*. Abu-l-Qasim al-Junayd *(raḏiya-Llaahu ʿanhu)* said:

> **This knowledge of ours is built of the Qur'an and *sunnah*** (al-Misri 864).

All the ethical guidelines that one could possibly need are available in the Qur'an and *sunnah*. These guidelines are not rigid rules, but rather a framework for a new/old ethic which I refer to as "evolutionary ethics." Evolutionary ethics reflect the readiness of the individual to grasp the next level of ethical potential, the next level of inner and outer freedom.

A History of Stagnation

The key to activating the framework of evolutionary ethics lies in placing the timeless guidance of Qur'an and *sunnah* in the context of our time, place, and circumstances.

History testifies to the failure of Muslim nations to keep up with a changing world. For more than 200 years after printing presses flourished across Europe, the *ʿulamaa'* (religious scholars) of the Ottoman empire considered printing to be *ḫaram,* for texts (especially sacred ones) were too precious to be mass produced. The first Islamic printing press was not established in the Ottoman empire until 1720. Moreover, this press was only granted permission to print secular and scientific books, further divorcing sacred Islamic texts from the rapidly modernizing world (Murad 4).

Some Muslims argue that it was colonization that stifled creative thought in the Islamic world. Contemporary scholar Ismail Serageldin observes that, in fact, Muslim leaders suppressed progressive thinking before the colonists arrived. This suppression helped open the way for colonization, which in turn furthered the deterioration of Islamic society (Serageldin 82).

Historic misinterpretations of the Qur'an and *Hadith* have given rise to stereotypes of Islam as rigid and backwards. Still today, some Muslims reinforce these stereotypes by rejecting technology, forbidding women from working outside the home, condemning non-Muslims, and castigating fellow Muslims.

Such attitudes deny Islam its rightful place in the ethical discourse of today. It falls to the people who are fluent in the *sharee'ah*, the *sunnah*, and *Tasawwuf—and* in the technology and vocabulary of our age—to present the teachings in ways that can make them a positive force for change.

Distrust of Organized Religion and Dangers of Catering to It

The challenges involved are enormous. The world is linked as never before by a global economy, communications technology, and environmental crises. We also are operating on new frontiers of consciousness, as scientists learn more about the human mind and brain. Many people question whether any religious tradition meets the needs of such a diverse and rapidly changing world. They argue that institutionalized religion is passé, and should be replaced by new forms of spiritual expression.

It can be tempting to cater to those who wish to be "spiritual" without having to be "religious." Add to this trend the widespread fear of Islam in the West, and it is not surprising that new strands of so-called Sufism should emerge, distant from the guidance of the Holy Qur'an, the *Hadith*, and the genuine traditions of the Way.

The guidance of an authorized *shaykh* is essential to success on this Path. Those who are rightly guided and who can guide others rightly are those who point students towards the Qur'an and *Hadith*, towards *sharee'ah*, towards *akhlaaq*, towards the essence of Islam.

Westerners who are drawn to Sufism are usually compelled by a personal search for inner realization, for meaning, for an understanding of their purpose in life. In many cases, they are dissatisfied with the belief system or religion with which they are raised. Wary of doctrine, institutions, and hierarchy, they adopt an intellectual and experiential approach to finding answers to their questions.

It is understandable that individuals who come to the Path in this way initially tend to gloss over the essence of Sufism: namely, Islam. But the longer they maintain this attitude, the greater the obstacle it poses to spiritual progress. Shaykh Ahmad ar-Rifa'i *(radiya-Llaahu 'anhu)*, founder of the Rifa'i Order, said, "The *tareeqah* (way of the Sufi) is the same as the *sharee'ah* (the laws of religion), and the laws of religion are the same as the *tareeqah*" (AICP 5). Hazrat Khwaja Abdul Khalique Ghujduwani *(radiya-Llaahu 'anhu)*, one of the Masters of Wisdom in the *silsila* of the Naqshbandiyya Order, wrote to a *mureed* (student):

> Adhere to the *sunnah*. Study the *fiqh* (the knowledge of the rules of the religion). Study the *Hadith* (the sayings of the Prophet *[salla-Llaahu 'alayhi wa sallam])*. Study *tafseer* (the commentary of the Qur'an), and beware and avoid those who are ignorant and claim to be Sufis (AICP 5).

The farther removed Sufism becomes from *sharee'ah*, the more it becomes labeled a New Age fad, as yoga has been. Sufism is not a fad. Sufism is the understanding of how to operate the archetype, the *naqsh* (design) within the human being, in the ever-renewing universe of consciousness and materiality. In all eras and places,

Sufism has purified the hearts of sincere seekers. It was the reality of experiencing "Know yourself and you will know your Lord" long before it had a name.

Certainly, we cannot solve ethical and social problems through unconscious litanies or rituals. When and where Islam has been reduced to such, its spiritual underpinnings must be revitalized. At the same time, we cannot effectively address ethics by creating a new religion or by diluting *Tasawwuf* so much that it no longer causes a seeker to stretch or to experience the treasures of submission *(islaam)*, faith *(imaan)*, and trust *(tawakkul)*.

Islaam, Imaan, and Tawakkul

Post-modern intellectuals dismiss submission as servile, faith as blind, and trust as naive. From a Sufic point of view, submission, faith, and trust are wakeful, mature, and premised upon insight and attentiveness to the moment. As the bird submits to the currents of the wind, so, too, seekers submit to the forces that can take them to their destination.

Every human being is submitted to something. We submit to our children's needs, and to cultural standards for attire and manners. We allow the media to shape our opinions. We submit to advertising campaigns. We submit to the law. Every day, we submit at least thirty or forty times (perhaps more!). We stop what we are doing when the phone rings or someone drops by. We remember something we meant to do yesterday, and switch to doing that. We spend our days, submitting again and again. Yes, that's life—*alhamduli-Llaah*, Islam is what life is all about!

Islam makes this minute-to-minute social submission purposeful, within a framework of *'aqeedah* (belief) and values. In contrast, many people operate from unconscious conditioning, even while they affirm "freedom of choice." They submit to the material world, to the demands of desire and convenience, rather than to a Higher Power. Allah *(Subhaanahu wa ta'aalaa)* observes in the Holy Qur'an:

> ***Al-haakumu-t-takaathur hattaa zurtumu-l-maqaabir.***
>
> **You are obsessed by greed for more and more until you go down to your graves** (102:1-2).

Along with such greed comes an attitude of ethical impunity. I remind you again of the people of Medina, confident of their merits while "flames of wrong actions" enveloped their city. So, too, modern-day societies, confident in their ethical underpinnings, suffer from environmental destruction born of their own consumerism. We fear nuclear, chemical, and biological weapons, bred of our own hunger for hegemony. We suffer disillusionment, depression, alcohol and drug dependencies in the wake of our own disregard for community values.

And so we find ourselves at a crossroads in thought and philosophy. The path that can take us toward solutions is not the one leading away from Islam, but rather the one that taps its evolutionary potential.

Sufic Islam as Process

Almost every aspect of *sharee'ah* points to process, as this saying sometimes attributed to the Prophet Muhammad *(salla-Llaahu 'alayhi wa sallam)* indicates:

> **Seek knowledge from cradle to grave.**[1]

Truth is revealed throughout the lives of individuals and societies as we are ready to see, hear, and understand it. All aspects of

Islam and *Tasawwuf* encourage this discovery by promoting flexibility and patience.

Consider Islam's approach to slavery. Slavery was a mainstay of Arabian society, and the Prophet Muhammad *(salla-Llaahu 'alayhi wa sallam)* never called for its immediate abolition. Instead, the Qur'an and *Hadith* provided new guidelines for the treatment of slaves. Slaves were to be dressed and fed in the same manner as their masters. If they embraced Islam, they stood shoulder to shoulder with their masters in prayer. To free a slave was a commonplace punishment for crime. Such guidelines inevitably led to the emancipation of many slaves.

Just as *sharee'ah* could progressively address slavery in seventh century Arabia, so, too, it is progressive enough to address key ethical issues today. Methods of adapting the Qur'an and *sunnah* to the needs of a particular place and circumstance include *ijtihaad* (the exercise of independent judgment), *qiyaas* (analogy), and *ijmaa'* (consensus). Volumes have been written on these subjects, and I do not have time to explore them today. But perhaps two brief examples can illustrate these processes.

Organ transplants obviously were not an issue in the Prophet's day. But the following statement in the Qur'an bears on this and other issues in medical ethics:

> ***...man ahyaahaa fa-ka'annamaaa ahya-n-naasa jamee'aa.***
>
> **...whoever saves a life, it would be as if he [or she] saved the life of all the people** (5:32).

The violation of a body is forbidden in Islam, a prohibition that governs the removal of organs. Yet, according to Islamic law,

"Necessities overrule prohibition," and "the lesser of two evils is to be chosen if both cannot be avoided." Combining these injunctions, one Muslim leader concludes that if a person is likely to die without a transplant, then the transplant should be undertaken (Organ).

Entering the debate over genetic engineering, the same scholar notes that

> Gene replacement is essentially transplantation surgery, albeit at the molecular level....[G]enetic engineering [could] open tremendous vistas in treatment of many illnesses and the possibilities in agriculture and animal husbandry might be the clue to solving the problem of famine the world over (Genetic).

These and other examples show the Qur'an and *sunnah* as frameworks for evolutionary ethics.

Such ethics are articulated and enacted by the individual, within a secure community. Both individual and community are essential to the process.

"Invelopment": Personal & Community Development through Involvement

Human beings have an inherent urge to become constructively involved in the lives of others. We want to play a useful part in the community (*ummah*). Appropriately directed, this urge creates a link between personal development and society's progress. I call this link "invelopment": personal and societal development through involvement.

"Invelopment" results when the innate desire to contribute to the community has a proper venue for expression. The more a person is involved in fostering the well-being of society, the greater his or her personal growth and the more rapid the spiritual evolution of society.

The Best (and Worst) Man of the Bani Isra'eel

Allah *(Subhaanahu wa ta'aalaa)* once commanded the prophet Musa (Moses) *('alayhi-s-salaam)* to ask the *Bani Isra'eel* to select the thousand men and women of the highest ethic among them. They did, and once the group was formed, they were asked to choose the top one hundred. From these they were to choose the top ten, and from the top ten, they were to pick the one with the highest ethic.

They selected a man of the most refined, kindly, and humble disposition. This man was then instructed to find the worst person among the *Bani Isra'eel* and to bring him or her to Musa *('alayhi-s-salaam)*.

After a few days, he came across someone who was notoriously immoral. He thought, "Surely no one could be worse than this!" But he decided not to be too quick to end his search.

A little while later, he came across someone whose acts were even more vile. Again he hesitated. He reminded himself that he was judging based only on outward appearances, and that God alone knew the depths of a person's heart. He was also becoming wary of his own pride in being "the best."

Finally, he decided that he could not pass judgment on anyone other than himself. He concluded that the worst person had to be he, because he knew how many faults he had.

He returned to Musa *(ʿalayhi-s-salaam)* and introduced himself as the worst person among the *Bani Isra'eel*.

God then revealed that this man was indeed the best. Because he considered himself worst, he would always work to improve himself, his relationship with Allah, and his relationship with other people (Jamnia, 60-61).

In order to make ethics real, we must look closely at our own behavior. The term *akhlaaq* encompasses both "ethic" and "character." Each of us must continue to refine our own character if we are to foster an ethical society.

ʿIbaadah and Adab

The person in the story was of high ethic because he remained conscious of Allah. He understood the full breadth of the Islamic concept of *ʿibaadah*, or worship.

As children, many if not most of us attended church, synagogue, or (in some cases) mosque. But few of us were taught to truly worship: to turn our entire lives into service of the Divine, always seeing around us the beneficence of Allah *(Subhaanahu wa taʿaalaa)*, and feeling humbled by that greatness. Other words from the same root as *ʿibaadah* include *ʿabada* (venerate) and *ʿubuudah* (humble veneration). This is *ʿibaadah*—worship, veneration, and humility.

ʿIbaadah requires *adabah* (a moral, ethical approach to life). We are all familiar with the related term *adab:* spiritual courtesy rooted in the heart. *Adab* is one of the most practical tools of ethics, for it curbs the human tendency to be self-centered rather than God-centered.

Traditional sources on *adab* include the guidelines for behavior in the *khanaqahs* of the Khwaja Khwajagan, the rules of the

Naqshbandi Order, the duties of brotherhood of Imam Abu Hamid al-Ghazali *(radiya-Llaahu 'anhu)*, and the principles of *futuwwah* (chivalry), among many others. Allow me to share a sampling of the treasures that these resources contain.

- According to Imam Abu Hamid al-Ghazali *(radiya-Llaahu 'anhu)*, "Concealing faults, feigning ignorance of them and overlooking them—this is the mark of religious people." "You should seek seventy excuses for your brother's [or sister's] misdeed, and if your heart will accept none of them you should turn the blame upon yourself..." (39, 67).

- Imam Al-Ghazali *(radiya-Llaahu 'anhu)* also reminded readers that "the Prophet Muhammad said: '...If a person gives up contention even when he [or she] is...right, a house will be built for that person in the loftiest part of the Garden [of Paradise]' " (45).

- Hazrat Muhammad ibn al-Husayn as-Sulami *(radiya-Llaahu 'anhu)* instructed students of the Way to "respond to cruelty with kindness, and do not punish for an error." "Be satisfied with little for yourself, and wish much for others." "Remember that you are a servant of Allah and should not regard yourself or your actions highly, nor should you expect a return for your actions" (37, 41, 43).

- And, finally, Shaykh Abu al-Najib al-Suhrawardi *(radiya-Llaahu 'anhu)* stated: "Association with ignorant persons should be with patience, good manners, and sympathy." And, further, "...one should not listen to indecencies and slander" (47, 49).

Earlier I posed the question, "Where does civilization end up if it continues in the direction it's headed today? Where else might it end up?" I invite you now to imagine one alternative:

a community and civilization centered around *adab, ʿibaadah, akhlaaq, ʿaqeedah.*

TOWARDS AN ECOLOGY OF ETHICS

This is the community of Islam: one filled with light (*nuur*) and kinship and affinity (*nisbah*). It is a community where each person recognizes her or his responsibility for the well-being of others, where people assist those who are in need, where everyone has a duty and finds joy in fulfilling it, no matter how humble the task. It is a community of "invelopment," where every individual is engaged in perfecting himself or herself, and, as part of that perfecting process, is serving the community at large.

The Prophet *(ṣalla-Llaahu ʿalayhi wa sallam)* said,

> **The believers, in their mutual love and affection, are as one body. When one member has a complaint, the rest of the body is united with it in wakefulness and in fever** (An-Numan bin Bashir/Bukhari).

Ethics are cultivated within this matrix of relationships, in the shared context of walking on a straight path (*siraaṯa-l-mustaqeem*) towards a goal that is within and beyond the gates of this life. They are affirmed by a *shareeʿah* that promotes economic equity, education, social justice, and the balanced fulfillment of material and spiritual needs.

Such an environment naturally creates an ecology of goodness and ethic. It provides the basis for a trust, morality, and honesty that is not imposed from the outside, but rather inspired from within.

Of course, breaches of ethics will occur even in the best community. The Prophet Muhammad *(salla-Llaahu 'alayhi wa sallam)* said:

> **One who amongst you sees something abominable should modify it with the help of his or her hand; and if he [or she] has not strength enough to do [so with the hand], then...with the tongue; and if he [or she] has not strength enough to do [so with the tongue], then he [or she] should abhor it from the heart, and that is the least of faith** (Abu Sa'id al-Khudri/Sahih Muslim).

In a community governed by *sharee'ah*, each person is an "officer of the law." But this law is not enforced with ethics investigations and media rampages. It is enacted with love, gentleness, and kindness; with sweet words, encouragement, and models of what it means to live a principled life while covering the faults of others.

> **A man came to the Prophet Muhammad *(salla-Llaahu 'alayhi wa sallam)* to confess a sin and receive the punishment due him. The Prophet *(salla-Llaahu 'alayhi wa sallam)* ordered him to free a slave. The man replied that he had no slaves to free.**
>
> **The Prophet *(salla-Llaahu 'alayhi wa sallam)* then said he should fast for two months. He said he was too weak to do that.**
>
> **The Prophet *(salla-Llaahu 'alayhi wa sallam)* instructed him to provide food for all the poor, but he said he did not have the means to do so.**

> **Then the Prophet** ***(salla-Llaahu 'alayhi wa sallam)*** **said, "Please wait here." After some time, a person came with a basket of dates for the Prophet** ***(salla-Llaahu 'alayhi wa sallam)*****. The Prophet** ***(salla-Llaahu 'alayhi wa sallam)*** **gave them to the man, telling him to use them to feed the poor. "Am I to give them to someone poorer than I?" the man asked. "For I swear by Allah, there is no one poorer than my family!"**
>
> **The Prophet** ***(salla-Llaahu 'alayhi wa sallam)*** **laughed, it was said, "until his eyeteeth showed." Then he told the sinner, "Give the dates to your family, and eat!"** (Abu Hurayra/Al-Muwatta).

On another occasion, the Prophet *(salla-Llaahu 'alayhi wa sallam)* said:

> **Do not hurt those who believe, and do not impute evil to them, and do not try to uncover their nakedness [meaning "faults"]...** (Abu Hurayra/Sahih Muslim).

As we well know, this is not the way in the Westernized world, literally or figuratively. Here, everything is to be brought out into the open, in order to get at "the truth of the matter."

But who among us is qualified to represent the Truth? As the man of the *Bani Isra'eel* realized, only Allah *(Subhaanahu wa ta'aalaa)* is *al-Haqq* (The Truth). We may have facts and information, but these do not equal truth. They may not even equal understanding. Understanding comes through the process of receiving with an open heart, filtering everything through *sharee'ah* and *sunnah*, and adjusting for personal and cultural biases. The person who understands can reject unethical behavior without judging or publicizing it. She or he does not mistake others' worst qualities for their only qualities.

> The Prophet Isa *(ʿalayhi-s-salaam)* (Jesus) was walking with his followers one day when they passed the rotting carcass of a dog. His followers cried out, "How terrible it smells!" But Isa *(ʿalayhi-s-salaam)* said, "How white its teeth are."

Disclosure (even when accurate) does not necessarily improve a person's behavior. Nor does humiliation. Wrongful acts can only be ameliorated in ways that are appropriate to the capabilities of the people involved.

The Prophet *(ṣalla-Llaahu ʿalayhi wa sallam)* offered dates as punishment for sin. Hazrat Umar *(raḏiya-Llaahu ʿanhu)* prescribed charity in the face of fire. Both understood that the key to ensuring ethical conduct lies in preserving the fabric of the community, and that that lies in the dignity of the individual.

This is the core of "involopment": to accept and act upon one's innate patience, tolerance, faith, and belief. Herein lies the foundation and the heart of Islam and Sufism.

Learning the Most from the Least Ethical Behavior

The Prophet *(ṣalla-Llaahu ʿalayhi wa sallam)* said:

> **Every person is born in *fiṯrah* [in a state of essential goodness and submission]. It is one's parents who make one a Christian, Jew, or Magian.** (Abu Hurayra/Bukhari)

Allah *(Subḫaanahu wa taʿaalaa)* has sown not only religious differences, but many other differences among human beings by the hands of their families and their environments. Despite the purity of our natural disposition, we find huge and frightening variations in definitions of good and bad, right and wrong, morality and immorality. Twenty years after he slaughtered more than a million Cambodians, Pol Pot said that his conscience was clear, for he had done it for the good of his people. What misery has ever been inflicted in the name of bad?

We give thanks to Allah *(Subhaanahu wa ta'aalaa)* that most individuals seem to resonate with the higher end of the spectrum. As for the people at the lower end, they underscore the message that we are all responsible for everyone's well-being. Until that message becomes a primary message to every child in the world, we will still have the confusion that comes of irrational actions undertaken in the name of "good" and "right." Until we and the generations after us know what it means to adore God *('ibaadah)* and to evoke the highest conduct through *adab* and service to others, ethics will remain the stuff of Senate investigations, CNN reports, Rush Limbaugh radio programs, and tabloid exposés.

This takes me to the final topic I would like to address: focal points for action. Let me turn to the subject of future generations as a departure, and a beginning.

FOCAL POINTS FOR ACTION

1. Global Demographics and Education

The hope for a real basis in Islamic ethics, free of many of the cultural overlays, lies in how we raise and educate our youths. Today the need for sensitive education in *akhlaaq* and *adab* is more pressing than ever. While Western populations are "aging and static...with stable, introspective political cultures," Muslim countries are experiencing a "youth bulge." Political and social turmoil frequently accompany growing percentages of youths in a society. The Protestant reformation and the rise of German fascism are two cases in point (Murad 10-11). More recently,

> The Islamic revival over the past few years has faithfully reflected this trend. One of the first Muslim countries to reach a peak proportion of youth was Iran, in the late 1970s ([when youth made up] around 22% of the population), and revolution occurred in 1979. ...in Algeria this proportion was reached in 1989, just when the [extremist Islamic Salvation Front, or] FIS, was winning its greatest support (Murad 11).

If we want our children to grow up with ethical principles, they have to be taught the Qur'an and *sunnah* properly from early in life. Young people need to understand the Qur'an and *sunnah* in the context of being part of a global society, understanding the terminologies of post-modern political and social discourse, participating in the information revolution, and being voices of tolerance, compassion, faith, trust, and reliability.

We have to look towards educating our youths to be strong Muslims and Sufis. What does this mean in the United States? How can we best use the texts, tools, and technologies that are available? After all, a failure to incorporate the Internet into our educational approaches could be as damaging as the Ottomans' disdain for the printing press.

In addition to working with our youths, a second focal point for action lies in acting as facilitators and models of dialogue.

2. Relations Among Muslims: Tolerance, not Takfeer

Both Muslim and non-Muslim societies today are fraught with schisms, contractiveness, and suspicion. Fear and the abandonment of basic human and spiritual principles characterize much of the content and style of communications among people of faith, be they Muslims, Christians, Jews, Hindus, Buddhists or others. One need spend only a short time on the World Wide Web to come across dialogues turned into diatribe. Any hope for reconciliation among our brothers and sisters is shrouded in doubt and *takfeer* (charges of unbelief).

It appears that the Sufis alone may be able to reconcile the disparity and celebrate the diversity of our community of faith. However, we can only manifest this ability if we truly agree upon and practice what Allah *(Subhaanahu wa ta'aalaa)* and the Prophet *(salla-Llaahu 'alayhi wa sallam)* have provided, bringing our unique methods, commitments, personal experiences, and, hopefully, Islamic unity to the critical task at hand. We must resist engaging in *takfeer*, and rather enjoin others to reflect the same tolerance and love that we experience among ourselves in gatherings such as this.

3. Expressing the New/Old Perspective Throughout Society

A third focal point for action lies in expressing the new/old perspective of Islam and *Tasawwuf* through our daily work.

Each of us who has benefited from the blessings of this Path has an obligation to share what we have gained. Some of us may do this on a local scale, working with just a small circle of neighbors. Others may attain international acclaim. Some of us may publicly identify ourselves as "Muslims" or "Sufis;" others may not. As Muslims, as Sufis, we work in both *dunyaa* (this world) and *akhirah* (the Hereafter). The criteria for our success neither excludes nor depends upon the criteria of the material world. Rather, we know that Allah *(Subhaanahu wa ta'aalaa)* is aware of our successes and failures. Remaining ever mindful of the Divine Presence in our lives, we strive each day to be able to answer "yes!" in response to the question: "Am I reflecting an Islamic and Sufic paradigm in my work, in my interactions, in every aspect of my life to the best of my ability?"

With Allah's mercy, the day we can say "yes!" is the day that our work will have profound effects for the betterment of our society... and of our world.

The attainment of this goal begins with turning attention to our inward state.

CHARACTER BUILDING AND MUHAASABATU-N-NAFS

Allah *(Subhaanahu wa ta'aalaa)* tells us in the Holy Qur'an:

> ***Qad aflaha man zakkaahaa. Wa qad khaaba man dassaahaa.***
>
> **Blessed indeed is [the one] who purifies it [his soul], and unsuccessful is [the one] who debases it** (91: 9-10).

In the pursuit of purification *(tazkiyah),* each of us must strive to recognize that all that is unhealthy and unwholesome in life is neither necessary nor, ultimately, desirable. *Tazkiyah* is acquiring what is healthy for us. It involves maintaining the physical surroundings, the psychological states, and the types of interactions that are purifying for us in *dunyaa* (the material world). It means supporting and encouraging the inclinations and aspirations that are spiritually fulfilling (Ahmed 1).

A key tool of character building is conscious reflection, encompassed in the Islamic concept of *muhaasabah,* which literally means to reckon, to reconcile, or to take an account of (as in balancing an organization's financial accounts). The Sufis practice *muhaasabatu-n-nafs* (accounting for one's self), as Shaykh ᶜAbdullaah Nooruddeen Durkee presents in his book, *'Insajaama.*

> ***Qaala Rasuulu-Llaah (salawaatu-Llaahi wa salaamuhu ᶜalayh) "Haasibu anfusakum qabla an tuhaasibu, wa zinu aᶜmaalakum qabla an tuzanu ᶜalaykum."***
>
> **The Messenger of Allah** ***(salawaatu-Llaahi wa salaamuhu ᶜalayh)*** **said, "Account for your 'selfs' (*anfus*) before you are accounted; weigh your actions before your actions become a weight upon you."**

Muhaasabatu-n-nafs entails the examination of one's self, of one's intentions, decisions, actions, and conscience. This is a practice of utmost significance. It forms a practical basis for change, for refocussing one's life and point of view, for beautifying one's character, for evolving and for "invelopment." Ultimately, this is the aim of every spiritual journey.

In sum, the Qur'an and *sunnah* provide an essential, flexible, and relevant framework for evolutionary ethics in today's world. In an ethical environment, everything is oriented first towards the community and the sustainability of that community. But this orientation can only be arrived at and maintained by making commitments and utilizing appropriate mechanisms for expressing one's own understanding of *'ibaadah* and building one's character as an individual Muslim and *mu'min*.

Islam speaks directly to each person's role, commitment, remembrance, and duty to others and self. It stresses a personal ethic (*akhlaaq*) which begins its development at home, in relationships with one's family and neighbors. It is refined through the mastery of *adab* and extends to self-observation and the understanding that "every action I perform affects the whole." As each of us learns how we can best express our inborn urge to contribute to the community, "invelopment" takes place: we become better people, and the community makes progress.

Let me end with a story, and an invitation to try one of the approaches I have just described.

Once a king decided that he wanted to have a lake of milk next to his palace. A hole was dug, and everyone in the kingdom was notified that they should bring a liter of milk and pour it into the hole on a particular night, so that the king could watch the sun rise over the lake the next morning. When the night finally arrived, the king lay awake in anticipation, listening to the footsteps and sounds of pouring. Finally, the first rays of light brightened his room. He rushed to the window, threw open the curtains, and looked out upon...a beautiful lake of water!

The king sent his wazir to find out what had happened. The wazir traveled far and wide, speaking to people throughout the king's dominions. After many weeks, he returned with an explanation. All of the king's subjects were so poor that each one had thought, "I have no milk to spare, so I'll bring water. After all, who will miss *my* little bucket of milk?"

A Sufi knows the value of his or her bucket of milk. A Sufi's concern for the well-being of others takes precedent over his or her concern for himself or herself—gladly, gratefully, humbly, and out of inner necessity.

With this story in mind, I remind you again of *muhaasabatu-n-nafs:* accounting for one's self. May I invite you to take a few moments now for private reflection.

Please relax. Breath deeply. Turn your attention to your heart, and recite the *Suuratu-l-Faatihah:*

> ***Bismi-Llaahi-r-Rahmaani-r-Raheem. Alhamdu-li-Llaahi Rabbi-l-ᶜaalameen, Ar-Rahmaani-r-Raheem. Maaliki yawmi-d-deen. Iyyaaka naᶜbudu wa'iyyaaka nastaᶜeen. Ihdina-s-siraata-l-mustaqeem, siraata-l-ladheena anᶜamta ᶜalayhim, ghayri-l-maghduubi ᶜalayhim, wa la-d-daaalleen. Aameen.***
>
> **In the Name of Allah, the Universally Merciful, the Singularly Compassionate, Praise be to Allah, the Lord of All the Worlds—the Universally Merciful, the Singularly Compassionate—Master**

> **of the Day of Judgment. You alone we worship, and You alone we ask for help. Guide us [to] the straight way, The way of those whom You have blessed, not [the way of] those on whom is [Your] anger, nor those who are astray** (Qur'an 1:1-7).

Then recite the following *du'aa'* both in Arabic and in translation.

> ***Qaala Rasuulu-Llaah** (salawaatu-Llaahi wa salaamuhu 'alayh)* ***"Haasibu anfusakum qabla an tuhaasibu, wa zinu a'maalakum qabla an tuzanu 'alaykum."***
>
> **The Messenger of Allah** *(salawaatu-Llaahi wa salaamuhu 'alayh)* **said, "Account for your 'selfs' (*anfus*) before you are accounted; weigh your actions before your actions become a weight upon you."**

Think over your day in detail, from the time you got up this morning, to this moment....

...reflect upon the real purpose of life and how you live it....

...ask yourself, "What could I have done more according to Allah's will today? How could I have changed my responses, words, thoughts, actions to be in harmony with Allah's will?"...

...make the internal commitment that can change nations, by changing yourself.

Jazaaka-Llaah khayr—thank you.

* * *

Wa-Llaahu lahu-l-haqqu wa huwa yahdi-s-sabeel.
Hasbuna-Llaahu wahdahu wa ni'mal-wakil.

Wa salli ʿalaa Sayyidina Muhammadin
wa aaalihi wa sahbihi ajmaʿeen
wa-l-hamdu li-Llaahi Rabbi-l-ʿaalameen.

Truth belongs to Allah; it is He who shows the way.
Allah, alone, suffices us, and what a fine guardian is He!
Blessings upon our Master Muhammad
and his family and companions altogether
and praise is due to Allah, Lord of the Worlds.

O Allah *(Subhaanahu wa taʿaalaa)* give peace, understanding,
and highest ethic to all those who are gathered here today.
Grant them the ability to worship You humbly,
to serve You, to have trust and rely upon You,
and to gain the deepest insight that is buried in their hearts.

Rabbanaa laa tu'aakhidhnaaa in-naseenaaa aw akhta'naa.
Rabbanaa wa laa tahmil ʿalaynaa israñ
kamaa hamaltahu ʿalaa-l-ladheena miñ qablinaa.
Rabbanaa wa laa tahammilnaa maa laa taaqata lanaa bih.
Waʿfu ʿannaa, wagh-fir lanaa warhmnaaa.
Anta Mawlaanaa fa-ñsurnaa ʿalaa-l-qawmi-l-kaafireen.

Our Lord! Condemn us not if we forget or miss the mark! Our
Lord! Lay not on us such a burden
as Thou didst lay on those before us!
Our Lord! Impose not on us
that which we have not the strength to bear!
Pardon us, absolve us, and have mercy on us,
Thou, our Protector, and give us victory
over the disbelieving folk (Qur'an 2:286).

Notes

1 The saying, "Seek knowledge from cradle to grave," is typically attributed to the Prophet Muhammad *(ṣalla-Llaahu 'alayhi wa sallam)*, although this specific wording is not found in *ḥadith* literature. However, other *hadith* are quite similar in language and meaning, such as, "Seeking knowledge is incumbent upon every Muslim," which was reported as a saying of the Prophet *(ṣalla-Llaahu 'alayhi wa sallam)* by Ibn Majah, Bayhaqi, and other scholars. Consequently, the former statement is regarded as part of the general wisdom of Islam, whether it was uttered by Muhammad *(ṣalla-Llaahu 'alayhi wa sallam)* or one of his early followers.

References

Abdulhadi, Fahhim. Statement Regarding Anti-Muslim Comments Made by Pat Robertson on October 27, 1997. Excerpts printed in *The AMC (American Muslim Council) Report*, Jan. 1998.

Ahmed, Kurshid. Some Aspects of Character Building. *The Muslim*. Oct./ Nov. 1970.

AICP (Association of Islamic Charitable Projects). Sufism: The Methodology of the True Sufis is Part of the Religion of Islam. Available on the internet at http://www.aicp.org/Graphics/Sufism/parti.htm.

Durkee, 'Abdullaah Nooruddeen *'Insajaama* or *Harmonic Flow*. Keene, VA: Green Mountain School, transmitted by Shaykh Nuuru-d-deen al Gharib.

Genetic Engineering. Printed by the University of Northumbria (UK) Islamic Student Society. Available on the internet at http://www.unn.ac.uk/ societies/islamic/about/modern/gen.htm.

al-Ghazali, Abu Hamid Muhammad. *The Duties of Brotherhood in Islam*. Translated by Muhtar Holland. Woodstock, NY: Overlook Press, 1976.

al-Misri, Ahmad ibn Naqib. *Reliance of the Traveller: A Classical Manual of Islamic Sacred Law*. Edited and translated by Nur Ha Mim Keller. Evanston, IL: Sunna Books, 1994.

Jamnia, Mohammed Ali and Mojdeh Bayat. *Under the Sufi's Cloak: Stories of Abu Sa'id and His Mystical Teachings*. Beltsville, MD: Writers', Inc., 1995.

Murad, Abdal Hakim. "Islam and the New Millennium, Part I." From a lecture delivered at the Belfast Mosque, March 1997. Available on the internet at http://www.iol.ie/~afifi/Articles/Millenium.htm.

Organ Donation and Transplantation. Printed by the University of Northumbria (UK) Islamic Student Society. Available on the internet at http://www.unn.ac.uk/societies/islamic/about/modern/organ.htm.

Serageldin, Ismail. Mirrors and Windows: Redefining the Boundaries of the Mind. *The American Journal of Islamic Social Sciences.* Volume 11, Number 1, Spring 1994: 79-107.

al-Suhrawardi, Abu al-Najib. *A Sufi Rule for Novices (Kitab Adab al-Muridin).* Translated by Menahem Milson. Cambridge, MA: Harvard University Press, 1975.

al-Sulami, Muhammad ibn al-Husayn. *The Book of Sufi Chivalry: Lessons to a Son of the Moment (Futuwwah).* Translated by Sheikh Tosun Bayrak al-Jerrahi al-Halveti. New York: Inner Traditions International, 1983.

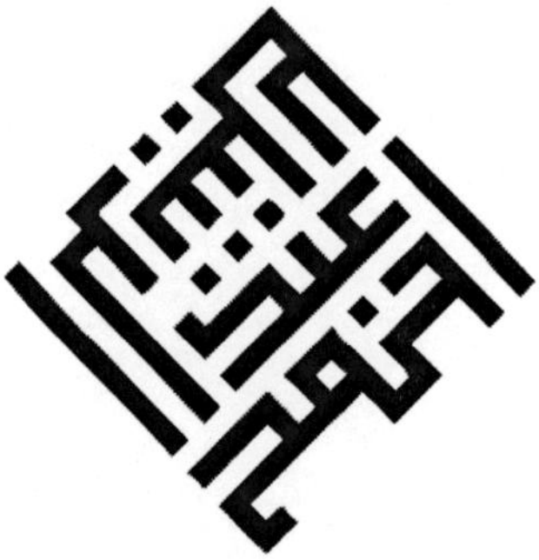

Discovering Extremism in Oneself in the Search for Moderation

Al-ḥamdu-li-Llaahi, muqaliba-l-quluubi wa-l-abṣaar.
Allaahumma thabit quluubana ʿalaa ṣiraaṭika-l-qaweem,
Wa-jʿalnaa li-wajhika muttajiheen,
wa ṣalli ʿalaa-sh-shafeeʿi-l-ḥabeeb,
raḥmatil-ʿaalameen, wa manaari-l-najiyeen, wa marsaa-l-ʿaarifeen

Praise be to Allah, the turner of the hearts and sight.
O Allah, fix our hearts on the best of Your ways,
and make us face You in our way,
and bestow blessings on the beloved intercessor,
the mercy of all the worlds,
the lighthouse of the survivors,
the harbor of the knowers.

Bismi-Llaah, Al-ḥamdu-li-Llaah
Allaahumma ṣalli wa sallim ʿalaa sayyidinaa Muḥammadin,
wa ʿalaa aaalihi wa saḥbih

Allah *(Subḥaanahu wa taʿaalaa)* reveals in the Holy Qur'an:

**Dhahara-l-fasaadu fi-l-barri wa-l-baḥri bi-maa
kasabat aydi-n-naasi liyudheeqahum-baʿda-l-
ladhee ʿamiluu laʿallahum yarjiʿuun**

Corruption *(fasaad)* appears on land and sea
because of [that] which people's hands have
done, that He [Allah] may make them taste

> **a part of that which they have done, in order that they may return** (30:41).

Some of the derivatives of the root F-S-D are *fasada*: "to become vicious, corrupt, depraved, perverted, vitiated, demoralized, depraved, degraded;" *fasaad:* "iniquity;" *mafsada*: "cause of evil, dirty tricks, malicious acts;" *ifsaad*: "undermining;" and *faasid*: "foul, vicious, empty, unsound."

How do we explain what we see in the world today? It is difficult to fully capture in words the relationship between what is happening in Iraq and the immoral, depraved, dissolute, destructive, undermining behavior of the people on both sides: the extreme behavior on the part of certain American soldiers in the prison, and the extreme behavior on the part of certain Iraqis. But delving into terms like *fasaad* can help us make some sense of today's events, for they suggest how selfishness, corruption, depravity, and social immorality keep proliferating.

Think about what people do in so-called "reality" TV programs. The producers stage all kinds of tests and frightening experiences that could be dangerous or psychologically disturbing, or they focus on physical attraction, sexuality, and contrasting social norms of "ugly" and "beautiful." Some of the humiliating things that are done for money or 15 minutes of fame, if forced would be considered assault, and if done to someone incarcerated would be considered torture. But do it for a million dollars, and it is considered "fun." That tells us something about the social mores of Western society.

Fasaad means the corruption, destruction, and undermining of society. The events in the news recently are symptomatic of the depravity of societies that will accept imperialism, wanton destruction, murder, and genocide. What are we witnessing? One answer, put forward by the television commentator Bill Moyers, is that we are seeing the moral end of America.

The extremism that is corrupting our society (and other societies around the world) comes from various political, economic, and social imbalances. Analogously, inside ourselves there are forces of extremism, arising from the deteriorating effect of the ego or *nafs ammaarah.* Is there really any difference between the conflicts and degradation being inflicted by groups and nations in the world around us, and what we do to ourselves, internally, every time we turn our attention away from Allah, away from truth, away from justice? Are we so different from the leaders on all sides of today's conflicts, who become heedless of the tendencies toward extremism and corruption within their own ranks, until those tendencies are brought back into their consciousness by some heinous acts?

But, just as we have within ourselves the *nafs ammaarah*, or unrepentant lower self and desire nature, so too we have the potential of the *nafs lawwaamah*: the reproaching self or conscience (Khan 2). When we look at the extremism that characterizes our world today, both outside of us and within us, we see not a clash of civilizations, but a clash of egos. Individual egos or collective egos (as when people stand behind individuals who are driven by their egos), the free rein granted to our lower natures, materials desires, attachments to *dunyaa*, unrepentant attitudes, and arrogance all encourage, initiate, and facilitate extremism. They all facilitate violence, and violence further feeds the *nafs ammaarah.*

Yet, the opportunity is always available to reduce the influence of the *nafs ammaarah.* Allah reveals in the Qur'an:

> ***Fa-mañ taaba mim-ba^cdi dhulmihee wa aslaha fa'inna-Llaaha yatuubu ^calayh; inna-Llaaha Ghafuurur-Raheem.***

> **But whoever repents** (makes *tawbah*) **after his wrongdoing and amends [things]** (brings about *salaah*), **lo! Allah will relent toward him. Lo! Allah is Forgiving, Merciful** (5:39).

Through repentance, through striving for *sulh* and all that it implies—peace, reconciliation, settlement, compromise, restoration, restitution, improvement, amelioration—we can (by Allah's Mercy) reach the stage of *nafs lawwaamah*: of humility and conscience, self-searching, repentance, peace, non-violence, cooperation, and reflection upon one's own self in *muhaasabah*.

In the Qur'an, Allah *(Subhaanahu wa ta'aalaa)* especially addresses the extreme actions of the *Ahl al-Kitaab*, warning believers not to follow those individuals in past generations who succumbed to excesses.

> ***Qul yaaa-ahla-l-kitaabi, laa taghluu fee deenikum ghayra-l-haqqi wa laa-tattabi'uu ahwaaa'a qawmiñ qad dalluu miñ qablu wa adalluu katheerañw-wa dalluu 'añ sawaaa'i-s-sabeel.***

> **Say, "O people of the Book! Do not exceed the bounds of truth in your religion, and do not yield to the fancies of those people who went astray before you; they misled many others and have themselves strayed from the right way"** (5:77).

Unfortunately, this warning seems to be falling on deaf ears, among members of the whole community of the *Ahl al-Kitaab*. Among Muslims, we witness extremes of two kinds. There is the person who pursues the worldly life, giving no thought to the *akhirah* and totally abandoning religion. On the other hand, there are those who become so engrossed in pursuing the *akhirah* that they think of nothing else but dying or preparing to die. In its worst form, the latter kind of extremism propels the fanatics who, in their own destruction, have destroyed the lives of thousands of innocents.

The Prophet *(salla-Llaahu ʿalayhi wa sallam)* consistently enjoined the path of moderation. He said,

> **Recite the Qur'an, and do good deeds .... Do not neglect it, nor be extreme in it...** *(Fiqh u Sunnah).*

The Prophet *(salla-Llaahu ʿalayhi wa sallam)* also taught us to **"make things easy, not difficult,"** and to **"beware of excessiveness in religion before you have perished as a result of such excessiveness in religion"** (Abu Hurayra/Bukhari).

We know from the Qur'an that the struggle between the potentials for good and evil is ongoing. Allah reveals:

> ***Am naj-ʿalu-l-ladheena aamanuu wa ʿamilu-s-saalihaati ka-l-mufsideena fi-l-'ard? Am naj-ʿalu-l-muttaqeena ka-l-fujjaar?***
>
> **Shall We treat those who believe and work deeds of righteousness *(ʿamilu-s-saalihaat)* the same as those who do mischief on earth *(al-mufsideen)*? Shall We treat the God-conscious in the same [way] as the wicked?** (38:28).

Historically, too, the confrontation between those who work for *sulh* and those who promote *fasaad* has also been ongoing. During the encounter with Firʿown, Musa *(ʿalayhi-s-salaam)* said,

> ***...inna-Llaaha laa yuslihu ʿamala-l-mufsideen....***
> **Allah does not further the work of those who**

> **do corruption...** [or, more literally, ...Allah *laa yuslih* — Allah does not make good, right, or useful — the work of *al-mufsideen*] (Qur'an 10:81).

The horrors of the Spanish Inquisition reflected this struggle, as did the rise of intolerant, moralistic attitudes in other times and places including the later years of the Ottoman Empire. In the ongoing effort to overcome *fasaad* and to uphold goodness *(ihsaan)*, justice *('adl)*, righteousness, peace, and reconciliation (*sulh*), and religious freedom, many people left their native lands and came to North America to establish this country. The abuses of the past gave rise to democracy and to all the associated rights and principles in which we believe, and for which (supposedly) we fight.

What kind of struggle—what kind of *jihaad*—characterizes today's world? According to a *hadith*, the Prophet *(salla-Llaahu 'alayhi wa sallam)* said:

> **Fighting is of two kinds: The one who seeks Allah's favor, obeys the leader, gives the property he values, treats his associates gently and avoids doing mischief, will have the reward for all the time whether he is asleep or awake; but the one who fights in a boasting spirit, for the sake of display and to gain a reputation, who disobeys the leader and does mischief in the earth will not return credit or without blame** (Abu Dawood 1037).

All along, Allah *(Subhaanahu wa ta'aalaa)* has been telling human beings to look beyond and to forgive unjust behavior toward us or toward others. Musa *('alayhi-s-salaam)* told it to the Jews, 'Isa *('alayhi-s-salaam)* told it to the Christians, the Prophet *(salla-Llaahu 'alayhi wa sallam)* tells it to the Muslims. Yet that fundamental, essential message becomes so sublimated that the forces of inhumane treatment have become dominant factors in conflict. Young "Muslims," young "Jews," and young "Christians" abandon this primary message of tolerance, peace, and forgiveness (Murad). In place of brotherhood and sisterhood there is angry rivalry between people. The concept of generosity has become so usurped by the idea of greed, power, and ambition that it is now considered weak to be tolerant, generous, and accepting.

Allah *(Subḥaanahu wa taʿaalaa)* reveals to us in the Qur'an:

> *Wa mina-n-naasi mañy-yaquulu aamannaa bi-Llaahi wa bi-l-yawmi-l-'aakhiri wa maa hum-bi-mu'mineen. Yukhaadiʿuuna-Llaaha wa-l-ladheena aamanuu: wa maa yakhdaʿuuna illaaa añfusahum wa maa yashʿuruun. Fee quluubihim-maraḍuñ fazaadahumu-Llaahu maraḍaa: wa lahum ʿadhaabun aleemum-bi-maa kaanuu yakdhibuun. Wa idhaa qeela lahum laa tufsiduu fi-l-'arḍi qaaluu innamaa naḥnu muṣliḥuun.*

> **Of the people there are some who say, "We believe in Allah and the Last Day," but they do not believe. They try to deceive Allah and those who believe, but they only deceive themselves and realize [it] not! In their hearts is a disease; and Allah has increased their disease and grievous is the penalty they [incur] because they are false [to themselves]. When it is said to them, "Make not mischief (fasaad) on the earth," they say, "Why, we are only makers of sulḥ"** (striving to bring about peace and reconciliation) (2:8-11).

Their reasoning makes sense, if one accepts the premise that there exists a clash of civilizations. But the case can be made that if one accepts this world view, it will become a "self-fulfilling prophesy," either because one will start to make decisions based on this, or because there may be people who want to incite such a clash, and so they demonize and degrade others, knowing that in this way they can sow the seeds for violent resistance. Either way—whether out of ignorance, or out of purposeful instigation—acting on the assumption of a clash leads to violence, and violence breeds hatred. It breeds destruction and negative values. Negative values are negative attitudes; negative attitudes are negative intentions, and negative actions follow. Situations become more complicated and problematic, and those who wish to spread corruption have more opportunities to exploit.

Enmity flourishes under violence. If the aim is to encourage peace and friendship, then we have to turn toward nonviolence. The events we are witnessing today are the antithesis of the principles of nonviolence and democracy which peaked in the mid- and late-20th century in the hands, minds, and efforts of people like Mahatma Gandhi, Khan Abdul Ghaffur Khan, Martin Luther King, Jr., Desmond Tutu, and others. They are the antithesis of non-violence as it was practiced by the Prophet *(ṣalla-Llaahu 'alayhi wa sallam)* for the first 13 years of his mission. He then engaged in a series of forced battles, yet after those, for the remainder of his life, he was again an advocate of non-violence.

Each one of us, or group of us, or communities of us are faced with problems, and the way people think they can solve them is by resorting to violence. No one is talking about peaceful means to solve the problem, in part because people tend to confuse peaceful means with passivity. But non-violence does not mean inaction or passivity. It means we do not commit violence. That is an action in and of itself, as Gandhi showed, and it is a more forceful kind of action than violence.

We read in the Qur'an:

> *Wa laa tastawi-l-ḥasanatu wa la-s-sayyi'ah; idfaʿ bi-l-latee hiya aḥsanu fa-idha-l-ladhee baynaka wa baynahuu ʿadaawatuñ ka'annahuu waliyyun ḥameem.*

> **Good deeds are not equal to the evil ones. Repel [evil] with that which is better *(aḥsanu)*; then will he between whom and you was hatred become as it were your friend and intimate!...** (41:34).

And the Prophet *(ṣalla-Llaahu ʿalayhi wa sallam)* observed, **"God grants to gentleness *(rifq)* what He does not grant to violence"** (Abu Dawood, 424/255).

Think about the treaty of Hudaybiyya. The Prophet *(ṣalla-Llaahu ʿalayhi wa sallam)* said (paraphrasing): "We won't enter Mecca this year, we'll wait a year." The next year, when the Muslims finally did enter Mecca, not one person died. Had the Muslims forced their way into Mecca a year earlier, there would have been a pitched battle. Instead, there was no fighting.

So, too, when the Mongols decimated the Muslim world from Samarkand to Aleppo, Islam apparently came to a standstill. Yet, in the long run, the majority of the Mongols converted to Islam. What the battles lost, Islam won (Khan 3).

According to a tradition, **"The master of a people is the one who serves them."** How does service leads to mastery? When one approaches situations from the point of view of peace, and one implements peaceful, constructive activities, instead of futile, continuous, armed interventions, one not only saves lives, but one also preserves social conditions, one preserves cultural integrity, ones preserves peoples' nobility and sense of honor. Most importantly, by preserving these aspects of individuals' well-being, one preserves their willingness to participate and work toward constructive change in their societies.

In the law of Allah *(Subhaanahu wa ta'aalaa)* as revealed to the *ambiyaa'* (the prophets), culminating in the Prophet Muhammad *(salla-Llaahu 'alayhi wa sallam)*, there is a kind of golden rule that governs human history, which is, to really win in the sense of establishing positive control, one has to remain generous and magnanimous. On a personal level, we know that if we are patient, tolerant, and generous in our interactions with others, those qualities can turn the tide of a discussion or disagreement. And so the principle of moral and ethical excellence is a two-edged sword. If it is *true* moral excellence, the outcomes are peace, tolerance, understanding, and positive growth or transition. If instead the effort to exert control is based on *feigned* moral excellence, then it can only be maintained through force, intimidation, coercion.

We need to begin to force ourselves, spiritually as well as intellectually, to deal in subtleties. If instead we speak in terms of black and white, then we reinforce the tendencies toward extremism, intolerance, and sweeping generalizations. We contribute to the view that Islam is anti-Western and anti-globalization, when in fact Islam is (or should be) a religion of globalization that recognizes common values and interests across barriers of religion, culture, language, and national interest.

From the Central Asian *shuyukh* we have a principle of "abstinence and restraint for the higher power." It is lawful, according to the

Qur'an, to extract revenge on a person who has wronged one, but that principle is restrained—and abstinence is considered the more meritorious course of action. Allah *(Subhaanahu wa ta'aalaa)* reveals in *Suuratu-sh-Shuuraa*:

> ***Wa-l-ladheena idhaaa asaabahumu-l-baghyu hum yañtasiruun. Wa jazaaa'u sayyi'atiñ sayyi'atum-mithluhaa: fa-man 'afaa wa aslaha fa-ajruhuu 'alaa-Llaah; innahuu laa yuhibbu-dh-dhaalimeen.***
>
> **...And who, when tyranny afflicts them, defend themselves. The recompense for an injury is an injury proportionate to it; but if a person forgives and makes reconciliation (*sulh*) he shall be rewarded by Allah; verily, He does not love evil doers** (*adh-dhaalimeen* - those who perpetuate *dhulm*) (42:39-40).

Here Allah *(Subhaanahu wa ta'aalaa)* tells us that the more noble act is to be patient, restrain oneself, and forgive. To exercise patience and self-restraint for the sake of Allah, even under extreme provocation, puts one at the highest level of moral and ethical excellence. It weakens the efforts of the perpetrator by showing a higher grade of moral excellence (Abu Saqib).

In addition to the concept of "abstinence and restraint for the higher power," three other rules of the Naqshbandi Order moderate extremism within the individual. These three rules—added by Shah Bahaudin Naqshband to the eight already-existing rules—are know as the three "pauses": time pause, heart pause, and number pause. Each helps to create balance or equanimity in a seeker's life by creating a "stop."

- Time Pause refers to taking the time to evaluate one's predisposition to lack of attention, to measure one's time in the journey towards the Divine Presence, and to look closely at one's efforts and evaluate them in *muḥaasabah*.

- Number Pause means to be aware of the number of recitations of *dhikr,* for the sake of protecting one's heart from distractions and realizing the necessity of remembering Allah *(Subḥaanahu wa taʿaalaa)* in all circumstances.

- Heart Pause enables the journeyer to avoid extreme thoughts and actions by directing her or his heart towards the Ever-Present and to experience that Presence everywhere, striving to see Allah *(Subḥaanahu wa taʿaalaa)* in everything, every circumstance, and to become reliant on Allah *(Subḥaanahu wa taʿaalaa)*.

I personally do not like to think about the *nafs ammaarah* as being as powerful, strong, and horrible as classical writers have said it is. I would rather think we are much more refined than that, that the *nafs ammaarah* is just that bothersome part of us that is still tempted to drink, swear, or engage in other, lesser infractions whose effects mostly impact the local level. But increasingly, it seems to me that the veneer of humanity, let alone humility, let alone humaneness, overlying our *nafs ammaarah* may be very thin. This explains why, in generation after generation, prophet after prophet, saint after saint, shaykh after shaykh, guru after guru, priest after priest, leader after leader in any religion from Zoroastrianism to Christianity has admonished his or her community to gentleness *(rifq)*, to patient perseverance *(ṣabr)*, to peace and reconciliation *(ṣulḥ)*, to justice and equity *(ʿadl)*, to that which is good, fair, beautiful, righteous, and kind *(ḥasan)*.

Anyone who has an air conditioner or heat pump knows that periodically, you have to change the filters. Similarly in life, we pick up dirt, and the way we keep the filter clean is by having gratitude toward Allah and by purifying ourselves through spiritual education (*tarbiyah*). As long as we live in this world, we need to try to purify ourselves. To the degree that we can remain uncorrupted in this world, the goodness, the *barakah*, the blessing, the pure expression of Allah's *Ruuh̲* flows into our minds, our bodies, and our souls, here in this world. As a result of that, and *only* as a result of that, we can be contented, happy, and fulfilled.

Tarbiyah and *tazkiyah* liberate people from the chains of their own ignorance, so that they could become genuinely free—not free to become *extreme*, but free to become *moderate*, or balanced, in the sense suggested in the Qur'an when Allah *(Subh̲aanahu wa ta'aalaa)* reveals:

> ***Wa-l-'ard̲a madadnaahaa wa alqaynaa feehaa rawaasiya wa ambatnaa feehaa miñ kulli shay'im-mawzuun.***
>
> **And the earth—We have spread it out wide, and placed on it mountains firm, and caused [life] of every kind to grow on it *in a balanced manner*** (in a manner that reflects the *meezaan*, the Balance established by Allah) (15:19).

The word "freedom" implies many possibilities and choices. It also implies a great deal of potential confusion and error. The freedom that we have to act in this world is like a franchise that one purchases, or like an *ijaazah* (license), granted to us by Allah *(Subh̲aanahu wa ta'aalaa)*, that says we have the ability to recognize that when we act in a harmonious way, in an efficient way, and when our intentions are good, then goodness comes from us. We receive a license from Allah *(Subh̲aanahu wa ta'aalaa)* to choose freely, and at the same time we are told that Allah *(Subh̲aanahu wa ta'aalaa)* knows what is right, what needs to be done, and how it needs to be done. Over time, then, we progress toward the point where we consciously and purposefully choose the only thing one can choose for success, the only thing one can choose for contentment, harmony, and happiness. When we achieve that, we know what needs to be done. We know how it needs to be done, and we know how success comes about, and we have no other choice than to go in that direction. Usually, that is a specific direction. People who have gained real insight know that the more knowledge one has, the less freedom one has, because the truth stands out from the untruth.

So in the statement often attributed to the Prophet *(salla-Llaahu 'alayhi wa sallam)*, **"Seek knowledge from cradle to grave,"** [1] he was not saying, go out and have no choice. He was saying, pursue knowledge, and as you do so, you will voluntarily limit yourself to more ethical behavior. You cannot just tell people to go out and "get" morality and ethics. Knowledge leads to being moral and ethical.

Every time we make a choice not to study, not to sit in meditation, not to make *du'aa*, not to be conscious of the Presence of Allah *(Subhaanahu wa ta'aalaa)*, we are choosing ignorance, not knowledge. We are saying, "I am at the stage in my life in reality where I do not want to give up the illusion of choices, even if it means I am going to abandon my duties and responsibilities, my knowledge, my heart, my soul, my everything. I am going to play a dangerous game of Russian roulette with God, and see if I can survive in ignorance, thinking I am free, while I am gambling away paradise, truth, and reality." The irony of that ignorance is that, during the last fifty to one hundred years, society has begun to represent it, to the point that the materialistic world view of today feeds this false concept of freedom and choice. Literally, it destroys us, our families, our relationships, and our societies. It destroys our characters or creates barriers to introducing the virtues of character elevation to our children, to our future society. It sublimates the character of Muslims as well as our predecessors: the Christians, Jews and Magians. People become socialized out of the essence of the *deen* and believe such character change is a sign of modernity and freedom. How wrong they are. Today's global situation is the proof of the degradation of the human potential, and the aversion to the Divine Presence. In the midst of this situation, we are challenged to remember the guidance given to us in the Holy Qur'an:

> ***Udᶜuu Rabbakum ta<u>d</u>arruᶜañw-wa khufyah; innahuu laa yu<u>h</u>ibbu-l-muᶜtadeen. Wa laa tufsiduu fi-l-'ar<u>d</u>i baᶜda i<u>s</u>laa<u>h</u>ihaa wa-d-ᶜuuhu khawfañw-wa <u>t</u>amaᶜaa; inna ra<u>h</u>mata-Llaahi qareebum-mina-l-mu<u>h</u>sineen.***
>
> **Call on your *Rabb* (Lord) with humility and in private, for He does not love the transgressors. Do not create *fasaad* (iniquity) in the land after it has been set in order. Pray to Him with fear and hope. Surely the Mercy of Allah is always close to those who do good to others *(al-mu<u>h</u>sineen)*** (7:55-6).

We are challenged to remember that fourteen hundred and twenty-four years ago, the Prophet *(<u>s</u>alla-Llaahu ᶜalayhi wa sallam)* repeated the warning to humankind against the type of devolution of ethics and morality that we are witnessing today. As he said to Aisha *(ra<u>d</u>iya-Llaahu ᶜanhaa)*,

> **Kindness (*rifq*) is not to be found in anything but that it adds to its beauty, and it is not withdrawn from anything but it makes it defective** (Sa<u>h</u>i<u>h</u> Muslim 1187).

As Wahiduddin Khan points out in an article on Islam and nonviolence, the Prophet Muhammad *(<u>s</u>alla-Llaahu ᶜalayhi wa sallam)* could have focused on challenging the Meccan authorities through force, or by trying to create terrorist cells to bring down the *Quraysh*. But he didn't. Allah revealed to him, "*Iqra*" (Read). *Iqra* became, and should have *remained*, the basis of Islam. It was a message of peaceful non-violence. It was not a challenge to Mecca's power structures; it was simply a call to learn the revelations of God, memorize them, and live them. This was hardly a political statement, especially coming from the young man who had replaced the black stone in the *Ka'bah*, which (at the time) housed 360 idols (Khan 2).

The teaching of the Prophet Muhammad *(salla-Llaahu 'alayhi wa sallam)* did not begin with destruction, nor did it end with destruction. In his *khutbah* during the Farewell Pilgrimage, the Prophet *(salla-Llaahu 'alayhi wa sallam)* enjoined the Muslims:

Hurt no one, so that no one may hurt you.

Through the twenty-three years of his mission, the Prophet's message was a call *not* to violence, but to Truth, to patience, to perseverance. It was a reminder that the more we strive to help others and to turn away from distraction, selfishness, disbalance, or intemperance, then the more we will find contentment. If instead we refuse to recognize our wrong actions, put off repenting, and allow the harms that we have done to remain un-remedied, we will fail to find fulfillment, and our attainments in *dunyaa* will be meaningless.

We refine our conscience in the sense of making it operative and effective by becoming conscious of the presence of God and the 99 Names of God, and by making *muhaasabah*. It is important to look at our desires and make them realistic, and to look at our intentions and translate them into good actions. As we do that, our lives will become more balanced. Our community will become more aligned with the description enjoined upon us by Allah *(Subhaanahu wa ta'aalaa)* in the Qur'an:

> ***Wa kadhaalika ja'alnaakum ummatañw-wasatal-li-takuunuu shuhadaaa'a 'ala-n-naasi wa yakuuna-r-rasuulu 'alaykum shaheedaa.***
>
> **Thus We made you a community of the middle way *(ummata wasata)*, that you might be a witness to the people, and the Messenger, a witness to you** (2:143).

In closing, as we look at the extremism that characterizes our world today, both on the outer, global level and within our own selves, may we remember the guidance provided by the Prophet *(salla-Llaahu 'alayhi wa sallam)* when he said:

> **He who alleviates the suffering of a brother from the afflictions of the world, Allah will alleviate his afflictions from the sufferings of the Day of Resurrection. He who finds relief for one who is hard pressed, Allah will make things easy for him in the Hereafter, and he who conceals [the faults] of a Muslim, Allah would conceal his faults in the world and in the Hereafter. Allah is at the back of a servant so long as the servant is at the back of his brother. He who treads the path in search of knowledge, Allah will make that path easy, leading to Paradise for him and those persons who assemble in one of the houses of Allah (mosques), recite the Book of Allah and learn and teach the Qur'an [among themselves]. There will descend upon them tranquility, mercy will cover them, the angels will surround them and Allah will mention them in the presence of those near Him...** (Sahih Muslim 1245).

* * *

Wa-Llaahu lahu ul-haqqu wa huwa yahdi-s-sabeel.
Hasbuna-Llaahu wahdahu wa ni'mal-wakil.
Wa salli 'alaa Sayyidina Muhammadin
wa aaalihi wa sahbihi ajma'een
wa-l-hamdu li-Llaahi Rabbi-l-'aalameen.

Truth belongs to Allah; it is He who shows the way.
Allah, alone, suffices us, and what a fine guardian is He!
Blessings upon our Master Muhammad
and his family and companions altogether
and praise is due to Allah, Lord of the Worlds.

Notes

1 The saying, "Seek knowledge from cradle to grave," is typically attributed to the Prophet Muhammad *(salla-Llaahu 'alayhi wa sallam)* although this specific wording is not found in *hadith* literature. However, other *hadiths* are quite similar in language and meaning, such as "Seeking knowledge is incumbent upon every Muslim," which was reported as a saying of the Prophet *(salla-Llaahu 'alayhi wa sallam)* by Ibn Majah, Bayhaqi, and other scholars. Consequently, the former statement is regarded as part of the general wisdom of Islam, whether it was uttered by Mohammed *(salla-Llaahu 'alayhi wa sallam)* or one of his early followers.

References

Abu Saqib, "Forgive and Overlook" Posted online. Accessed 13 April 2004.

Khan, Maulana Wahiduddin. Non-Violence and Islam. Online. Available at http://www.alrisala.org/Articles/papes/nonviolence.htm. Accessed 1 March 2001.

Murad, Abdul Hakim. The Fall of the Family. Courtesy of Belfast Masjid. Downloaded from the Internet in May 2001.

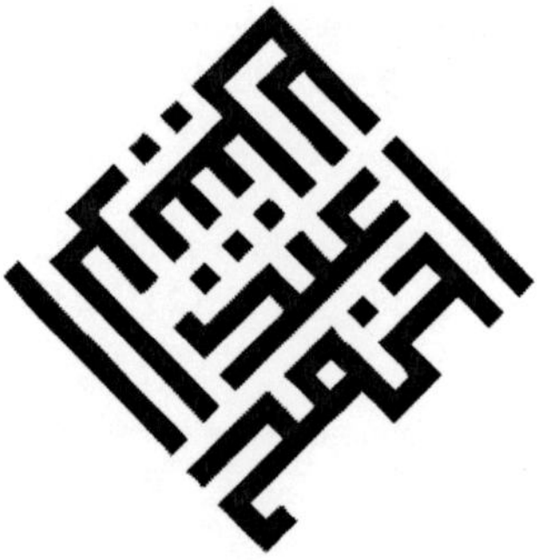

بسم الله الرحمن الرحيم

Peace Making with Islam

Bismi-Llaah, Al-hamdu-li-Llaah
Allaahumma salli wa sallim ʿalaa sayyidinaa Muhammadin,
wa ʿalaa aaalihi wa sahbih

Greetings of Peace for a Celebration of Peace: The ʿEidu-l-Adhaa

"As-salaamu alaykum!" I greet you as Muslims greet one another, by saying, "peace be with you."

In a sense, this entire evening is dedicated to peace, for it honors the occasion of *ʿEidu-l-Adhaa* —a time when people of all nationalities, all languages, all ethnic groups and races gather together peacefully in the *hajj* (the pilgrimage) to Mecca.

The *hajj* is a truly global event. We can safely say that Islam, as characterized in the *hajj,* is one of the earliest and most lasting examples of globalization. It reunites diverse members of the human family under the banner of One Truth, One God, One Purpose, symbolizing the truth revealed by Allah *(Subhaanahu wa taʿaalaa)* when He said:

> ***Yaaa-ayyuha-n-naasu innaa khalaq-naakum-miñ dhakariñw-wa uñthaa wa jaʿalnaakum shuʿuubañw-wa qabaaa'ila li-taʿaarafuu;***
>
> **O humanity, We created you from a single male and a female, and made you into nations and tribes, so that you may know each other** (Qur'an 49:13).

Malik el-Shabbazz (Malcolm X) wrote of the *Hajj:*

> For the past week, I have been utterly speechless and spellbound by the graciousness I see displayed around me by people of all colors. ...You may be shocked by these words coming from me. But on this pilgrimage, what I have seen, and experienced, has forced me to rearrange much of my thought-patterns previously held, and to toss aside some of my previous conclusions (Haley 346-47).

Hajj forges a harmony, dignity, and courtesy of returning to one's Source. It awakens attitudes of *adab* (spiritual courtesy): of caring for others, looking after the elderly, speaking in ways that can be understood across language and cultural differences, and setting aside quarrels. In so doing, it reminds us of the harmony that can be achieved in our communities—and in our world.

The *hajj* also symbolizes the hardships entailed in finding peace. Pilgrims retrace the footsteps of the founder of Mecca: not some mighty warrior, but a faithful, loving mother—Hajar *('alayha-s-salaam)*. They gather where Ibrahim *('alayhi-s-salaam)* brought Hajar and Isma'eel *('alayhimma-s-salaam)*, in the valley, once desolate, where Hajar *('alayha-s-salaam)* called after her husband, "O Ibrahim! Where are you going, leaving us in this valley, where there is neither any person nor anything else to [help us] survive?" She repeated this to him many times, we are told, but he did not look back. Then she asked, "Has Allah instructed you to do so?" He replied, "Yes." That was sufficient for Hajar . She knew it was the Divine Will, and she said, "Then God will not neglect us" (based on a *hadith* narrated by Ibn Abbas and compiled by Bukhari).

Allah *(Subhaanahu wa ta'aalaa)* did not neglect Hajar and Isma'eel

(ͨalayhimma-s-salaam). The angel Jibreel *(ͨalayhi-s-salaam)* appeared, and the spring of ZemZem emerged from the desert.

We can all learn from the love, service, loyalty, and humility of H̲ajar *(ͨalayha-s-salaam)*. Like the faithful mother, left with her son in the desert, we too can reflect upon the trust that Allah *(Subh̲aanahu wa taͨaalaa)* has given us—whether we stand on the plain of ͨArafat in Arabia, or on the plain of ͨArafat in our hearts.

The *ͨEidu-l-Ad̲h̲aa* also reminds us of Ibrahim *(ͨalayhi-s-salaam)*, who loved God so much that he was willing to sacrifice his son. Allah *(Subh̲aanahu wa taͨaalaa)* narrates in the Qur'an:

> ***Fa-lammaa balagha maͨahu-s-saͨya qaala yaa-bunayya innee araa fi-l-manaami annee adh-bah̲uka fa-ñ-d̲h̲ur maadhaa taraa? Qaala yaaa-abati-f-ͨal maa tu'mar: satajidunee iñ shaaa'a-Llaahu mina-s̲-s̲aabireen.***
>
> **And when [his son] was old enough to walk with him, [Ibrahim] said: "O my dear son, I have seen in a dream that I must sacrifice you. So look, what do you think?" He said: "O my father! Do that which you are commanded. Allah willing, you will find me of the steadfast"** (37:102).

Ibrahim and his son *(ͨalayhimma-s-salaam)* epitomize the peace of *H̲ajj*: a peace born of the willingness to set aside all else but trust in God. This is the peace achieved when our love for Allah *(Subh̲aanahu wa taͨaalaa)* and our understanding of the Divine presence in our lives is so great that we dedicate ourselves fully to Allah *(Subh̲aanahu wa taͨaalaa)*, as did Ibrahim, Isma'eel, Ish̲aaq, H̲ajar and Saara; Muusa, 'Isa, the Prophet Muh̲ammad, and all the other righteous guides and messengers (may Allah's peace be upon them all).

Going Beyond the Images of Pilgrim and Militant

In contrast to the peaceful images and traditional stories of *hajj* and *ʿEidu-l-Adhaa*, we find today other images and stories of Islam: confusing, often violent. In the media we hear about Muslims making pilgrimage—but even more often, we hear about Muslims in the context of oppression, terrorism, and conflict.

Sharply disparate images challenge our efforts to put together a cohesive picture of Islam. We are drawn towards the image of the pilgrim, clad in white, bowing in prayer, in harmony with the Lord and with his or her fellow human beings. Yet, we cannot ignore the other, disturbing images: the sword-brandishing or gun-wielding militants of nineteenth century European paintings, twentieth century movies, and sometimes (regrettably) twenty-first century newscasts.

My goal is to take us beyond images, to facilitate understanding of realities. I will explain why, out of these two sets of pictures, the pilgrims reflect the more accurate view. But I also will explore the nuances of Islamic teachings on peace, including those that govern legitimate uses of force. Above all, I hope to encourage each of you—Muslim or non-Muslim—to reflect on the real meaning of peace as it pertains to our shared identity as members of the human community.

A Case Study in Nonviolence: The Prophet Muhammad (Salla-Llaahu ʿalayhi wa sallam) at Hudaybiyyah

My exploration of Islam and peace centers around a story. The story's setting is Arabia, on a plain called Hudaybiyyah, outside Mecca. The time is 628 C.E.—year 6 A.H. of the Islamic calendar—and then, as during present-day pilgrimages, a crowd of Muslims eagerly awaits entry to Mecca. But in 628 C.E., idol-worshipers still control the city and they refuse to let the Muslims in. Faced with a choice of going home or attacking, the Muslims under the leadership of the Prophet Muhammad *(salla-Llaahu 'alayhi wa sallam)* choose a third alternative: they remain peacefully at Hudaybiyyah.

As a consequence, the Meccans face an awkward situation. Their prestige and their profits depend upon welcoming worshipers of diverse gods to their city. Denying entry to a peaceful band of pilgrims is likely to damage their reputation for hospitality. On the other hand, allowing Muslims to enter will jeopardize the status of the numerous idols stationed at the *Ka'bah.*

Finally, to get the Muslims to leave, the Meccans sign a treaty. They agree that if the Prophet *(salla-Llaahu 'alayhi wa sallam)* and his companions will return to Medina this year without entering Mecca, then next year the group will be permitted to make pilgrimage. Both sides also agree to a ten-year truce.

Many Muslims are infuriated by the treaty. Why should they agree to being turned away from the *Ka'bah?* But Allah *(Subhaanahu wa ta'aalaa)* reveals to the Prophet Muhammad *(salla-Llaahu 'alayhi wa sallam)*,

Innaa fatahnaa laka fat-ham-mubeenaa...

Lo! We have given you a clear victory... (Qur'an 48:1).

In today's jargon, we might call this revelation an attempt at "spin"! But the treaty of Hudaybiyyah did in fact constitute a clear victory, for it enabled Islam to grow. In subsequent years the religion flourished, as the believers could focus on spreading the teachings rather than defending themselves from the Meccans' attacks. In addition, the truce allowed a time and space for the Meccans themselves to reflect upon what they had heard about

Islam and its adherents, and many came to accept monotheism through inner recognition of its truths (Khan).

As a result, when the Quraysh tribe of Mecca broke the treaty two years later and the Muslims marched on Mecca, the Quraysh simply "opened the city gates, and Muhammad *(ṣalla-Llaahu 'alayhi wa sallam)* took [the city] without shedding a drop of blood" (Armstrong 23).

Linguistic Foundations in Peace and Reconciliation

The late Shaykh Ahmed Kaftaro *(raḫmatu-Llaahi)*, Grand Mufti of Syria, once noted in a conversation that "the Prophet Muhammad *(ṣalla-Llaahu 'alayhi wa sallam)* said, **'I have been raised as a teacher, to complete the structure of moral values.'** The Prophet *(ṣalla-Llaahu 'alayhi wa sallam)* did not say, 'I have been raised for militancy' or 'for fighting' " (Kaftaro 2001).

Peace building is so important in Islam that the religion is named for it. The word "Islam" comes from the same root as *salaam*, meaning peace. Literally speaking, the term "Muslims" may be defined as "those who actively work for peace, security, safety, and well-being."

Reconciliation also is a central theme of Islam. Derivatives of the Qur'anic word for righteousness (*ṣalaaḫ*) connote reconciliation, settlement, and peace making. In sum, piety in Islam is inseparable from the establishment of peace.

Islamic Principles that Promote Peace through Prevention

The Islamic commitment to peace begins with social structures and attitudes that seek to prevent conflict from establishing roots.

Conflicts do not begin when two sides start shooting. They begin months, years, even decades before fighting breaks out, in the enmities and resentments that grow from poverty, from not having a voice in government, from injustice and ignorance. The origins of conflict may stretch back centuries, rooted in cultural prejudice. The Qur'an and the *sunnah* (the teachings and example of the Prophet Muhammad *[ṣalla-Llaahu ʿalayhi wa sallam]*) address each of these social ills.

- To reduce poverty, Muslims are enjoined to assist the poor. The Prophet Muhammad *(ṣalla-Llaahu ʿalayhi wa sallam)* said, **"He is not a man of faith who eats his fill when his neighbor is hungry"** (Buhkari).

- To ensure that the common people have a voice in government, Islam calls for consultation and consensus in community affairs.

- To prevent injustice, Allah *(Subḫaanahu wa taʿaalaa)* guides Muslims to

  ...kuunuu qawwaameena bi-l-qisṯi shuhadaaa'a ... wa law ʿalaa añfusikum awi-l-waalidayni wa-l-'aqrabeen. Iñy-yakun ghaniyyan aw faqeerañ fa-Llaahu awlaa-bihimaa. Fa-laa tattabiʿu-l-hawaaa añ taʿdiluu...

  ...be steadfast in justice, witnesses...even though it be against yourselves, your parents or your relatives. It does not matter whether the party is rich or poor—Allah is well wisher of both. So let not your selfish desires swerve you [from justice]... (Qur'an 4:135).

- To reduce ignorance, Muslims are guided to **"seek knowledge from cradle to grave"** (a saying attributed to the Prophet *[ṣalla-Llaahu ʿalayhi wa sallam])* and to transmit their knowledge to others.

- To reduce prejudice, Islam promotes ethnic and racial tolerance, and teaches religious tolerance. Allah *(Subhaanahu wa ta'aalaa)* states in the Qur'an:

  Inna-l-ladheena aamanuu wa-l-ladheena haaduu wa-n-nasaaraa wa-s-saabi'eena man aamana bi-Llaahi wa-l-yawmi-l-'aakhiri wa ᶜamila saalihañ fa-lahum ajruhum ᶜiñda Rabbihim...

  Those who believe—the Jews, the Christians, and the Sabaeans—whoever believes in God and the Last Day and does good—surely their reward is with their Lord... (2:62).

Clearly, not all Muslim societies are living up to ideals of economic and social equity, justice, tolerance, and educational opportunity. According to the 1999 *State of the World Atlas*, among countries where Islam is the state religion, roughly four out of five have yet to establish functioning democratic governments; approximately 75% are reported by Amnesty International as allowing extra-judicial executions, arbitrary arrests, or unfair trials; and in more than half, the illiteracy rate stands at 30% or higher (Smith 52-53, 64-65, 70-71).

These are significant problems that Muslims must address in fulfilling Islam's commitment to peace. But while acknowledging the issues, we can also find inspiration in communities where Islamic principles have operated and have helped to ensure peace.

Ultimately, peace depends on more than social principles. It depends on establishing peace *within* human beings.

"In Remembrance of Allah do Hearts Find Rest"

What allows people to engage in tyranny and oppression is a limited world-view that omits God from the picture. So drawn are human beings to status and wealth that they debase their humanhood with genocide and war, with destruction and wanton disregard for human rights. Such stubborn conceits harden the heart to the point that people cannot even conceive of the kind of faith that enabled Ibrahim *(ʿalayhi-s-salaam)* to agree to sacrifice his son.

Peace depends on remembrance of the Divine. Only through frequent remembrance of Allah *(Subhaanahu wa taʿaalaa)* can we correct our shortcomings and attune ourselves to the role that Allah *(Subhaanahu wa taʿaalaa)* intends us to play in creation.

Allah *(Subhaanahu wa taʿaalaa)* says in a *hadith qudsi*, **"I am a sitting companion for those who sit in My remembrance."** Shaykh Kaftaro has given the following analogy: "One who sits with the fire receives its heat and ashes, and whoever sits with ice gets some of its coldness. Similarly, one who remembers Allah *(Subhaanahu wa taʿaalaa)* is the one who is sitting with Allah *(Subhaanahu wa taʿaalaa)*. As long as that person is near Allah *(Subhaanahu wa taʿaalaa)*, the signs of perfection start to show on him or her" (Kaftaro 2000).

Striving to perfect ourselves is the highest form of *jihaad.* The word *jihaad* literally means "struggle" (not "holy war," as it is frequently translated). Once when the Prophet *(salla-Llaahu ʿalayhi wa sallam)* was returning to Medina after a battle, he told his companions:

> **We are returning from the lesser *jihaad* to the greater *jihaad*** (Jabir/Bayhaqi).

The Prophet *(salla-Llaahu ʿalayhi wa sallam)* understood that striving against outer enemies may be easier than striving inwardly to improve the self. The highest form of courage comes forth not on the battlefield, but within us. The Prophet *(salla-Llaahu ʿalayhi wa sallam)* said:

> **A strong person is not the one who throws his**

> **adversaries to the ground. A strong person is the one who controls himself when he is angry** (al-Muwatta).

A self-centered or aggressive person looks for excuses to be self-centered or aggressive. Conversely, a person of inner peace approaches life with a perspective that gives rise to peaceful solutions. In the Qur'an, we read:

> ***...inna-Llaaha yudillu many-yashaaa'u wa yahdee ilayhi man anaab, al-ladheena aamanuu wa tatma'innu quluubuhum-bi-dhikri-Llaah; Alaa bi-dhikri-Llaahi tatma'innu-l-quluub.***
>
> **...Allah sends whom He will astray, and guides to Himself all who turn [to Him], who have believed and whose hearts have rest in the remembrance of Allah. Verily, in the remembrance of Allah do hearts find rest!** (13:27-28).

"Rest" in this *ayat* implies not only repose, but a sense of calmness, tranquility, and security; a feeling of being reassured; a state of confidence, certainty, and equanimity born of trust. When our selfishness is put to rest, we become better able to accept graciously what God has given us, be it gold or iron, poverty or wealth. We find refuge in patience (*sabr*) and trust in Allah *(Subhaanahu wa ta'aalaa)*. We stop blaming others, and start seeing our own faults and repenting. We begin to consider others' needs before our own.

On *hajj*, pilgrims experience these attitudes as they re-set their course and speed toward consciousness of Allah's Presence. Many other aspects of Islam—hearing the call to prayer; pausing five times a day for *salah* (prayer); fasting during *Ramadaan*; engaging in *dhikr* (remembrance), *muhaasabah* (accounting for ourselves), and *muraaqabah* (meditative reflection)—all these practices bring us back to remembering a Higher Power. In so doing, they cultivate the inner attitudes that enable outer peace making.

The Use of Force in Islam

The Islamic guidelines for applying force relate to the topic of remembering Allah *(Subhaanahu wa ta'aalaa)*, as I will explain shortly. But first, let me touch on more facets of Islam's early history.

In 610 C.E., the Prophet Muhammad *(salla-Llaahu 'alayhi wa sallam)* first received from Allah *(Subhaanahu wa ta'aalaa)* revelation affirming the existence of only One God. This belief was not unknown to the peoples of Arabia at this time, and the Prophet himself *(salla-Llaahu 'alayhi wa sallam)* had always worshiped God alone, but most Arabs of the era honored multiple gods. Indeed, the Meccans were such avid polytheists that initially the Prophet *(salla-Llaahu 'alayhi wa sallam)* dared share the teachings only with his closest friends and family. But three years after the revelations began, Allah *(Subhaanahu wa ta'aalaa)* directed him to preach publicly.

Most Meccans greeted his message with rage. For the next ten years the Prophet *(salla-Llaahu 'alayhi wa sallam)* and his followers endured the hostility of their neighbors, particularly the tribe of Quraysh. Muslims were physically abused, tormented, stoned, and killed. The first to be killed was a woman, tortured to death for affirming "there is no god but God." Many Muslims fled to Abyssinia, where the Christian king respected their faith and gave them asylum. The Meccans then launched an economic and social boycott against the Muslims, forbidding even the sale of basic foodstuffs to them.

How did the Prophet *(salla-Llaahu 'alayhi wa sallam)* respond to such persecution? Nonviolently. Never during those ten years did he authorize armed resistance, even in self-defense. The only resistance he offered was to continue teaching the message of the Qur'an.

Finally, the Quraysh decided to kill the Prophet Muhammad *(salla-Llaahu 'alayhi wa sallam)*. Again, he did not raise arms against them. Instead, he slipped out of the city at night, beginning his *hijrah* (emigration) to Medina—and eluding, with Allah's aid, a band of assassins gathered in the dark outside his home.

Even after the Prophet *(salla-Llaahu 'alayhi wa sallam)* reached Medina, he did not launch a campaign against the Quraysh immediately. He waited, until—roughly twelve years after the Quraysh had begun their attacks—God sent a new revelation, authorizing Muslims to respond with force.

I mentioned that the use of force in Islam is connected to the remembrance of Allah *(Subhaanahu wa ta'aalaa)*. The link between the two is articulated in the following *ayat*, which was the first revelation to authorize forceful responses to oppression.

> ***Udhina-li-l-ladheena yuqaataluuna bi-annahum dhulimuu...Al-ladheena ukhrijuu miñ diyaarihim-bi-ghayri haqqin illaaa añy-yaquuluu Rabbuna-Llaah; wa law laa daf-'u-Llaahi-n-naasa ba'dahum-bi-ba'dil-lahuddimat sawaami'u wa biya'uñw-wa salawaatuñw-wa masaajidu yudhkaru feeha-s-mu-Llaahi katheeraa.***
>
> **Permission is given to those who fight because they have been wronged...those who have been driven from their homes unjustly only because they said, "Our Lord is God." For had it not been for God**

repelling some people by means of others, monasteries and churches and synagogues and mosques, in which the name of God is often remembered, would surely have been pulled down. (Qur'an 22:39-40).

What are Muslims instructed to defend? The right to remember and worship God. Are they to defend only Muslims' right to worship? No. Jews, Christians, and others who believe in One God must also be protected.

Allah *(Subhaanahu wa ta'aalaa)* states:

Kutiba ᶜalaykumu-l-qitaalu wa huwa kurhul-lakum: wa ᶜasaaa an takrahuu shay'anw-wa huwa khayrul-lakum; wa ᶜasaaa an tuhibbuu shay'anw-wa huwa sharrul-lakum; wa-Llaahu yaᶜlamu wa antum laa taᶜlamuun.

Fighting is prescribed for you, and you dislike it. But it is possible that you dislike a thing that is good for you, and that you love a thing that is bad for you. Allah knows, and you know not (Qur'an 2:216).

Wa-q-tuluuhum haythu thaqiftumuuhum wa akhrijuuhum-min haythu akhrajuukum wa-l-fitnatu ashaddu mina-l-qatl...

Kill [those who fight you] wherever they confront you in combat and drive them out of the places from which they have driven you; for though killing is bad, oppression is worse... (Qur'an 2:191).

Even within the Gandhian philosophy of nonviolence, there is acknowledgement that "conditions could be so extreme that those who stood for truth were faced with the necessity of choosing between violent resistance and none at all. Gandhi said that in these cases 'vengeance is any day superior to passive and helpless submission' " (Juergensmeyer 106).

Allah *(Subhaanahu wa ta'aalaa)* asks in the Qur'an:

> ***Wa maa lakum laa tuqaatiluuna fee sabeeli-Llaahi wa-l-musta<u>d</u>ᶜafeena mina-r-rijaali wa-n-nisaa'i wa-l-wildaani-lladheena yaquuluuna Rabbanaaa akhrijnaa min haadhihi-l-qaryati-<u>dh</u>-<u>dh</u>aalimi ahluhaa; wa-j-ᶜal-lanaa mil-laduñka waliyyañw-wa-j-ᶜal lanaa mil-laduñka na<u>s</u>eeraa.***
>
> **And why should you not fight in the cause of Allah and of those who, being weak, are ill-treated [and oppressed]?—men, women, and children whose cry is, "Our Lord! Rescue us from this town, whose people are oppressors, and raise for us out of Your grace a protector; raise for us out of Your grace one who will help!** (4:75).

The limited use of force in Islam to defend "basic human rights—security, [life] and property, freedom of thought—corresponds to what [we might call] 'humanitarian intervention' " (Boisard 181). Like humanitarian intervention, it must meet strict criteria.

First, it must be for the sake of religion, not politics. Once in the midst of the civil strife that followed the death of the caliph 'Ali *(ra<u>d</u>iya-Llaahu 'anhu)*, some of the combatants were trying to enlist the support of the eldest remaining companion of the Prophet *(salla-Llaahu 'alayhi wa sallam).* They quoted Qur'an to him, trying to prove that he was obligated to take part. But he replied that the Qur'an calls for battling religious coercion—not for political infighting (Khan 6).

Second, those who resort to force in defending human rights may do so only in proportion to the offense committed.

> ***Wa'in 'aaqabtum fa-'aaqibuu bi-mithli maa 'uuqibtum-bih; wa la'iñ sabartum la-huwa khayrul-li-s-saabireen.***
>
> **If you have to retaliate, let your retaliation be commensurate with the wrong which was done to you; but if you endure with patience, the best reward indeed is for those who endure with patience** (Qur'an 16:126).

Muslims must not themselves become oppressors. Abu Bakr *(radiya-Llaahu 'anhu)*, the first Caliph, instructed a commander of the campaign against the Romans in Syria as follows:

> Do justice and keep away from tyranny and oppression, because a community that engages in tyranny does not prosper, nor does it win victory over the enemies.... Do not kill the [enemy's] children, old people, and women. Do not approach their date palms, nor burn their harvest, nor cut the fruit bearing trees. Do not break the promise once you have made it, and do not break the terms of a treaty once you have entered it. You will meet on your way people in monasteries, the monks engaged in the worship of Allah: leave them alone. Do not disperse them, do not destroy

the monasteries, and do not kill the monks. May the peace of Allah be upon you (Doi 446 [grammar revised]).

Finally, the use of force must cease as soon as possible. Muslims are to stop fighting as soon as the situation that necessitated intervention has been rectified. Allah *(Subḥaanahu wa taʿaalaa)* commands in the Qur'an:

> *Wa qaatiluu fee sabeeli-Llaahi-lladheena yuqaatiluunakum wa laa taʿtaduu; inna-Llaaha laa yuḥibbu-l-muʿtadeen....Wa qaatiluuhum ḥattaa laa takuuna fitnatuñw-wa yakuuna-d-deenu li-Llaah; fa-ini-ñ-tahaw fa-laa ʿudwaana illaa ʿala-ḏẖ-ḏẖaalimeen.*

> **Fight in the way of Allah against those who fight you, but do not go beyond the limits. Allah does not love those who go beyond the limits....Fight them until there is no more tumult or oppression and there prevail justice and faith in God. If they cease, there should be no enmity toward any but wrongdoers (2:190, 193).**

Furthermore, all peace offers are to be accepted. Allah *(Subḥaanahu wa taʿaalaa)* revealed:

> *Fa-ini-ʿtazaluukum fa-lam yuqaatiluukum wa alqaw ilaykumu-s-salama fa-maa jaʿala-Llaahu lakum ʿalayhim sabeelaa.*

> **If they withdraw from you and fight you not, but send you [guarantees of] peace, then Allah**

> **allows no way for you [to war] against them** (Qur'an 4:90).

Even if one questions the motives behind a peace offer, one must accept it, according to the Qur'an:

> ***Wa'iñy-yureeduuu añy-yakhda'uuka fa'inna hasbaka-Llaah…***
>
> **And should they seek but to deceive thee [by their show of peace]—behold, Allah is enough for you!...** (8:62).

FROM JIHAAD TO NONVIOLENCE

To summarize: in those rare instances when a Muslim can or must apply force, it must be what Shaykh Kaftaro calls, "belligerency for the sake of peace" (Kaftaro 2001).

Once 'Ali *(radiya-Llaahu 'anhu)* was wielding his sword over an enemy soldier when suddenly the man spit on him. 'Ali *(radiya-Llaahu 'anhu)* withdrew his sword. He could not, in that moment, kill the man: for personal anger and retribution is a form of violence, not justifiable force. The restraint shown by 'Ali *(radiya-Llaahu 'anhu)* so impressed the soldier that he embraced Islam. As this incident illustrates, enemies may be overcome in a number of ways, some of which transform rather than take life.

Other anecdotes further illustrate the power of restraint. When the Muslims entered Mecca, many former enemies of Islam swiftly embraced it. Among them was a woman named Hind, who years earlier had arranged for the Prophet's uncle (Hamza *[radiya-Llaahu 'anhu]*) to be killed and had personally mutilated his body. When she approached the Prophet and embraced Islam, the Prophet—recognizing her for who she was—simply said, "Welcome" (Lings 301).

The Qur'an grants the right of the oppressed to take "an eye for an eye," but it stresses that forgiveness is more praiseworthy.

> ***Wa jazaaa'u sayyi'atiñ sayyi'atum-mithluhaa: fa-man ᶜafaa wa aslaha fa-ajruhuu ᶜalaa-Llaah; innahuu laa yuhibbu-dh-dhaalimeen. Wa la-mani-ñ-tasara baᶜda dhulmihee fa-ulaaa'ika maa ᶜalayhim-miñ sabeel. Innama-s-sabeelu ᶜalaa-l-ladheena yadhlimuuna-n-naasa wa yabghuuna fi-l-'ardi bi-ghayri-l-haqq; ulaaa'ika la-hum ᶜadhaabun aleem. Wa lamañ sabara wa ghafara inna dhaalika la-min ᶜazmi-l-umuur.***
>
> **The repayment of a bad action is one equivalent to it. But if someone pardons and puts things right, his reward is with Allah. Certainly He does not love wrongdoers. But if people do defend themselves when they are wronged, nothing can be held against them for doing that. There are only grounds against those who wrong people and act as tyrants in the earth without any right to do so. For such there will be a grievous penalty. But if someone is steadfast and forgives, that is the most resolute course to follow** (42:40-43).

Elsewhere in the Qur'an, Allah *(Subhaanahu wa taᶜaalaa)* enjoins peaceful responses as the route to ending enmity.

> ***Wa laa tastawi-l-hasanatu wa la-s-sayyi'ah; idfaᶜ bi-l-latee hiya ahsanu fa-idha-l-ladhee baynaka***

> ***wa baynahuu ʿadaawatuñ ka'annahuu waliyyun ḫameem.***
>
> **The good deed and the evil deed are not alike. Repel [the evil deed] with that which is better; then will he, between whom and you was hatred, become as it were your friend and intimate!** (41:34).

We know that violence breeds hatred. It sows destruction on physical, emotional, and mental levels, as is evident when we look at what has happened to the people of Bosnia and Herzegovina, Kosovo, Iran, Kurdistan, Palestine, Chechnya, and Iraq, among many other places in the world. In contrast, choosing nonviolence inspires people to re-make their lives (Khan 2).

One of the most successful modern-day practitioners of nonviolence was the Muslim leader Khan Abdul Ghaffar Khan, who in the 1930s and 1940s mobilized the Pathans of the North-West Frontier into a nonviolent army on behalf of Indian independence. He wrote to his followers, "I am going to give you such a weapon that the police and the army will not be able to stand against it. It is the weapon of the Prophet *(ṣalla-Llaahu ʿalayhi wa sallam)*, but you are not aware of it. That weapon is patience and righteousness. No power on earth can stand against it" (Easwaran 117).

Khan Abdul Ghaffar Khan's efforts reflect the *hadith*: "**Allah grants to gentleness what He does not grant to violence"** (Abu Dawood).

Real peace-building depends on addressing more than geo-political issues. The accords that emerge from Camp David, Dayton, or Belfast, from the United Nations or the Hague, may lead to a cessation of violence. But lasting peace depends on the reconstruction of society and on a willingness to co-exist.

Reconstruction and co-existence will only come about in an atmosphere of security, where trust, love, faith, and understanding can develop. These are the qualities around which Islam grew and toward which Islam guides us today.

Hajj: The Return to Peace

Every religion (Islam included) has people who misuse its teachings to support selfish ends or narrow points of view. But we must not let extremists and militants block the aspirations of those who long for peace.

'Alija 'Ali Izetbegovic, president of Bosnia and Herzegovina and a former Muslim dissident who spent years in prison under the communists, wrote:

> The human influence on the course of history depends on...the spiritual strength of the partaker[s] in events. Man, if he found himself among lions, would be lost, but this evident law does not apply to a lion tamer. History is a continuing story about small groups of decisive, courageous and clever people who have left an indelible stamp on the course of historical events and managed to change their flow (Izetbegovic 232-33).

Each of us is shaping history. Each of us can help to direct the course of the future: toward greed, self-centeredness, and violence—or toward peace, security, and well-being for all.

Life, like *hajj*, is a journey. In the Qur'an, we read, **"To Allah we belong, and to Him we shall return *(Innaa li-Llaahi, wa innaaa ilayhi raaji'uun)*"** (2:156).

How are we traversing this journey? In what state will we return to our Lord? Allah *(Subhaanahu wa ta'aalaa)* knows best; but as we honor the *'Eidu-l-Adhaa*, we can aspire to live up to the example of the pilgrims who—discarding prejudice and pride, status and enmity—meld into a tapestry that affirms the One Creator. Offering complete trust as Hajar *('alayha-s-salaam)* did in the desert, offering their total submission as Ibrahim *('alayhi-s-salaam)* did in his willing sacrifice, the pilgrims join in waves of seeking and of remembering Allah *(Subhaanahu wa ta'aalaa)*. Muslim or non-Muslim, all can join that movement. We too can come to know and live in the peace of Allah *(Subhaanahu wa ta'aalaa)*, of *as-Salaam.*

* * *

O Allah *(Subhaanahu wa ta'aalaa)*,
we pray that we may learn better how to trust in You.

O Allah *(Subhaanahu wa ta'aalaa)*,
we pray that we may build better understanding among all peoples, and work together to help society.

O Allah *(Subhaanahu wa ta'aalaa)*,
we pray to you to bring us to a more peaceful world,
and to make this earth
truly a place for the good life (the *hayaat-i-tayyibah)* for all people.

O Allah *(Subhaanahu wa ta'aalaa)*, remind us, moment to moment,
to reflect—not only on ourselves and our actions,
but on the needs of others.

O Allah *(Subhaanahu wa ta'aalaa)*, we pray to you
in the name of all the prophets and righteous guides to humanity
for peace and reconciliation,
so that in this world we may have a better place,
and we may prepare a better place in the world to come.

Wa Llaahu lahu ul-haqqu wa huwa yahdi-s-sabeel.
Hasbuna-Llaahu wahdahu wa ni'ma-l-wakeel.
Wa salli 'alaa sayyidinaa Muhammadin
wa aaalihi wa sahbihi ajma'een
wal-hamdu li-Llaahi Rabbil-'aalameen.

Truth belongs to Allah; it is He who shows the way.
Allah, alone, suffices us, and what a fine Guardian is He!
Blessings upon our leader Muhammad
and his family and companions altogether
and praise is due to Allah, Lord of the Worlds.

References

Armstrong, Karen. *Islam: A Short History.* New York: Random House, 2000.

Boisard, Marcel. *Humanism in Islam.* Indianapolis: American Trust Publications, 1988.

Doi, 'Abdur Rahman I. *Shari'ah: The Islamic Law.* London: Ta Ha Publishers, 1984.

Easwaran, Eknath. *A Man to Match his Mountains: Badshah Khan, Nonviolent Soldier of Islam.* Petaluma, CA: Nilgiri Press, 1984.

Haley, Alex. *The Autobiography of Malcolm X.* New York: Ballantine Books, 1964.

Izetbegovich, 'Alija 'Ali. *Islam Between East and West.* Second edition. Indianapolis: American Trust Publications, 1989.

Juergensmeyer, Mark. *Fighting with Gandhi.* San Francisco: Harper & Row, 1984.

Kaftaro, Shaykh Ahmed. Comments during telephone conversation with Shaykh Ahmed Abdur Rashid, 26 November 2000, Damascus/Bedford.

Kaftaro, Shaykh Ahmed. Comments during telephone conversation with Shaykh Ahmed Abdur Rashid, 5 March 2001, Damascus/Bedford.

Khan, Maulana Wahiduddin. Non-Violence and Islam. Online. Available at http://www.alrisala.org/Articles/papers/nonviolence.htm. Accessed 1 March 2001.

Lings, Martin. *Muhammad (peace be upon him): His Life Based on the Earliest Sources.* Kuala Lumpur: A.S. Noordeen, 1983.

Smith, Dan. *The State of the World Atlas.* Sixth edition. New York: Penguin Putnam, 1999.

بسم الله الرحمن الرحيم

Atonement: The Process of Healing and Reconciling of Differences

Bismi-Llaahi-r-Rahmaani-r-Raheem

Bismi-Llaah, Al-hamdu-li-Llaah
Allaahumma salli wa sallim 'alaa sayyidinaa Muhammadin,
wa 'alaa aaalihi wa sahbih

The Sweetness of Repentance

One of my favorite stories of atonement (or repentance, as I tend to call it) is an account of a conversation with the eleventh century Muslim scholar Imam al-Ghazali *(rahmatu-Llaahi 'alayhi)*, based on a well-known *hadith qudsi.*[1] Someone asked the imam, "What happens if I sin?" He replied, "The angel will write it down, and you will be called to account for it on the Day of Awakening."

The person then asked, "What happens if I repent of that sin?" Imam al Ghazali said, "Allah *(Subhaanahu wa ta'aalaa)* will erase it."

The man went on, "And what happens if I repeat the same sin?" Replied the imam, "The angel will write it down again."

"And again, if I repent of it?"

"Allah *(Subhaanahu wa ta'aalaa)* will erase it."

"How long does this go on?" the man asked. Imam al-Ghazali replied, "Until you forget to repent."

From an Islamic point of view, our sins are the lapses, faults, and slips of the developing human being. They are a natural part of our growth. Even sin has a purpose in bringing us nearer to Allah *(Subḥaanahu wa taʿaalaa)*.

> The Prophet *(ṣalla-Llaahuʿalayhi wa sallam)* told his companions: "Verily the servant will commit a sin, and through that sin it is possible he will enter Heaven."
>
> "How is that, O Messenger of Allah?" one of them asked.
>
> He replied, "The person concentrates his attention on repentance and the avoidance of sin until he enters Heaven."

Repentance, and the forgiveness that follows, are keys to the door of fulfillment. They are not just ways to escape the punishments of Hell or the wrath of God. They are a doorway to the sweet vision, nearness, taste, hearing, scent, and Presence of the Divine. We go through that door, and we feel the Divine Presence, because nothing is blocking it.

Allah *(Subḥaanahu wa taʿaalaa)* Himself calls to us:

> *Yaaa ayyuha-l-ladheena 'aamanuu tuubuuu ila-Llaahi tawbatan-nasuuhaa. ʿAsaa Rabukum añy-yukaffira añkum sayyi'aatikum wa yud-khilakum jannaatin tajree miñ taḥtiha-l-anhaaru...*
>
> O believers! Turn to Allah in sincere repentance. It may well be that your Lord will remove from you your sins and admit you to gardens beneath which rivers flow... (Qur'an 66:8).

When we make our prayer, the segment of time from the last prayer to that prayer is like standing before Allah *(Subhaanahu wa ta'aalaa)* on the Day of Awakening. If we prepare inwardly and fill our lives with the radiance of repentance, then there is hope. If we think we can get through one day without feeling some repentance, we're wrong. We are degrading our lives, our souls, and the community around us. No good can come without dependence on God. As we enlist Allah's *(Subhaanahu wa ta'aalaa)* aid in the struggle against the forces of darkness within us; as we turn our lives from selfishness to service; as we strive to correct our wrong actions and attitudes, we uplift our families, our communities, and humanity. We begin to think Islamically.

Not all Muslims think Islamically. By "thinking Islamically," I mean suffusing our lives with the attributes of Allah *(Subhaanahu wa ta'aalaa)*: the Compassionate, the Merciful, the Gatherer, the Just, the Forgiver, the Protector. Islamic thinking evolves from our good actions. We only begin to be that way through our *'ibaadah* (worship), repentance, sincerity, service—through changing our attitudes and habits.

When we think Islamically, we think with an attitude of confidence, tolerance, and patience. Compassion and mercy accompany everything we do and say. We also know that as we come to be more compassionate and merciful, there are times when we succumb to one flash of anger or frustration, and feel as if we have lost all the progress we had made. But, let us rest assured that when we have repentance, Allah *(Subhaanahu wa ta'aalaa)* will always place us back on the path, at the place where we deviated.

Once the Prophet Musa *('alayhi-s-salaam)* prayed, "O Lord, I want to meet the most abominable of your creatures." A voice came to him and said, "Go see the first man at the riverbank in the morning." So, he went down to the river the next day, and there he found a surly man with bloodshot eyes, mumbling and cursing and beating his donkey, obviously hung over from the previous evening's cavorting and libations.

The Prophet Musa *('alayhi-s-salaam)* went back to prayer. This time, he prayed to see the best of God's creations. Allah *(Subhaanahu wa ta'aalaa)* said, "Return to the river tomorrow morning." Musa *('alayhi-s-salaam)* went, and lo and behold, he encountered the same man. This time, the man was sweet and kind, and being gentle with his donkey. Musa *('alayhi-s-salaam)* thought, "How can this be?" In search of an explanation, he visited the man's house and spoke to his wife.

He told her all that he had seen. After listening carefully, she said, "Yesterday, my husband came home, and I served him dinner, and he began cursing me as usual. Then he demanded that I massage his feet. As I was doing that, I asked if I could ask him a question. He said, 'Yes.'

"I said, 'What is greater than the earth?' He answered, 'The seas.' I asked, 'What is greater than the seas?' 'My sins,' he replied. I asked, 'What is greater than your sins?' And he said, with tears of gratitude pouring from his eyes, 'Allah's forgiveness.' From that moment on, he has been as you see."

If we, like the man in the story, long to experience the forgiveness of Allah *(Subhaanahu wa ta'aalaa)*, then we need to take stock of how well we are forgiving our fellow human beings.

Extending Forgiveness to Others

Allah *(Subhaanahu wa ta'aalaa)* says:

> ***Wa-l-ya'fuu wa-l-yasfahuu; alaa tuhibbuuna añy-yaghfira-Llaahu lakum? Wa-Llaahu Ghafuurur-Raheem.***

> **Let them forgive and overlook. Do you not wish that God will forgive you? For God is All-Forgiving, Most-Merciful** (Qur'an 24:22).
>
> ***Yaquuluuna Rabbana-gh-firlanaa wa li-ikhwaanina-l-ladheena sabaquunaa bi-l-eemaani wa laa taj-ʿal fee quluubinaa ghillal-li-l-ladheena aamanuu...***
>
> **...[they] say: "Our Lord! Forgive us and our brethren who came before us into the faith and leave not in our hearts rancor** (or sense of injury) **against those who believe!"...** (Qur'an 59:10).

If we expect forgiveness from God, how can we not give it to others? Too often, we choose to be harsher than Allah *(Subhaanahu wa taʿaalaa)*. Rather than forgiving, we hold grudges and punish people. Never mind that Allah *(Subhaanahu wa taʿaalaa)* has said, **"My Mercy overpowers My Anger"** (Abu Hurayra/Bukhari); in our lives, we replace the Mercy of Allah *(Subhaanahu wa taʿaalaa)* with our judgments, our blame, our desire to avenge past wrongs.

To earn the forgiveness of Allah *(Subhaanahu wa taʿaalaa)*, we have to let go of all that. We have to accept that whatever happens to us, happens with the permission of Allah *(Subhaanahu wa taʿaalaa)*.

The Prophet *(salla-Llaahu ʿalayhi wa sallam)* advised Ibn Abbas *(radiya-Llaahu ʿanhu)*:

> **...If you ask, ask only Allah *(Subhaanahu wa taʿaalaa)*. If you seek refuge, seek refuge only with Allah *(Subhaanahu wa taʿaalaa)*. And learn that if all people meet and agree to do something useful for you, they will not do that except by the wish of Allah *(Subhaanahu wa***

> ***ta'aalaa);* and if they decide to harm you, they will not do that except by the wish of Allah *(Subhaanahu wa ta'aalaa).***

We need to move towards that place where we can say, *"Alhamduli-Llaah"* (praise be to Allah) no matter what happens to us, rising above attitudes of blame or doubt, even violence and hate. As we do that, we realize that all good that comes to us comes from Allah *(Subhaanahu wa ta'aalaa)*, and all that heretofore we thought was bad, comes from our own self.

> ***Maaa asaabaka min hasanatiñ fa-mina-Llaahi wa maaa asaabaka miñ sayyi'atiñ fa-min-nafsik.***
>
> **Whatever good happens to you is from Allah; but whatever evil happens to you is from your [own] self** (Qur'an 4:79).

The catalyst—the way we get to this realization—is to turn to Allah *(Subhaanahu wa ta'aalaa)* in our hearts, our minds, and our words and to atone of our wrong actions. This builds the strength to accept that all things come from Allah *(Subhaanahu wa ta'aalaa)*. Neither atonement nor the forgiveness that follows is a sign of weakness. Rather, both are indications of strength. Real forgiveness is when we have the power to take revenge, and we choose not to. The Prophet *(salla-Llaahu 'alayhi wa sallam)* said:

> **The strong person is not the one who overcomes people by his strength, but the one who controls himself when he is angry.** (Abu Hurayra/Bukhari)

On another occasion, the Prophet *(salla-Llaahu 'alayhi wa sallam)* said,

> **The best deed before Allah is to pardon a person who has wronged you, to show affection for relatives who have broken ties with you, and to act generously towards a person who has deprived you** (Uqah b. Amir/Baihaqi).

You may have heard about the recent murder case in Iran. A teenage boy quarreled with another young man, fatally stabbed him, and was sentenced to be executed by public hanging. The morning of the execution, a crowd of people gathered, crying and pleading for the boy to be spared. He was already on the platform with the noose around his neck when the father of the victim intervened. He stopped the execution, saying that he had forgiven the boy.

Later, somebody asked the father why he forgave his son's murderer. He said, "I realized that killing him wouldn't bring back my son." He also said he thought about the honor of Islam, and that if he forgave, then people around the world would see that Islam teaches forgiveness (Valinejad).

Sometimes you have in your heart a willingness to forgive, seeking to forgive, wanting to forgive, even though you know you cannot forgive. You may have in your heart forgiveness, but the social mores and laws dictate some act of punishment. Or, you might value forgiveness, but not feel forgiving towards a certain person yet.

We need to understand that forgiveness is reached progressively. Even if you cannot forgive right away, you can try to approach the situation with forgiveness in your heart, seeking the means to forgive.

In fact, the laws and rules of behavior, punishment, and reward that Allah *(Subhaanahu wa ta'aalaa)* commands us to observe (that is, the *sharee'ah*) encourage the progression towards forgiveness. The evolution indicated by Islamic thought on the theme of "an eye for an eye and a tooth for a tooth" lies in Qur'an, where Allah *(Subhaanahu wa ta'aalaa)* states:

> ***Wa jazaaa'u sayyi'atiñ sayyi'atum-mithluhaa: fa-man ᶜafaa wa aslaha fa-ajruhuu ᶜala-Llaah; innahuu laa yuhibbu-dh-dhaalimeen.***
>
> **The recompense for an injury is an injury equal thereto and to degree. But a person who forgives and makes reconciliation, his reward is due from God, for He loves not those who do wrong** (42:40).
>
> ***Wa laa tastawi-l-hasanatu wa la-s-sayyi'ah; idfaᶜ bi-l-latee hiya ahsanu fa-idha-l-ladhee baynaka wa baynahuu ᶜadaawatuñ ka'annahuu waliyyun hameem.***
>
> **The good deed and the evil deed are not alike. Repel [the evil deed] with one which is better, then lo! he who was your enemy [will become] as though he were a close friend** (41:34).

Reconciliation

Sharee'ah guides us towards conciliation, towards having concern for both parties, so that we can bring people back to a moral, ethical consciousness—to make people human again. It is Shaytan who lures our humanity away. No truly humane being could commit terrible wrongs against another person. But Shaytan lures our humanity away by appealing to our lower nature—power, greed, fear, doubt, desires—and we start acting inhumanely. We need to remember that we have the higher road, because we are the believers in Ibrahim *(ᶜalayhi-s-salaam)*, Musa *(ᶜalayhi-s-salaam)*, ᶜIsa *(ᶜalayhi-s-salaam)*, and Mu<u>h</u>ammad *(<u>s</u>alla-Llaahu ᶜalayhi wa sallam)*. We are the people who believe in peace. We greet one another with *"as-salaam ᶜalaykum* (peace be with you)." We must mean it, and we must live it.

And so, we must remain near to those people who feel offended when others are offended, and who feel harmed when others are harmed. These are the people who are good in their hearts and souls, who are good Muslims, who are guided and not misguided.

Whoever reconciles brother with brother, sister with sister, parent with child, neighbor with neighbor, community with community, or nation with nation will be rewarded by Allah *(Sub<u>h</u>aanahu wa taᶜaalaa)*. The mere fact that the effort has been made is rewarded. Allah *(Sub<u>h</u>aanahu wa taᶜaalaa)* gives credit to the person who says, "I will try. I will seek the way to make peace and understanding"—even if the person dies in the effort.

Allah *(Sub<u>h</u>aanahu wa taᶜaalaa)* also recognizes that sometimes, the best way to work for peace is in private. We read in the Holy Qur'an:

> ***Laa khayra fee katheerim-min-najwaahum illaa man amara bi-<u>s</u>adaqatin aw maᶜruufin aw i<u>s</u>laa<u>h</u>im-bayna-n-naas; wa mañy-yaf-ᶜal dhaalika-b-tighaaa'a mar<u>d</u>aati-Llaahi fa-sawfa nu'teehi ajran ᶜa<u>dh</u>eemaa.***
>
> **There is no virtue in most of the secret counsels of the people; it is, however, good if one secretly enjoins charity, kindness, and reconciliation among people; the one who does this to please Allah, will soon be given a mighty reward** (4:114).

FORGIVING, NOT FORGETTING

None of this means that reconciliation is easy. When the oppression, the killing, the rapes, the injustice, and the destruction have gone on for generations, it is very difficult to reconcile. People who have suffered worry that if they forgive, if they make peace, then history might repeat itself.

I have worked for more than twenty years in the field of dialogue—between Palestinians, Israeli Arabs and Israeli Jews; Spaniards and Basques; Northern Irish Catholics and Protestant; Abkhazians and Georgians; and others. In a discussion this past summer, a Bosnian youth said to me, "I can forgive, but I can never forget." I replied that there are two kinds of not forgetting. One kind is repeating "I won't forget!" with bitterness, and handing down hatred generation after generation. The second kind of not forgetting is remembering that what happened was terrible, and teaching our children that it should never happen again: that all children—Bosnian, Albanian, Chechen, Serb, Kosovar, Palestinian, Israeli, white, black, yellow, brown, Jewish, Christian, Muslim—should learn patience, tolerance, and to reach out to one another and promise the next generation, "no more fighting."

It is our duty to teach our children to reconcile differences not only by gaining greater knowledge of issues and "making a better argument," as the Qur'an says; but also and just as importantly, by opening their hearts, understanding others' points of view, and relying on the power of tolerance, patience, justice to extend across all barriers of nation, race, and religion. Impatience for change is understandable, but there is an aspect of arrogance when we want or expect to see the results of our efforts "right away," or even within our lifetimes. **"*Inna-Llaaha maʿa-s̱-s̱aabareen*"—surely, Allah assists those who are patient** (Qur'an 2:153).

Yet, change is constant and even rapid when there is deep, abiding faith and effort.

Islam guides us to identify, first and foremost, with an overriding culture based on faith. Allah *(Subhaanahu wa ta'aalaa)* tells us:

> ***Inna haadhihee ummatukum ummatañw-waahidatañw-wa ana Rabbukum...***
>
> **Verily, this community of yours is a single community, and I am your Lord and Cherisher...** (Qur'an 21:92).

Allah *(Subhaanahu wa ta'aalaa)* also says that He divided us into different groups for a reason.

> ***Wa law shaaa'a-Llaahu laja'alakum ummatañw-waahidatañw-wa laakil-li-yabluwakum fee maaa aataakum fa-s-tabiqu-l-khayraat; ila-Llaahi marji'ukum jamee'añ fa-yunabbi'ukum-bimaa kuñtum feehi takh-talifuun.***
>
> **If Allah had willed, He could have made [humanity] one community. But He willed to test you by means of what He has given you. So, strive to excel one another in good deeds** (Qur'an 5:48).

Some sense of ethnic, racial, or national identity can be constructive, in that it bonds people together and gives them a common goal. But focusing on race, ethnicity, or national origin in the long run ends up creating walls between people. It is one thing for a group—

whether Pakistani or African, European or Indonesian, Jewish or Muslim—to be put in a ghetto against its will. It is quite another if we ghettoize ourselves, building our own walls and keeping ourselves behind them.

Earlier, I spoke about atonement in terms of repentance. Let me return again to the idea of atonement, from a different perspective.

The word "atone" shows us the need to break down walls. Look at the word itself: "at-one-ment." Until we understand not only our relationship with Allah *(Subhaanahu wa ta'aalaa)*, but the relationship that Allah *(Subhaanahu wa ta'aalaa)* wants us to have with our fellow human beings, we will not be atoning or repenting fully.

Atonement means coming to "at-one-ness," setting aside the attitudes that keep us separate from the truth, the beauty, the sweetness of Allah *(Subhaanahu wa ta'aalaa)* and of Allah's *(Subhaanahu wa ta'aalaa)* creation. When you look at a mountain or beautiful landscape from a distance, there are different elements within it: a peak, a clump of trees, a bird in the sky. But viewing the scene in its entirety, you see one beauty, one majesty. So it is with humanity: we come from different races, nations, and ethnic backgrounds, but we are all part of a greater picture, a greater whole. Islam embraces the uniqueness of each of our groups, while enabling all of us to find strength in unity with one another.

In most parts of the Islamic world, Muslim communities are mono-cultural, mono-lingual, and mono-racial. Muslims in the United States are not. We come from many cultures and races, and speak many languages. Living in such a multicultural society is causing dramatic shifts among immigrant Muslims. The first generation of immigrants are Pakistani Muslims, Nigerian Muslims, Indian Muslims, Persian Muslims, Indonesian Muslims, and so on; but their children and grandchildren see themselves as American Muslims.

The same holds true for the African American Muslim community. There has to be a merging of their Islamic character, a development of Islamic thought based in Islamic belief, family duty, social activism, and community responsibility.

Racial and ethnic diversity are among the espoused values of this country. If we as Muslims do our part to make those values lived instead of just talked about, then we can bring to completion the dismantling of the inequalities that have been part of our country's fabric since its founding. Over the past 50 years, these inequalities have begun to be torn down. Yet, there still exist attitudes and policies that target certain ethnic, racial, and religious groups. To change these—to complete the process of establishing true equality—we ourselves must guarantee the rights of others. Lack of atonement and lack of forgiveness blocks our ability to reach out to everyone through Islam.

Moreover—just like the early Muslims whose way of life inspired others to embrace Islam—we, too, have a new frontier to which we can bring the values and the proven methods of Islamic life. All of us who are sincere and who are striving to be good Muslims/ Mu'mins have something to offer the larger society. We have experiences and knowledge in community development; in raising healthy, well-adjusted children; in promoting education and social responsibility (among other areas). We have had many successes in inspiring both believers and non-believers, overcoming disabling social and psychological ills, and creating viable businesses. Islam requires that successes within one's own community should be shared. It is time to reach out to other Muslims and non-Muslims with two hands: one hand to give, and one hand to receive. We need to reach out with open minds and open hearts.

Although there is much that we should not forget, forgiveness (which is the key to progress and understanding and transmitting the Truth of Islam) must be practiced. For that to happen, we must be willing to look closely at ourselves, to measure ourselves daily against the values, the practices, and the Truth of Islam.

MUHAASABATU-N-NAFS

Every day we are encouraged to pause:

> ***Haasibuu anfusakum qabla an tuhaasabuu wa zinuu a'maalakum qabla an tuzanuu 'alaykum.***
>
> **Account for yourselves before you are accounted; weigh your actions before your actions become a weight upon you.** [2]

Every day, we need to look at how well we take advantage of the gifts of Allah *(Subhaanahu wa ta'aalaa)*. When we look honestly at ourselves, we discover the ways we waste our time and talents, without discipline, not taking the guidance of the Qur'an and the teachings of the Prophet Muhammad *(salla-Llaahu 'alayhi wa sallam)*. The way of submission is the way of security, here and hereafter.

A respected imam said, "That person is not among our people who does not call himself to account every day. If he has done wrong, he asks for forgiveness and turns in repentance to Allah *(Subhaanahu wa ta'aalaa)*." Part of repentance is disciplining ourselves to correct the faults we detect. This is what the Prophet *(salla-Llaahu 'alayhi wa sallam)* called the *Jihaadu-l-akbar*, the greater struggle. It is harder to address our own bad habits and mistakes than to engage in armed battle. But *alhamduli-Llaah*, Allah *(Subhaanahu wa ta'aalaa)* promises us in the Holy Qur'an:

Wa-l-ladheena jaahaduu feenaa la-nah-diyannahum subulanaa; wa inna-Llaaha la-maᶜa-l-muhsineen.

...those who struggle hard for Us, We shall certainly guide them to Our paths, and Allah is definitely with those who do good (29:69).

Once when Hazrat Umar *(radiya-Llaahu ʿanhu)* was with some of his companions, he pointed out a man walking nearby and said, "That person is a great soul, a lover of Allah, one who spends much time in awareness of his Lord." Curious, one of the companions approached the man, told him what Umar *(radiya-Llaahu ʿanhu)* had said, and asked how he had earned such praise.

The man said, "I do three things. First, every night when I go to bed, I pray to be forgiven by anyone I harmed that day. I ask Allah *(Subhaanahu wa taʿaalaa)* to forgive me for all my thoughts that were directed against Him or any of His creatures, and for anything I did in disbelief." He went on, detailing all the things he asked forgiveness for.

"Second," he said, "I think that if anyone offered me all the riches, fame, and power in the world, I would reject them without being tempted in the least.

"Third, I think that if I had all the kingdoms of the earth, and then someone took them away, I should give them up without feeling any loss."

This philosophy is as useful today as it was 1400 years ago. Before we go to sleep each night, we can review how we spent our day, and what we could have done differently. We can reflect upon our sins, ask forgiveness from Allah *(Subhaanahu wa taʿaalaa)*, and resolve not to repeat them. We can consider the good deeds that we should have done, but didn't, and promise Allah *(Subhaanahu wa ta'aalaa)* to try to do them the next day. We can review the good acts we did do, thanking Allah *(Subhaanahu wa ta'aalaa)* for the insight that allowed us to do them and seeking His protection against pride. We can think about death—how it could come upon us at any moment—and intend to be prepared, and pray to have enough time left in life to correct what we have neglected so far.

Through this practice, our thoughts and actions will come closer to the example of the Messenger of Allah, the Prophet Muhammad *(salla-Llaahu 'alayhi wa sallam)*. We will become Muslims of high character and deep knowledge.

In conclusion, if we seek atonement, forgiveness, reconciliation, and inner and outer peace, even for a moment, then we must pass through one of the most difficult doorways of human existence. It is easy to be angry. It is easy to keep ourselves apart from others. It is easy to avoid seeing ourselves, and never bother to ask forgiveness. It is easy to think that we are right, and others are wrong. But can we be forgiving? Really forgiving? Can we set aside our differences? Can we face our own faults, and admit that we need to change?

The spiritual essence of Islam begins with the light that Allah *(Subhaanahu wa ta'aalaa)* created this world with. It is up to us to unveil that light inside ourselves. Allah *(Subhaanahu wa ta'aalaa)* is "as near as our jugular vein"; but as long as we hold ourselves or others hostage with anger, resentment, bias, or mistrust, we will not feel His nearness. We will never open the doorway to the sweet Presence of the Divine.

The future of the Muslim community lies in the creativity that comes from the hearts and minds of those who repent, who forgive others, who make peace. Let us affirm that all of us will try our best to live in harmony. Let us pray that Allah *(Subh̲aanahu wa taʿaalaa)* guides and keeps us on the straight path, and let us ask Allah's forgiveness. Let us ask Allah *(Subh̲aanahu wa taʿaalaa)* to make us forgiving people, and to help us to understand that repentance is an opportunity, for forgiveness will cleanse our souls.

* * *

Allaahumma-shrah̲ suduuranaa li-l-Islaam.
Allaahumma h̲abbib ilaynaa-l-eemaan wa zayyinhu fee quluubinaa
wa karrih ilaynaa-l-kufra wa-l-fusuuqa wa-l-ʿisyaan.
Allaahumma-j-ʿalnaa mina-r-raashideen.
O Allah! Open our hearts for Islam.
O Allah! Make faith something cherished for us,
and embellish with that our hearts,
and make repulsive and hateful for us
unbelief, immorality, and transgression.
O Allah! Make us of those who are rightly guided.

Allaahumma baaʿidu baynee wabayna khataayaaya
kamaa baaʿidta bayna-l-mashriqi wa-l-maghrib.
Allaahumma naqqinee min khataayaaya
kamaa tunaqqaa-th-thawba-l-abyadu mina-d-danas.
Allaahumma-ghsilnee min khataayaaya bi-maa'a wa-th-thalji wa-l-barad.

O Allah, cause a separation between me and my sins
as much as You caused a separation between the east and the west.
O Allah, purify me from my sins
as You make pure the white cloth from filth.
O Allah, wash me with water, snow and hail from my sins.

Laa ilaaha illa anta, subh̲anak,
Allaahumma inna nas'alak al-ʿafwa min khatayaana,
wa nas'alak ar-rah̲mah.

Allaahumma laa tazigh quluubinaa
baʿda idh hadaytana, wahdina min ladunka rahmah innaka anta-l-Wahhab.

There is no god but You, glory be to You,
O Allah! we ask Your pardon for our sin
and we ask You for Your mercy.
O Allah! do not cause our hearts to deviate (from guidance)
after You have guided us,
and grant us mercy from Yourself;
surely, You are the Grantor.

Wa Llaahu lahu-l-haqqu wa huwa yahdi-s-sabeel.
Hasbuna-Llaahu wahdahu wa niʿma-l-wakeel.
Wa salli ʿalaa Sayyidina Muhammadin
wa aaalihi wa sahbihi ajmaʿeen
wa-l-hamdu li-Llaahi Rabbil-ʿaalameen.

Truth belongs to Allah; it is He who shows the way.
Allah, alone, suffices us, and what a fine guardian is He!
Blessings upon our leader Muhammad
and his family and companions altogether
and praise is due to Allah, Lord of the Worlds.

Thank you very much.
Assalaamu ʿalaykum wa rahmatu-Llaahi wa barakaatuhu.

Notes

1 The *hadith qudsi* upon which the story of Imam al-Ghazali *(rahmatu-Llaahi 'alayhi)* is based is recounted by Abu Hurayra *(radiya-Llaahu 'anhu)* as follows:

> **I heard the Prophet *(salla-Llaahu 'alayhi wa sallam)* saying, "If somebody commits a sin and then says, 'O my Lord! I have sinned, please forgive me!' his Lord says, 'My slave has known that he has a Lord who forgives sins and punishes for it, I therefore have forgiven my slave (his sins).'**
>
> **"Then he remains without committing any sin for a while and then again commits another sin and says, 'O my Lord, I have committed another sin, please forgive me,' and Allah says, 'My slave has known that he has a Lord who forgives sins and punishes for it, I therefore have forgiven my slave (his sin).'**
>
> **"Then he remains without committing any another sin for a while and then commits another sin (for the third time) and says, 'O my Lord, I have committed another sin, please forgive me,' and Allah says, 'My slave has known that he has a Lord Who forgives sins and punishes for it. I therefore have forgiven My slave (his sin), he can do whatever he likes.' "**

The Qur'anic foundation for this *hadith* is:

> ***...illaa mañ taaba wa aamana wa 'amila 'amalañ saalihañ fa-ulaaa'ika yubaddila-Llaahu sayyi'aatihim hasanaat; wa kaana-Llaahu Ghafuura-r-Raheem.***
>
> **...save him who repents and believes and does righteous work; as for such, Allah will change their evil deeds to good deeds. Allah is ever Forgiving, Merciful** (25:70).

2 The statement which begins "Account for yourselves before you are taken into account..." is usually attributed to the companion of the Prophet *(salla-Llaahu 'alayhi wa sallam)* and later imam Umar Ibn Khattab *(radiya-Llaahu 'anhu)*, as Imam Ghazali indicates in his book Ihya 'Ulum ad-Din. Although it lacks a clear chain or transmission, by tradition many Sufis and scholars have attributed the saying and/or the wisdom behind it to the Prophet *(salla-Llaahu 'alayhi wa sallam)*.

References

Valinejad, Afshin "Iranian teen pardoned seconds before hanging." Nando Times. Online. Posted at http://www.nandotimes.com/noframes/story/…,7,5001149278-500181455-500740977-0,00.html. Accessed 5 January 2000.

بسم الله الرحمن الرحيم

Accepting One's Choices: Sufic Islam, a Life Changing Experience

Bismi-Llaah, Alẖamduli-Llaah
Allaahumma s̱alli wa sallim ʿalaa Sayyidinaa Muhammadin,
wa ʿalaa aalihi wa saẖbih

Introduction: Sufic Islam's Potential to Heal Cultural/ Ethnic Conflicts

Fourteen hundred and thirty years ago (by the Islamic calendar), two tribes of Arabia were locked in civil war. Centuries of living side by side had failed to integrate their blood-lines; on the contrary, feuds had multiplied. Then, remarkably, they heard about a man who taught a new way of thinking: a man who had erased the lines between clan and clan, slave and master, black and white, rich and poor, calling all to equality in the name of one God. A small group of visionary men and women of both clans approached this man to see if he would consider emigrating to their area to bring peace to their warring peoples. He agreed.

With that emigration, the city now known as "Medina" emerged from the ashes of age-old violence—and Islam, under attack from tribal factions in its place of origin, finally came into its own as a way of life that transcends all differences of ethnicity.

Fourteen centuries later, where do we stand? What are we to make of the ethnic violence among Hutus and Tutsis? West Bank Palestinians and Israeli settlers? Northern Irish Catholics and Protestants? Serbians and Kosovars?

The theme of this symposium is self-discovery. Clearly, "self" can be understood in different ways. From the time of the Prophet Muhammad *(salla-Llaahu 'alayhi wa sallam)* until today, some people have held images of self that engender fragmentation, self-centeredness, ethnocentricity, and conflict. Others—including the Prophet *(salla-Llaahu 'alayhi wa sallam)*—have understood the self in ways that transcend cultural limitations. This is the understanding of self that reconciled the clans of Medina. This is the understanding of self that can heal the conflicts in our world today. This is the understanding of self that comes through the path of Sufic Islam.

Peace, equity, co-existence, tolerance, forgiveness, and partnership are fundamental principles of Islam. Allah *(Subhaanahu wa ta'aalaa)* tells us in the Holy Qur'an:

> ***Yaaa-ayyuha-l-ladheena aamanuu laa ta'kuluuu amwaalakum-baynakum-bi-l-baatili illaaa añ takuuna tijaaratan 'añ taraadim-miñkum: wa laa taqtuluuu añfusakum; inna-Llaaha kaana bikum Raheemaa.***
>
> **O ye who believe! Do not eat up your property among yourselves in vanities: but let there be amongst you traffic and trade by mutual good-will: nor kill [or destroy] yourselves, for verily God hath been to you Most Merciful** (4:29).
>
> ***Innama-s-sabeelu 'ala-l-ladheena yadhlimuuna-n-naasa wa yabghuuna fi-l-ardi bi-ghayri-l-haqq; ulaaa'ika la-hum adhaabun aleem. Wa lamañ sabara wa ghafara inna dhaalika la-min azmi-l-umuur.***

> **The blame is only against those who oppress people with wrong-doing and insolently transgress beyond bounds through[out] the land, defying right and justice: for such there will be a grievous penalty. But indeed if any show patience and forgive, that would truly be an exercise of courageous will and resolution in the conduct of affairs** (42:42-43).
>
> ***Wa iñ janaḫuu li-s-salmi fa-j-naḫ lahaa wa tawakkal ʿala-Llaah.***
>
> **And if [your enemies] incline to peace, incline thou also to it, and trust in Allah...** (8:61).

The Sufis have refined the means of attaining to and sustaining these principles in our lives here and hereafter. If more people were practicing Islam and Sufism, the world would not be in the miserable state it is in today.

Redefining Terms / Redefining Our Lives

There is no lack of people who call themselves "Muslim" and "Sufi." But identifying oneself as "Muslim" or "Sufi" does not guarantee that one is understanding, let alone practicing, *Taṣawwuf* and Islam. One may equally well be trying to make *Taṣawwuf* and Islam fit one's own definitions, or "pouring the ocean into a cup." Perhaps a cup of ocean is better than no ocean at all, but just think how much more is gained by experiencing the real thing!

Newcomers to Sufic Islam in the West often assume that they can understand *Taṣawwuf* in intellectual or psychological terms. Moreover, like most novices eagerly venturing into unknown territory, they may be too quick to assume that they already have the tools needed for the journey.

For example, every English speaking adult can define the terms "trust," "faith," "belief," "submission," "duty," and "responsibility." Yet, all these terms change their meanings as we pursue knowledge. To plumb the realms of self-discovery, the seeker has to embrace this process of change.

The terms *"Taṣawwuf"* and "Islam" are among the first that need to be re-defined in many seekers' vocabularies. Basic misunderstandings of both terms have led some people to think that they can define them independently. In fact, there is no *Taṣawwuf* without Islam. What is Islam? In Arabic, the word means "to affirm peace, safety, and security; to be unimpaired, faultless, certain, and established; to submit and hand oneself over to a higher power." What is *Taṣawwuf*? It is the process of developing and refining the character of an individual for the sole purpose of perfecting the worship, service, and trust of Allah *(Subḫaanahu wa ta'aalaa)* and, as a result, creating a more balanced and harmonious world for today and future generations, as well as creating our place and role in the hereafter. Once one grasps these definitions of the terms, one clearly recognizes that Islam and *Taṣawwuf* are inseparable.

Integrating new or broader meanings (such as those I have just given) equips the seeker to comprehend greater subtleties of self-discovery. Two stages are involved, requiring different levels of development and spiritual commitment. First, we understand new definitions conceptually; next comes the more challenging task of accepting them.

In the Holy Qur'an, Allah *(Subḫaanahu wa ta'aalaa)* comments on those people who,

> ***Wa la'iñ sa'altahum-man khalaqa-s-samaawaati wa-l-ar<u>d</u>a wa sakh-khara-sh-shamsa wa-l-qamara la-yaquulunna-Llaah: fa-annaa yu'fakuun.... Wa la'iñ sa'altahum-man-nazzala mina-s-samaaa'i maaa'añ fa-a<u>h</u>yaa bihi-l-ar<u>d</u>a mim-ba'di mawtihaa la-yaquulunna-Llaah; quli-l-<u>h</u>amdu li-Llaah; bal aktharuhum laa ya'qiluun. Wa maa haadhihi-l-<u>h</u>ayaatu-d-dunyaaaa illaa lahwuñw-wa la'ib; wa inna-d-daara-l-aakhirata la-hiya-l-<u>h</u>ayawaan, law kaanu ya'lamuun.***
>
> **... And if you were to ask them, "Who created the heavens and the earth, and constrained the sun and the moon [to their appointed work]?" they would say, "God." How, then, are they turned away?.... And thus it is: if you ask them, "Who is it that sends down water from the skies, giving life thereby to the earth after it had been lifeless?"—they will surely answer, "God." Say: "[Since this is so,] all praise is due to God [alone]!" But most of them will not use their reason: for, [if they did, they would know that] the life of this world is nothing but a passing delight and a play—whereas, behold, the life in the hereafter is indeed the only [true] life: if they but knew this!** (29:61, 63-64).

To change our definitions means changing not only the way we speak and interpret others' speech, but the way we think. Ultimately, it means redefining the context in which we live our lives. It means redefining the very terms of our existence. This takes contentment, confidence, and courage. The Prophet Musa *('alayhi-s-salaam)* prayed,

> ***Rabbi-shrah̲ lee s̲adree. Wa yassir-lee amree. Wa-h̲-lul ʿuqdatam-mi-l-lisaanee. Yafqahuu qawlee.***
>
> **O my Lord, open for me my chest [grant me self-confidence, contentment, and boldness], and ease my task for me, and loose the knot [defect] from my tongue, that they may understand my speech** (Qur'an 20:25-28).

Those who are drawn to the spiritual path feel inwardly compelled toward a deeper understanding of self, and thus of Allah's creation and purpose for us.

> ***Man ʿarafa nafsahu, faqad ʿarafa Rabbahu***
>
> **Know yourself and you will know your Lord.** [1]

In coming to know ourselves, our selves are transformed. At a certain point in the journey, each of us must accept that our choice to travel the path of *Tas̲awwuf* is life changing. This choice eventually alters every aspect of our thinking, feeling, sensing, reasoning, and planning. It changes each of us so drastically that sooner or later, we find ourselves reflecting back on who we used to be, and hardly recognizing that person.

Some seekers find the prospect of major life changes threatening. They postpone them for as long as possible. They may go through the external changes, but put off the internal ones. Or, they are receptive to internal changes, but deny the need to make external ones. Most often, they reluctantly accept the necessity of guidance, but resist the multiple levels of trust required to understand the comprehensiveness of Islam.

At the opposite end of the spectrum are those who desire life-changing experiences too much. They declare anything that is spiritually-charged to be "life-changing," and go out collecting such experiences, as long as those experiences support their self-image and provide ample emotional and ego stimulation.

Self-discovery requires overcoming both fearful and over-eager reactions to life-altering experiences. Resisting change out of fear, or chasing change because it feels good, keeps one in the mode of "I want, I need, I can, I can't." To make progress, one must relate to "I" in a different way. One must start to seriously consider the questions, "Who am I? What am I? Where am I? And why am I?"—and to align one's answers with the choice to pursue this Path.

In the Qur'an, Allah *(Subhaanahu wa ta'aalaa)* contrasts two types of people:

> ***Wa mina-n-naasi mañy-yu'jibuka qawluhuu fi-l-hayaati-d-dunyaaa wa yush-hidu-Llaaha 'alaa maa fee qalbihee, wa huwa aladdu-l-khisaam. Wa idhaa tawallaa sa'aa fi-l-ardi li-yufsida feehaa wa yuhlika-l-hartha wa-n-nasl; wa-Llaahu laa yuhibbu-l-fasaad.... Wa mina-n-naasi mañy-yashree nafsahu-b-tighaaa'a mardaati-Llaah; wa-Llaahu Ra'uufum-bi-l-'ibaad.***
>
> **Now there is a kind of person whose views on the life of this world may please thee greatly, and [the more so as] he cites God as witness to what is in his heart and is, moreover, exceedingly skillful in argument. But whenever he prevails, he goes about the earth spreading corruption and destroying [humanity's] tilth and progeny: and God does not love corruption....But there is**

> **[also] a kind of person who would willingly sell his own self in order to please God: and God is most compassionate towards His servants** (2:204-5, 207).

Ask, "Who am I?" "I am a Muslim and an aspiring Sufi." No; dive deeper. "Who am I, as an aspiring Sufi and as one who identifies himself or herself as a Muslim? Where am I in this process? What are the implications and responsibilities of this identity?"

Ask yourself, "Where am I?" The answer is not just, "At the Sufism Symposium." Nor is the answer simply, "I am on the path of Sufism" or "I am a Muslim." If that is the extent of your response, you are avoiding the active aspect of your life journey and avoiding many inner and outer commitments that are necessary for real progress.

It is not enough to ask, "What am I?" "I am a teacher...a therapist... a parent...a doctor...." Go further: "What kind of a teacher? What kind of a parent?" Are you one who exemplifies a clear and specific value system, beyond self-interest? Are you a sincere and humble seeker of Truth, wherever it may take you inside and outside your "self"? Are you willing to own that identity, and not just your image of it? Are you ready to understand and accept unequivocally what it gives to you and demands of you, as a partisan of Allah *(Subhaanahu wa ta'aalaa)*?

The questions do not stop here. As we meet, people elsewhere in the world are fleeing "ethnic cleansing," starving, wandering homeless. Each of us must ask, "What part of history am I in? Where am I standing in the universe as a Muslim in the truest sense of the word?" Then, turning our attention back to this Symposium and to all our other day-to-day circumstances, we must reflect, "Who am I in this specific situation, and what is my relationship to others of like name and identity, as well as to the rest of humanity who are my fellow beings, created and sustained by Allah *(Subḫaanahu wa ta'aalaa)*?"

SELF-REFERENCING OR ALLAH-REFERENCING?

Although these questions sound psychologically-based, for the Sufi aspirant, they come from a spiritual yearning and paradigm. Therefore, the answers lead to different kinds of realizations and transformations. (Please note that I use the word "psychological" in its most common sense [referring to the secular science of mental processes, behaviors, and emotions], rather than in its philosophical sense.)

There is little possibility that a psychological approach to self-discovery will yield deep spiritual awareness, although spiritual understanding does result in deep personal awareness of one's psychological nature. The person of spiritual insight sees no need to reconcile spirituality with secularism, or a self-centered paradigm with a paradigm which is centered on Allah and our responsibility to Allah *(Subḫaanahu wa ta'aalaa)* and the purpose of His creation. For Allah *(Subḫaanahu wa ta'aalaa)* guides us in the Holy Qur'an:

> ***Wa maa khalaqtu-l-jinna wa-l-iñsa illaa li-ya'buduun.***
>
> **And I have not created the jinn and human beings to any end other than that they may [know and] worship Me** (51:56).

To increase the seeker's attunement to this Divine purpose, the Shaykh guides him or her to refine subtle centers of perception (which we call the *laṯaa'if* and which have many dimensions to them, too complicated to explore in this talk[2]). The awakening of the *laṭaa'if* makes possible degrees of self-discovery that are inaccessible by any other means.

People seek out psychological counseling in hopes of becoming more self-aware, improving their relationships, understanding the circumstances of life, learning to feel good about themselves. From the point of view of the Sufi, these goals are secondary to the purpose of human life. Indeed, their fulfillment is a natural consequence of sincere effort and faith. But they are not meant to be the focus of the spiritual journey.

The real spiritual journey is designed to catapult us out of incessant self-referencing. It is to free us from self-absorption so that we might praise and serve Allah *(Subḥaanahu wa taʿaalaa)* and create a better environment for future generations to do the same. Allah's *(Subḥaanahu wa taʿaalaa)* favorite name is " ʿAbd Allah," meaning "servant of Allah." Through *Taṣawwuf,* every one of us may transform our self into ʿAbd Allah.

THE DYNAMIC NATURE OF NAFS

What is this self that we are seeking to transform? *Nafs,* the Arabic word for "self," connotes "soul, psyche, or spirit." It is also defined as "a living creature, a human being"; as "the essence or nature"; as "inclination or desire." *Nafs* is derived from the same root as *nafusa,* meaning "to be valuable, precious." Related verbs mean "to compete or strive" and "to breathe." *Nifaas* means "childbirth." *Nafas* means "freedom or liberty."

So, then, we can say that *nafs* is the dynamic force which is breathed into the physical body at childbirth. It is the precious essence that differentiates the living from the dead. It is deeply connected to a sense of liberty and freedom.

As you listen to me and others speaking at the Symposium, you might find it interesting to plug in different meanings of *nafs*. When I talk about personal identity, for example, you could substitute the word "essence." As people refer to "essence," you could put in the word "self." If I mention what the self is inclined toward, you might recall that "inclination" is a definition of self.

Striving, competing, breathing, giving birth: clearly, the self that we are trying to discover not only exists, but is active. It is moving, evolving. It has traveled from *ghayb* (the unseen) to *dunyaa* (the material world), and it will return again to *ghayb*. In the course of its journey, it rarely stays still for long.

Do you aspire to be a better person? Are there aspects of your character that you would like to improve? Do you long for greater clarity?

Why would we have these feelings, unless our *nafs* inclines towards and has the ability to change? Our selves can be changed. In fact, they are changing right now, right before our very eyes.

What are we changing into? What should we be changing into? The answer is *ʿAbd Allah*.

From Nafs to ʿAbd: Fulfilling the Human Design to Serve and Worship

ʿAbd is commonly defined as "servant" or "slave," most frequently in the context of serving Allah. But it also may mean "human being." By definition, human beings are servants and slaves of the Divine.

The verbs based on the root letters of *ʿabd* indicate the type of servants we are to be. *ʿAbada* means "to worship, to venerate, to adore." Human beings are constructed not just to serve, but to be servants who worship, venerate, and adore.

Where are we to worship, serve, and venerate? In the *ma*ʿ*bad*: the "place of worship or house of God." Remember, *ma*ʿ*bad* comes from the same root as ʿ*abd* (human being). Allah *(Subhaanahu wa ta*ʿ*aalaa)* says in the Qur'an,

> ***...Nahnu aqrabu ilayhi min habli-l-wareed.***
>
> **...We are as near to you as your jugular vein** (50:16).

Where is this house of God? Here, in us, in human beings. It is not *where* we pray. It is where we *pray*: in ourselves. For this reason, Muslims may pray anywhere—in a house, under a tree, in a car, in an airplane—because we carry our house of worship with us.

However, if one's house is filled with ego and self-importance, then no matter where one is, one has no space to serve the Divine. A portion of the Qur'anic verse that Muslims most frequently repeat in prayer states,

> ***Iyyaaka na*ʿ*budu wa iyyaaka nasta*ʿ*een.***
>
> **You alone we worship; You alone we ask for help** (1:5).

How often, when we pray, do our thoughts remain concentrated on our own selves? What happens when we turn our full attention towards the Truth, and really live "You alone we worship"?

We begin to fulfill that which Allah *(Subhaanahu wa ta*ʿ*aalaa)* has designed us to do. We are transformed from physically-oriented beings to limitless seekers of our origins.

Until that time, we struggle with the self in every situation, instead of being ourselves: humane beings, seekers, and Muslims in the true meaning of the term. When we can be ourselves in every situation, we will no longer struggle with ourselves.

This is the life-altering change that results from accepting the choice to pursue the Path of *Tasawwuf*. This is a deeper meaning of "submission" in Islam: to perfect our humanness as servants, worshipers, and lovers of Allah *(Subhaanahu wa ta'aalaa)*; to become who we can be.

> ***Afamañ sharaha-Llaahu sadrahuu li-l-Islaami fa-huwa 'alaa nuurim-mir-Rabbih?***
>
> **Could, then, one whose bosom God has opened wide with willingness towards self-surrender unto Him, so that he is illumined by a light [that flows] from his Sustainer [be likened to the blind and deaf of heart]?** (Qur'an 39:22).

This illumination through the surrendering of one's self is the reciprocal of the creative intention of Allah *(Subhaanahu wa ta'aalaa)* that gave us life—***"kun fa-yakuun*** (be and it became)" (Qur'an 36:82).

THE ORGANISM OF HUMANITY

Kun fa-yakuun is the link that binds all human beings, beyond differences of culture and ethnicity. Just as one egg, when fertilized, grows into a single organism, so too Allah's *(Subhaanahu wa ta'aalaa)* intention created a unified organism. This organism is humanity. We are all cells of the same body.

On an individual level, if one part of your body gets wounded or infected, your whole body responds. You respond emotionally; you call a doctor; you try this or that medicine. You respond physiologically: your immune system sends corpuscles to fight infection and promote healing.

Our natural state is to resist disease and destructive forces. Our immune system is the physical analog to our *lataa'if*: that is, it is the recipient on the physical level of the transmissions of the intent (*niyyah*) of our Creator so that our body can and will serve well our spiritual purpose. But we must make choices to bring harmony between our inner self and our outer circumstances; to create a developed, balanced, harmonious life and spiritual center for the worship (*'ibaadah*), praise (*hamd*), and glorification (*subhaana*) of Allah *(Subhaanahu wa ta'aalaa)*—in a sustainable and harmonious way.

On a global level, the average person neither perceives nor responds to humanity as an organism. He or she regards himself or herself as a separate entity, connected only loosely (if at all) to "those other people over there." Humanity's immune system has been suppressed for so long that when one part of the body is engulfed in crisis, the other parts either fail to notice or are too paralyzed to respond. The blood vessels are clogged; the synapses are not striking.

Re-activating our Capacity to Respond

Mevlana Jalaluddin Rumi wrote, "It is through necessity that the means of perception are developed. Therefore, O man, increase your necessity."

Necessity has a way of increasing itself if we do not take the initiative. We are all too familiar with the pattern: human rights violations occur in one part of the world. The rest of the world turns a blind eye. The violations escalate. Other nations still fail to respond. Finally, the violations reach such proportions that other societies are compelled to respond, if only for self-interest or protection. Necessity has refined humanity's organs of perception: the world wakes up and takes action. But by now, the genocide, war, or devastation has spread like an untreated infection. Far stronger measures are needed to stop it than might have been required at an earlier stage.

How can we increase our necessity sooner? How can we wake up before nightmares of human bloodshed jolt us to consciousness? We have to see the necessity of "those other people" to be our necessity. We have to not block our innate sense of interconnectedness. Look at the refugees streaming across our television screens, the children starving in Iraq, the victims of riots in Indonesia. Look at the faces of the people—look at their eyes—and get upset. That may be one of the last tools we have before we stop caring altogether.

Perhaps some of us feel that our burdens are so great we cannot possibly take on another's weight. But just think: if our bodies operated that way, we would all have died from the first infection we ever got!

Levels of Response, from Long-Distance to Right at Home

According to a *hadith*:

> **Allah will ask on the Day of Awakening, "O child of Adam, I fell ill and you did not visit Me." He will reply, "O my Lord! How could I have visited Thee when Thou art the Lord of all the worlds?" Allah will say, "Did you not know that so and so among My servants**

> **was sick, but you did not visit him? And did you not know that if you had visited him, you would surely have found Me with him?"**
>
> **Again, Allah will say, "O child of Adam, I asked for food from you, but you did not give Me food." He will reply, "O my Lord! How could I have fed Thee, when Thou art the Lord of all the worlds?" Allah will say, "Did you not know that so and so of My servants asked you for food, but you did not feed him? Did you not know, that if you had fed him, you would surely have found Me with him?"** (Karim 274-275).

As we come to recognize the inextricable bonds between our individual selves, our fellow human beings, and the Divine, we cannot not respond. The question then becomes, how? On a personal level, the options seem to fall into two categories. We can offer long-distance support, sending money or other items to organizations who are directly assisting those in need. Or, we can offer hands-on aid, volunteering our skills and energies in places like Macedonia, Kosovo, Bosnia, and Rwanda.

Both venues are essential. Both express and reinforce our understanding that all human beings are cells of the same organism. Both reflect the guidance of the Qur'an and the *sunnah* of *Nebi* Muhammad *(ṣalla-Llaahu ʿalayhi wa sallam)*. Obviously, giving hands-on aid requires a greater investment of ourselves. Writing a check is not the same as handing out bags of rice, carrying water, hauling beds to makeshift infirmaries, working for days without sleep.

But an even greater investment of self is necessary if one wants to end the kinds of tragic situations that the world suffers from today. To bring lasting resolution and healing, one has to do all that—and more. One has to engage in *tarbiyah*: spiritual education and the gaining of knowledge.

The processes of *Taṣawwuf*—that is, the processes whereby the Shaykh guides the seeker to become an *ʿAbd Allah*—send transmissions to the global society. If we give the time and make the effort; if we are sincere about our prayers, meditation, and our love for humanity; if we are self-sacrificing without any caveats or back-pocket excuses, we can develop potential within us that can transform ourselves and our communities, and thereby become a powerful spiritual magnetic force that sends out a vibration to humanity. People who are in tune with it will resonate with it, like a male moth who, as soon as he detects one pheromone of scent from a female moth ten miles away, turns around and immediately flies towards her. If we can become one-pointed enough to overcome the destructive tendency to be eclectic and never satisfied, if we can accept what our role and duty is, we will pick up the scent (*dhawq*), the inclination, the responsiveness, and head towards the source. If enough people do that, it can send out a transmission that will change the direction of humanity.

We have no trouble recognizing the negative effects of products that are corrupting, destructive, and disunifying: the mass market toys, video games, television shows, and so on. Nor do we doubt the power of the intentions of manufacturers and media moguls, who sell people what they want to buy, while simultaneously shaping their preferences through the products and images being sold to them. If we so readily acknowledge the power of greed, how can we doubt that efforts based on compassion, mercy, forgiveness, tolerance, patience, understanding, and service to one's brothers and sisters (whether or not they are our friends or allies) can shift the paradigms of the world?

Our prayers and intentions do make a difference. Even more importantly, our thoughts and actions make a difference. If you say a kind word to someone here, then a border guard says a kind word to someone passing through the border, or refrains from shooting someone.

Realizing that "My Way of Being has Global Impacts"

You can believe this because you think spiritual people are supposed to believe such things, or you can believe it based on experience. I recommend the latter.

Islam evokes from us the experience and the active responsibilities that are necessary for the transformation of self and society. One experiences the non-local effects of one's prayers, actions, and intentions through meditation.[3] Our *shuyukh* speak of the necessity of "adding spirituality to your Islam." By this they refer to the absolute necessity of adding *muraaqabah* (meditation, contemplation) and *dhikr* (remembrance) to the standard Islamic practices of Qur'an reading and daily prayers. The Prophet himself *(salla-Llaahu 'alayhi wa sallam)* set the example for these voluntary expressions of love for the Divine, doing prolonged prayers and other forms of meditation that are extensions of the prescribed practices of Islam.

When one sits in meditation and does *dhikr* for long periods of time with all sincerity, one comes to perceive reality in a different way, a way that is more accurate, more spiritual, and more in tune with recent developments in science. Scientists have found evidence of non-local experiences. But most of us were trained in the old paradigm of linear and reductionist science. This has a profound effect on how we think about social and spiritual issues. If we had been taught from childhood that our thoughts and actions have profound effects outside our small circle of friends and family, we would act and think in different ways today.

One cannot redo one's childhood education. But, through proven methods, one can change one's mindset now. Meditation and contemplation bring to consciousness one's cellular intuition of the interconnectedness of humanity. It enables one to experience the reality that everything one does, everything one thinks, and everything one says has far-reaching effects.

If the terms of one's life have not changed before one reaches this stage in meditation, they definitely change afterwards. One realizes that the choice to commit to a spiritual path entails refining the self until one's deeds, thoughts, and words have only constructive effects.

Life Changing Experiences that can Change the World (i.e., Methods for Refinement)

In the last few minutes of my talk, let me offer some brief suggestions for how to refine the self. My first suggestion pertains to love.

Method #1: Cultivate Love for the Divine

The inborn instinct of the human being is to love the Supreme, the Absolute, the beauty and perfection of Allah. Unfortunately, love of the material world blocks this inherent attraction. Meditation alone rends the veil between *dunyaa* and *ghayb*, between the physical world and the non-physical reality. The deeper and longer one meditates, the closer one comes to perfect consciousness of the presence of the Divine.

The *shuyukh* say, "Humans fall in love, and in spirituality, we rise in love." In the rapture of spiritual love, we realize that Allah *(Subhaanahu wa tá aalaa)* alone is the Doer, the Owner, the One Who Controls. What, then, is our relationship with Allah's *(Subḥaanahu wa tá aalaa)* creation? It must be one of loving it. What else is there? If I do not own it or control it, and I am enthusiastically working for the One who does, the only relationship I could possibly have is love.

Such love liberates our minds and hearts from the illusion of self-importance. It moves us from the complacency born of our prosperity, safety, and security to activism based on the responsibility that comes with prosperity, safety, and security.

The flame of love for Allah *(Subḥaanahu wa tá aalaa)* is kindled through meditation, remembrance, and the reading of Qur'an. Once lit, it must continue to be stoked by these same practices. This brings me to my second suggestion.

Method #2: Be Prepared to Re-affirm Your Faith and Commitment Moment to Moment

Allah *(Subḥaanahu wa tá aalaa)* tells us in the Holy Qur'an:

> *Aḥasiba-n-naasuañy-yutrakuuuañy-yaquuluuu aamannaa wa hum laa yuftanuun?*

> **Do people imagine that they will be left [at ease] because they say, "We believe," and will not be tested with affliction?** (29:2).

> *Wa mina-n-naasi mañy-yaᶜbudu-Llaaha ᶜalaa ḥarf: fa-in aṣaabahuu khayruni-t-ma'anna bih: wa in aṣaabat-hu fitnatuni-ñ-qalaba ᶜalaa wajhih: khasira-d-dunyaaa wa-l-aakhirah...*

> **And there is, too, among people many a one**

> **who worships God on the border-line [of faith]: thus, if good befalls him, he is satisfied with Allah; but if a trial assails him, he turns away utterly, losing [thereby both] this world and the life to come...** (22:11).

You do not just love God once and then you are a Sufi. You do not just believe once and from that time on, you are a believer. You believe, and then the test and trial comes, and still you believe. Then the test and trial comes again, and you believe.

How do you not run out of belief? By maintaining your *muraaqabah, dhikr,* and study of Qur'an. These are the doorways to *"laa hawla wa laa quwwata illaa bi-Llaahi-l-ᶜAliyyu-l-ᶜAdheem"* ("there is no strength nor power but in Allah, the Most Powerful, the Almighty"). Through these means, one gains patience and steadfastness (*sabr*), and one's tests and trials become merely the polishing of the heart.

Method #3: Dive into the Creative Possibilities of Islam, Within the Parameters of Shareeᶜah

I realize that "the creative possibilities of Islam" may strike some people as a contradiction in terms, and that mention of "the parameters of *shareeᶜah*" may evoke fears of the kind of stultifying dogma that many have turned to Sufism to escape.[4]

But Islam is not meant to be upheld by narrow-minded authorities, not does it restrict creativity, access to information, or dialogue. Allah *(Subhaanahu wa taᶜaalaa)* instructs us in the Holy Qur'an:

> ***...Fabash-shir ᶜibaadi-l-ladhiina yastamiᶜuuna-l-qawla fa-yattabiᶜuuna ahsanah; ulaaa'ika-***

l-ladheena hadaahumu-Llaahu wa ulaaa'ika hum ulu-l-albaab.

...Give, then, this glad tiding to [those of] My servants who listen [closely] to all that is said, and follow the best of it: [for] it is they whom God has graced with His guidance, and it is they who are [truly] endowed with insight! (39:17-18).

...Maa ja'ala 'alaykum fi-d-deeni min haraj...

...[Allah] has laid no hardship on you in [anything that pertains to] religion... (22:78).

Therefore, one need not fear, reject, or try to universalize Islam, or attempt to de-Islamicize Sufism.

Historically, authoritarian structures and restrictions have been imposed in the name of Islam on certain people and societies, creating negative impressions of Islam among Muslims and non-Muslims alike. But why should educated individuals remain passive victims of these stereotypes, and why should they be rejectionist? Those who fail to see Islam as a dynamic and organic process are not doing the things that will illuminate their Islam. They are not studying Qur'an and *Hadith*, they are not meditating, they are not making *dhikr*, and they are not placing others before themselves.

Studying and absorbing a set of values-based guidelines frees us from habituated patterns and expands our tools for self-discovery. Indeed, by experiencing Islam in its essence, we can generate new energy, new outlooks, new ideas, new institutions and discoveries that can and will revitalize our global civilization. Those who are drawn towards Sufism but reject the prayer, *zakat* (charity), fasting, or pilgrimage will never know this potential. Those who accept *shareeʻah* will progressively discover its meaning and benefit from its transforming power.

This brings me to my fourth and final suggestion.

Method #4: Humble Oneself Through Supplication

Let me share with you an excerpt from a traditional prayer known as *Duʻaa' Kumayl.*

> O Allah, my Master, many a fault You have overlooked. Many a hardship You have mitigated. Many an error You have prevented. Many an ordeal You have averted, and my beautiful praise, [which] I did not deserve, you have made known. O Allah, worst is my distress; intense is my discomfort; few are my virtues; chains pull me down. My far-fetched desires keep me from my gains. I have been deceived by the wily world and by my dishonest, unwary self. ...O my God, guilty of acts of omission and commission against my own self, I have come to You, and I stand before You, apologetic, repentant, humble and debased, asking mercy, confessing my sins, confiding in You, disclosing my faults.

We live in a world where that type of prayer is considered unacceptable, because it seems to be self-deprecating. As people have turned away from religion and toward a populist/modernist, self-referencing, self-aggrandizing, and psychologically-oriented lifestyle, they have lost understanding of the positivity of acknowledging one's sins and imploring forgiveness. Even the terms "sin" and "imploring" are dismissed as mindless litany. How does one get beyond one's reactions, and, in so doing, allow oneself to experience the beneficence and generosity of the

Creator, the Compassionate, the Merciful—Allah *(Subhaanahu wa ta'aalaa)*? One must recognize the pollutants of the world around us; acknowledge one's conditioning, past, limited definitions, prejudices, and developmental handicaps; and see the need to constantly cleanse ourselves. Dependence on Allah *(Subhaanahu wa ta'aalaa)* is not demeaning, but clarifying and purifying.

The *du'aa'* continues:

> If you put me away with Your enemies, join me with the condemned and separate me from Your adorers and friends, then suppose, O my God, my Chief, my Master, my Lord, that I may patiently bear with Your punishment. But how will I put up with Your separation? I may hold on patiently to the burning heat of the fire, but how will I endure the painful deprivation of not beholding Your clemency?

Many of us have been conditioned to recoil from and reject those images. But how can we not see the simplicity and sweetness, the purity and faith in such a supplication?

Contemplate the power of repentance as embodied in this *du'aa'*. The repentance expressed here is more than saying "I'm sorry" because one is expected to say it, or "I'm sorry" because one has a momentary bout of remorse. It is a heartfelt evaluation of self (*muhaasabatu-n-nafs*) based on faith and submission. Such repentance brings one to a level of honesty that guarantees protection and security.

When Islam is understood, lived, presented, and experienced as the safe, secure, tolerant, and forgiving Truth that it is, progress towards breaking the cycle of revenge around the globe—as well as towards overcoming one's own selfishness or self-deprecation—is guaranteed. Think of the doorways that can be opened to forgiveness and patience, towards setting aside the egotism of seeing oneself as authorized by Allah *(Subhaanahu wa ta'aalaa)* to punish others in the name of Truth. Think of what it would mean if even a small number of those involved in the crises raging today could come to see themselves as nothing more than *'abd Allah*, servants of Allah *(Subhaanahu wa ta'aalaa)*, no better than anyone else. Think of how many lives could be saved if, instead of judging, condemning, resenting, and attacking, some tiny proportion of the world's people could learn to look one another in the eyes and say, "I am of the same origin as you; our duties and our responsibilities are the same; so, too, are our hopes."

This was the healing brought 1420 years ago to the warring tribes of Medina by the Prophet Muhammad *(salla-Llaahu 'alayhi wa sallam)*. This is the healing available today, when we accept the life-changing experience of Sufic Islam and embark upon the real discovering of the self and its purpose. It is a discovery to be found by those who would strive in the way of Allah, the way of Truth and Compassion: by those who would commit themselves (and their selves) to service, praise, and worship of the One who alone is worthy of worship.

Jazaaka-Llaah khayr.

* * *

Wa Llaahu lahu ul-haqqu wa huwa yahdi-s-sabeel.
Hasbuna Llahu wahdahu wa ni'ma-l-wakeel.
Wa salli 'ala sayyidina Muhammadin
wa aaalihi wa sahbihi ajma'een
wal-hamdu li-Llaahi rabbil-'aalameen.

Truth belongs to Allah; it is He who shows the way.
Allah, alone, suffices us, and what a fine guardian is He!
Blessings upon our leader Muhammad
and his family and companions altogether
and praise is due to Allah, Lord of the Worlds.

Notes

1 There is considerable controversy about the origin of the widely quoted statement, "one who knows oneself knows his Lord." Some believe it was a statement of the Prophet, although it does not appear in *hadith* literature. Some attribute it to a close companion, Imam Ali *(radiya-Llaahu 'anhu)*. The respected scholar and Sufi Ibn Arabi said "This *hadith*, although it is not proved by way of narration, is proved to us by way of *kashf* (inner vision)," while other scholars reject Arabi's method of verification as extremely dangerous. Imam Suyuti wrote a beautiful essay about it, demonstrating that even if it can not be traced back directly to the Prophet *(salla-Llaahu 'alayhi wa sallam)* its meaning is still true. In keeping with Sufic literature, the statement is respectfully included here.

2 For a deeper intellectual understanding of the lataa'if and the Naqshbandi methodology, please see Professor Arthur Buehler's comprehensive and important work, *Sufi Heirs of the Prophet* (Columbia, SC: University of South Carolina Press,1998).

3 Understanding of the non-local effects of one's prayers, thoughts, and actions may also be gained through direct transmission from the spiritual guide to the seeker.

4 Winifred Gallagher astutely describes the mixed feelings towards religion that are common among Westerners.

> As middle age looms, as it does for 75 million baby boomers, certain questions grow more insistent: Is this all there is? What's the point of life? Smart and well-educated in the rationalistic, scientific worldview, [these "neo-agnostics"] think of religion as belief in the unbelievable, upheld by suffocating authorities....Put off by the institutional connotations of organized religion, they prefer to focus on spirituality: religion's juicy, good parts, minus the doctrines and hierarchies.

References

Translations of *Du'aa' Kumayl* are available at www.duas.org and www.al-islam.org.

Gallagher, Winifred. New Breed of Spiritual Seekers: Looking for God Beyond the Borders of Organized Faith. Special to MSNBC. April 1, 1999.

Karim, Fazlul. *Al Hadis: An English Translation and Commentary of Mishkat-ul-Masabih.* Book I. Lahore: The Book House, undated.

Weiss, Rick. Sixth Sense: What Your Immune System Knows. *Washington Post,* April 19, 1999:A3.

Glossary of Terms

ʿabd – servant, slave

ʿabd Allah – servant of God; favorite name of the Prophet Muhammad *(saw)*

adab – spiritual courtesy

adhaan – call to prayer

ʿadl – justice and equity

ahl al-kitaab – people of the Book, adherents of revealed religion such as Christians and Jews

akhirah – the Hereafter

akhlaaq – ethic; disposition

ʿalayhi-s-salaam/ ʿalayha-s-salaam/ ʿalayhimma-s-salaam – peace be upon him/her/both of them

al<u>h</u>amduli-Llaah – praise be to Allah

ʿalim – (plural *ʿulamaa'*) – religious scholar

amaanaat – trust, charge

ʿaqeedah – tenets of belief; creed; includes the Five Pillars of Islam and the Six Articles of Belief

al-Asmaa' al-<u>H</u>usnaa – the Ninety-Nine Beautiful Names of Allah

ambiyaa' (sing. ***nebi***) – the prophets

araada – to will or aim

as-salaam ʿalaykum – peace be with you

awliyaa' (plural of *waliy*) – literally, "those who are close to, close associates, friends"; in a religious context, those who are near to God

ayat (pl. ***aayaat****)* – sign, Qur'anic verse

baa<u>t</u>in – inner realm

Bani Isra'eel – the Children of Israel

barakah – blessings of God

Bismi-Llaahi-r-Ra<u>h</u>maani-r-Ra<u>h</u>eem – the invocation that begins every surah of the Qur'an (except Surah 9) translated means, "In the name of Allah, the Merciful, the Bestower of Mercy."

daa'i – one who calls to Islam, or responds to the call of the heart to Islam

da'eef – the categorization of a hadith authority as "weak"

dar-as-salaam – the abode of peace

dars – lectures

da'wah – a call or an invitation

da'wah al-kubraa – greater *da'wah*

deen – religion

dhaalimeen – those who perpetuate *dhulm*

dhaahir – outer realm

dhawq – scent

dhikr – literally, remembrance; in the Sufic context, generally refers to recitations that evoke remembrance of Allah

dhikr jalee – *dhikr* aloud

dhikr katheer – "remembering [Allah] much," a practice enjoined in the Qur'an

dhikr khafee – *dhikr* silently

dhikru-Llaah – the remembrance of Allah *(Subhaanahu wa ta'aalaa)*

dhulm – transgressions and oppression

du'aa' – supplication

dunyaa – the material world

'Eidu-l-Adhaa – the feast of sacrifice; a major holy day of Islam that falls on the 10th day of the last month of the lunar calendar, following the rites of the *hajj*

fard – obligatory

fasaad – the corruption, destruction, and undermining of society

fee sabeeli-Llaah – for the sake of Allah, for the cause of Allah

Five Pillars of Islam – These are as follows: the *kalima* (There is no god but God and Muhammad *(saw)* is his Prophet), *salah* (the obligatory five times a day prayers), *zakat* (charity), *sawm* (fasting in the month of *Ramadaan*), *Hajj* (pilgrimage to Mecca).

fikr – contemplation, reflection

fiqh – Islamic jurisprudence

firaasa – perspicacity, acumen, discrimination, or minute observation
fitrah – natural disposition, innate character
fuqaraa' – (plural of *faqeer* - poor) mendicant dervishes
futuwwah – Sufic chivalry
Ghafuur – The All-Forgiving (one of the Ninety-Nine Beautiful Names of Allah)
ghayb – the unseen, the non-physical reality
gellabia (also ***jellaba***) – a loose, long shirt-like garment, worn by North African and Middle Eastern men and women
hadith (pl. ***ahaadith***) – statement(s) of the Prophet Muhammad
hadith qudsi – sayings of the Prophet Muhammad (*saw*) where the wording is that of the Prophet, while the meaning and content are from Allah
hadrah – Sufic circle for *dhikr* and accompanying movement
hafiz – one who commits to memory the entire Qur'an
hajj – the pilgrimage to Mecca; one of the Five Pillars of Islam incumbent upon every capable Muslim once in his/her lifetime
hakeem – doctor, shaykh
hamd – praise
haneef – a believer in one God
haqeeqah – truth; elevated awareness of Divine Essence
al-Haqq – The Truth (one of the Ninety-Nine Beautiful Names of Allah)
haram – forbidden or prohibited
hasan – that which is good, fair, beautiful, righteous, and kind
hayaat-i-tayyibah – the good life
al-Hayy – The Living (one of the Ninety-Nine Beautiful Names of Allah)
himma – yearning
hijaab – literally "barrier"; refers to women's headcovering, sometimes extending to face, hands and body
hijrah – the emigration from Mecca to Medina by the Prophet *(saw)* and the Muslims
hikmah – wisdom

ᶜibaadah – worship

iḫsaan – "goodness"; the state of doing what is beautiful; defined in a Hadith as, "It [*iḫsaan*] is to worship Allah as if you see him and if you can not [see him] then remember that He is seeing you."

ijaazah – license

ijmaaᶜ – consensus

ikhtiraam – sacredness and respect

imaan – faith

inshaa'a-Llaah – if Allah wills

iqra – read

al-Islaam – the way of submission; the religion of Islam as a way of life

Israa' Miᶜraaj – refers to the Prophet's *(saw)* night journey from Mecca to Jerusalem and his ascent to the highest Heavens

ijtiḫaad – logical deduction; the process of making a legal decision by independent interpretation of the sources of the law: the Qur'an and the *sunnah*

isnaad – a chain of authorities who guarantee a statement by transmitting the words verbatim to each other at times and places that can be historically confirmed

jadhb (jadhbah) – attraction

jaahiliyah – "the time of ignorance"; refers specifically to pre-Islamic Arabia

jamaal – beauty

jalaal – majesty

jazaaka-Llaah khayr – May Allah reward you

jiḫaad - literally "struggle"; most often refers to struggling with one's own lower self; also, struggling with external forces of oppression

Jiḫaadu-l-akbar – the greater struggle

***kaafir** (pl. **kaafiruun**)* – disbeliever(s); those who knowingly cover up the truth

Kaᶜbah – the sacred house of Allah re-built by Ibrahim and Ishmael located in the middle of the mosque in Mecca to which all Muslims turn to pray

kashf – visions; spiritual insight received by removing the veil of illusions

kalaam – speech, discussion

ʿilm al-kalaam – scholastic theology

khalifah – successor, deputy, vice-regent

khanaqah – a spiritual community with a living Sufi teacher and a consciously designed environment dedicated to applying the teachings in daily life

khidmah – service

Khidr – a mystic sage mentioned in the Qur'an (16:65-82) and often referred to as the patron saints of Sufis

khuṯbah – Islamic sermon

Khwaja Khwajagan – Masters of Wisdom; title referring to the tradition of Sufi teachers

kun fa-yakuun – be and it became

Laa ilaaha illa-Llaah – There is no god but Allah

laṯeefah** (pl.* ***laṯaa'if) – subtle center of consciousness

madh-hab – an Islamic school of law. There are four main madh-habs within the Sunni branch of Islam: Maliki, Hanbali, Hanafi, and Shafi'i. Shi'a Muslims follow the 'Jafari madh-hab.

maʿiyat-i-ḫubbi – accompaniment with love

majlis – council meeting; communal gathering; parliament

maqaam – station

maʿrifah – knowledge, gnosis

mash-huud – what is seen

masjid – mosque, Muslim place of worship

meezaan – balance

mu'min (pl. ***mu'minuun***)– believer

muḫajjab – wearing ḫijaab

muḫaasabah (muḫaasabatu-n-nafs) – reflecting upon and taking account of one's self

mujaahid – one who struggles inwardly in the cause of Allah; one who fights oppression

mujaamalah – refers to a type of exaggerated courtesy, politeness specific to Arab cultures

mujaddid – reviver

munaafiq *(pl.* ***munaafiquun****)* – hypocrite(s)

munaasabah – congenial relationship usually referring to that between a shaykh and mureed

muraad – the sought

mureed (fem. ***mureeda,*** pl. ***mureeduun***) – student of a shaykh

murshid – spiritual guide, shaykh

muraaqabah – literally, contemplation; in Sufic terms, meditation

mushaahadah – seeing, witnessing

nafs – self; one of the *lataa'if*

nafs ammaarah – the uncultivated self

nafs lawwaamah – the reproaching self or conscience

naqsh – design

nisbah – spiritual affinity; different levels of relationship with Allah

niyyah – intention

nuur – light

qalb – heart; one of the *lataa'if*

qareen – evil spirits, personal demons

qawwali – devotional music of Subcontinental Muslims

Qayyuum – The Everlasting (one of the Ninety-Nine Beautiful Names of Allah)

qiblah – direction faced during prayer

qiyaas – analogy

Quraysh – a tribe of Mecca

quwwata-l-baatin – the power of inner awakening

Rabbi-l-ᶜaalameen – Lord of the Universes, Sustainer of the Worlds

radiya-Llaahu ᶜanhu/ᶜanhaa/ᶜanhum/ᶜanhumma – May Allah be pleased with him/her/them/both of them

ar-Raheem – The Merciful (one of the Ninety-Nine Beautiful Names of Allah)
ar-Rahmaan – The Compassionate (one of the Ninety-Nine Beautiful Names of Allah)
rahmat – compassion, mercy
Rahmatu-Llaahi ʿanhu – May Allah's mercy be upon him
ar-Raqeeb – the Source of all regulating, all monitoring (one of the Ninety-Nine Beautiful Names of Allah)
Ramadaan – the month of fasting (one of the Five Pillars of Islam)
rifq – gentleness, kindness
ruuh – soul; one of the *lataa'if*
sadaqah – alms, charity
sabr – patient perseverance
sahaabah – the companions of the Prophet *(saw)*
saheeh – the categorization of a hadith authority as authentic
Salafiya – an orthodox movement in Sunni Islam that seeks to revive a practice of Islam that closely resembles the religion during the time of the Prophet Muhammad (*saw*)
salah – five daily prayers obligatory for Muslims; one of the *Five Pillars of Islam*
salaah – righteousness
salaam – peace, safety, security, wholeness, well-being
saleem – free, flawless, healthy, whole
salla-Llaahu ʿalayhi wa sallam *(abbr: "saw")* – "Peace and blessings of God be upon him." Muslims add this phrase when referring to the Prophet Muhammad *(saw)*.
sayr-i anfus – inner journey
sayr-i aafaaq – outer journey
seerah – life of the Prophet *(saw)*
ash-Shaafee – The Healer (one of the Ninety-Nine Beautiful Names of Allah)
shahaadah – profession of faith
shaheed – witness, seer
shareeʿah – religious law

shirk – polytheism; associating anything as an equal partner with God
shuuraa – consultation, taking counsel
shuyukh (plural of *shaykh*) – mystical teachers
silsila – a non-linear spiritual genealogy of Sufi masters connected by *nisbah* rather than by blood that traces back to the Prophet Muhammad *(saw)*, often referred to as the Golden Chain
s̲iraat̲a-l-mustaqeem – straight path
subh̲aana – glorification
Subh̲aanahu wa ta'aalaa *(abbr: "swt")* – "Glorified is He"; expression Muslims use to glorify God
sulh̲ – peace and reconciliation
sunnah – way or tradition of the Prophet *(saw)* that Muslims emulate to lead a life that is pleasing to God. The basic source of the *sunnah* is the *h̲adith.*
suurah – chapter of Qur'an
tafakkur – remembrance and contemplation
tafseer – the commentary of the Qur'an
takfeer – accusing other Muslims of disbelief
tajalli – irradiation
taqwah – piety
tarbiyah – education, upbringing; teaching instruction
t̲areeqah – Sufic order
Tas̲awwuf – Sufism
tasleem – handing over, presenting, greeting, concession, assent approval
tawajjuh – spiritual attention; transmission from Shaykh to *mureed*
tawakkul – trust
tawbah – repentence
tazkiyah – purification
topi – a cap worn by men in parts of the Muslim world
'ulamaa' (plural of *'alim*) – religious scholars
'uluum (plural of *'ilm*) – sciences
ummah – nation, community
ummata wasat̲a – middle nation, community of the middle

ustadh – master, teacher or expert in a subject who can teach or guide others in that subject
wuduu' – ritual ablution performed before prayer
zakat – obligatory alms-giving

Applied Sufism:
Classical Teachings for the Contemporary Seeker

Shaykh Ahmed Abdur Rashid

The present volume frames these teachings in the form of a response to those seeking, in the midst of a world torn by social and political turmoil, a whole and integral path, a unity of form and meaning, self-effacing comportment, and intimate knowledge of God. The intimate portrayal of conscience afforded the reader in the exposition of these principles imbues these lectures with a light that is at once familiar and rare. In short, Shaykh Ahmed Abdur Rashid, in his person, as an exemplar and spiritual mentor, and in his teaching legacy, to which these lectures testify, has provided us with a timeless criteria, clear and coherent, of the theoretical and practical aspects of the timeless spiritual discourse of traditional Islam.

Dr. Kenneth Honerkamp - Associate Professor of Religion - University of Georgia

The Circle Group
1329 Prosperity Drive
Bedford, VA 24523 USA
e-mail: mail@circlegroup.org
www.circlegroup.org

CPSIA information can be obtained at www.ICGtesting.com
Printed in the USA
LVOW040818240912
300016LV00001B/4/A

9 781595 941213